150

MINISTERS TO
THE SOLDIERS OF SCOTLAND

MINISTERS TO
THE SOLDIERS OF SCOTLAND

*A History
of the Military Chaplains of Scotland
prior to the War in the Crimea*

ALEXANDER CRAWLEY DOW
M.C., M.A., Ph.D.

OLIVER AND BOYD
EDINBURGH AND LONDON

OLIVER AND BOYD LTD.

Tweeddale Court
Edinburgh

39a Welbeck Street
London, W.1.

First Published 1962

Printed in Great Britain by
Robert Cunningham and Sons Ltd.
Alva, Scotland

PREFACE

THIS BOOK seeks to fill part of a gap in religious and military history by tracing the development of the Army Chaplains of Scotland from the earliest Christian times to the outbreak of the War in the Crimea.

Considerable space has been given to the period of the Civil Wars for it was then that the Scots Kirk tried to set up a system of Church Courts within the Army, seeking to establish a Kirk Session in each regiment under the jurisdiction of a Presbytery of the Army.

Notice has also been taken of the ministers who served with mercenary regiments on the Continent of Europe and of those who attached themselves to various rebel armies at home.

On examination the Regular Chaplains of the 18th century proved to have been rather better than they are usually esteemed, they were not all guilty of neglect of duty nor were they all 'sanctified sots'.

Some 600 of the clergy who ministered to the Soldiers of Scotland before 1856 have been identified but it did not prove practical to include short biographies of all of these in this volume. It may yet prove possible to incorporate them in a larger list which would honour all those who have so served.

The considerable course of reading involved in this study was made possible by the courtesy of the Library staffs of Aberdeen, Aldershot, Belfast, Edinburgh, Glasgow and London and sincere thanks are also due to the Carnegie Trust for the Universities of Scotland for their generous contribution towards the expense of publication.

I am greatly indebted to the late Very Rev. G. D. Henderson, D.D., D.LITT. and to the Very Rev. Hugh Watt, D.D., D.LITT. for their encouragement and skilled guidance throughout. The co-operation of the Rev. J. A. Williamson, C.B.E., M.A. and of the Rev. T. N. Fraser, Q.H.C., M.A. during their respective terms of office as Assistant Chaplain General did much to ease my path.

It is my hope that, if the cares of a busy parish permit, I may bring this history up to the present day as a token of regard for all who have been Ministers to the Soldiers of Scotland.

TO MY WIFE

CONTENTS

Ministers to the Soldiers of Scotland

I	BEFORE THE REFORMATION	I
II	DURING THE REFORMATION	29
III	EMPLOYED BY OTHER NATIONS	49
IV	THE CIVIL WARS (1)	77
V	THE CIVIL WARS (2)	108
VI	IN IRELAND	137
VII	THE RESTORATION AND THE REVOLUTION	153
VIII	WILLIAM III AND ANNE	176
IX	THE JACOBITE REBELLIONS	195
X	THE HOUSE OF HANOVER	223
XI	AFTER 1796	252
	BIBLIOGRAPHY	274

I

BEFORE THE REFORMATION

ROBERT BAILLIE, scholar and Minister of the Church, wrote a letter from the camp of the Scottish army, in 1639, which could be the Apologia of every Army Chaplain.

> If it be the will of God in this voyage that I doe not returne, I am weel pleased to offer up my Life for the honour of my God, and the defence of my Countrie, which I apprehend to be in great hazard both of religion and liberties. I trust to die in the faith of Christ and heartie love of King Charles.[1]

He states the case for all the clergy who have gone soberly to war, for a cause they deemed righteous and with malice toward none. Their number has been legion, for the presence of the priest on the battlefield was accepted before the walls of Jericho fell.

If, however, we confine our attention to the Christian era, we find the Emperor Charlemagne ruling that the clergy who accompanied his army should do so in their proper capacity as priests or chaplains. The passage in Du Cange reads:

> Sanxit ut nullus in posterum sacerdos in hostem pergeret nisi duo vel tres episcopi electione caeterorum propter benedictionem populique reconciliationem, et cum illis electi sacerdotes qui bene scirent populis poenitentias dare, missas celebrare, etc.[2]

This was at once a counsel of perfection and an indication of a less happy state.

In Scotland, although the Druids had been excused service in war,[3] the Christian clergy made an early appearance on the battlefield, both as priests and as combatants.

The Father of the Scottish Church, Columba, himself served in both these capacities. In addition to his defeat of Diarmait at Cooldrevny, which occasioned his banishment from Ireland, he is said to have fought a battle at Coleraine against St Comgall of Bangor.[4] Adamnan asserts that Columba assumed a more priestly office also, for

> in the terrific clashings of battles he obtained this from God by the power of his prayers, namely, that some kings should be conquered, while other rulers should come off conquerors.[5]

In these ancient days the priest who came with the army to pray was not held to be privileged. A simpler faith or clearer logic regarded him as a protagonist, as Bede shows in his account of a battle near Chester, in 607.

There were, he says, many priests with the Welsh army, who

> after three days fasting had come with the others to the aforesaid army to pray for the soldiers ... and when King Ethelfrith had understood the cause of their coming thither, he said, 'Then if these men cry and call upon their God against us, truly though they themselves have no armour, yet they fight against us, who pursue us with curses to bring evil upon us.' Accordingly he commanded his soldiers to assault these men first. ... It is reported that there were slain in that battle, of them which had come to pray, about 1200 men and that only 50 escaped by flight.[6]

The ecclesiastical historian records this slaughter with a certain gusto, for these Welsh priests were heretical.

To reinforce the prayers of the clergy in time of battle, relics of the saints were carried with the army on the march, and through the ranks when drawn up for the fight. The Crozier of St Columba was thus carried into battle by the men of Alba, or Scotland. It was known as the Cath Bhuaidh, or Battle-Victory, and was used as a 'vexillum', or Ensign. The ancient annals tell of its power to bring victory.

About the same time (A.D. 918) the men of Fortrenn and the Lochlanns fought a battle. Bravely, indeed, the men of Alba fought this battle, for Columcille was aiding them; for they had prayed to him most fervently because he was their Apostle.[7]

The tale goes on to tell how, once more, the Crozier brought them victory.

It is unfortunate that the Chronicles, which are the chief source of history for these ancient days, are more apt to dwell upon the deeds or death of a Warrior-Bishop, than upon the less spectacular service of those who came to pray. Of the Battle of Brunanburh, in 934, they say that among the slain were two Bishops and many nobles, and, 'a countless multitude of the rabble of either side'.[8]

There are suggestions, however, that there was contemporary criticism of the priest as a soldier. The Anglo-Saxon Chronicle, for example, says of Leofgar, Bishop of Hereford:

He wore his knapsack in his priest-hood, until he was a bishop.
He abandoned his chrism and his rood—his ghostly weapons
—and took to his spear and his sword, after his bishop-hood;
and so marched to the field against Griffin the Welsh king.
But he was there slain and his priests with him.[9]

Such a tale leaves no doubt of Leofgar's purpose, but it is not always so easy to determine with what motive the priest came to the war. There is an account of the Battle of Carham, which took place about 1018, which illustrates this difficulty. In that famous battle between the Northumbrians and the Scots, nearly the whole of the former army was destroyed:

and among them were also eighteen priests (*sacerdotes*) who had inadvisedly mixed themselves up with the war.[10]

Surely a delightful phrase, which yet fails to tell us whether they fought with their ghostly weapons alone.

There is a grim story of the defence of Glasgow against Sumerled, the 'regulus' of Argyle, which helps us to a better understanding of these clerical warriors. The news that the semi-barbaric army from the remoter corners of the land was advancing terrified the people of Glasgow into flight. Inspired by St Kentigern, however, Bishop Herbert came forward as their leader, and:

> the defenders, hearing of the bishop's arrival, became very bold, like dragons or lions; although Sumerled and a thousand enemies were ready for battle against a hundred of the innocent, yet [the latter] advanced and made an attack upon the ranks of the treacherous men of Argyle ... and in the first cleft of the battle the baleful leader fell. A priest cut off the head of the unfortunate leader, Sumerled, and gave it to the bishop.[11]

Over against such tales of clerical prowess for worthy or unworthy causes must be set the evidence which shows that the clergy did have a recognised function as military chaplains. For instance, when Roger, who became Bishop of Salisbury in 1107, was an obscure priest in Normandy, his service was casually attended by Henry, brother of William Rufus, with some of his soldiers. Roger performed the service so expeditiously, that the Prince, between jest and earnest, invited him to go along with them, as a fit and proper chaplain for the army.[12] It would seem that the military taste for short sermons is of long standing.

There is, therefore, evidence for the presence of the clergy with the army, in two, or even in three capacities. They appear as warriors, they are present to pray for victory, and they attend as custodians of the sacred relics. All of these functions were illustrated on a grand scale in 1138, at the Battle of the Standard. The Church Militant was headed by the Archbishop of York, who levied the army of the northern counties to resist the Scottish invaders. The priests and the Holy Relics were included in the levy, for, although the Archbishop was prevented by age from personal attendance, he commanded:

> the priests of every parish within his diocese, to come out in procession with their crosses, banners and holy relicks; he enjoined all men capable of bearing arms to repair to the

general rendezvous of the barons, 'in defence of Christ's church against the barbarians'. He promised victory to the English if they were penitent, and salvation to those who should fall in battle. . . . On Cutton Moor, in the neighbourhood of Northallerton, the English standard was erected. It was the mast of a ship, fitted into the perch of a high four-wheeled carriage; from it were displayed the banners of St Peter of York, of St John of Beverley, and St Wilfred of Ripon; on the top of this mast there was a little casket containing a consecrated host.[13]

The Scottish invaders were also accompanied by their clergy, for Abbot Aeldred declares that, just before the battle, the clergy of both armies, in their white robes, with crosses and relics of the saints, were shriving the soldiers. He also suggests that the Scottish armour and weapons were of poor quality, and that their army was accompanied by Jesters, Buffoons and Dancers, both male and female (*histriones, saltatores et saltatrices*).[14] In the event the Scots were defeated and lost some of their sacred relics to the victors.

These years of fable and folk-lore give place slowly to an age whose story is partly supported by documentary evidence, and in which the clergy continue to appear on the battlefield as soldiers or as chaplains. It becomes evident too, that the clergy were sometimes forced into the role of men-at-arms. For example, the laws of the Marches or Debatable-land, between Scotland and England, sometimes called for a decision by the ordeal of single combat. These laws made no exception in the case of the clergy, and a bishop or an abbot must fight in person like a layman. Early in the thirteenth century this was forbidden, on pain of excommunication, but it died slowly.[15]

If there is increasing evidence that the clergy continued to give willing or unwilling service as soldiers, there are also proofs that they did do their spiritual duty to the army of Scotland. The reign of Alexander II yields an interesting example of such service. It appears that the Pope, anxious to secure King John and his heir upon the throne of England, had sent Gualo as his legate to that country. The legate, in pursuit of this policy, secured from Pope Honorius a rescript which declared:

> all the prelates of Scotland excommunicated forasmuch as they had given the Communion to the king of Scotland and his army who had fallen under the ban pronounced at the Lateran Council wherin were excommunicated all King John's enemies and their abettors.[16]

When peace was made between the nations, this ban was lifted from the King of Scotland and the laity, but the legate reserved to himself the absolution of the chaplains of the Scottish army, all the clergy who had

> either taken part in the war or had in any way ministered unto the combatants.[17]

The Scots had the support and the spiritual assistance of other clergy than those of their own land. This is shown in a complaint addressed to the Pope by Henry III of England, dated 26th April 1216. In it he declares that

> the Canons of Carlisle, favourers and adherents of the King of Scotland, and others the enemies of the Pope and King, despising the Legate's authority, irreverently and comtumaceously celebrated divers offices in forbidden places, in presence of his enemies and excommunicated persons.[18]

Matthew Paris also bears witness to the zeal of the Churchmen with the army of Alexander. He says that that King was beloved by his people, and that his army was

> all unanimous, all animated by the exhortations of the clergy and by confession courageously to fight and resolutely to die in the just defence of their native land.[19]

One prelate, at least, would be in attendance upon that army as the keeper of a sacred relic. The monastery at Aberbrothock had received from William the Lion the custody of the 'Brecbennoch' and, with it, the lands of Forglen given to God and St Columba and to the Brecbennoch, they making therefore the service in the army with the said Brecbennoch which is due to me from the said lands.[20]

Thereafter the Abbot would be expected to appear on all martial occasions, with the revered relic. He may have had to carry it three times round the host before they marched, and in their midst on the expedition, as was done with the Cathach, or Psalter of St Columba. The abbot parted with this honourable but dangerous duty, and it was performed by the Irvines of Drum until about the year 1500. A reliquary with long associations with Monymusk is still preserved. It may be the casket in which the Brecbennoch was carried to the ancient Scottish wars.[21]

The reign of Alexander III was comparatively peaceful, but it did not pass without the mustering of armies. The rival claims of Scotland and of Norway to control the Islands off the west coast of the former came to a head in this reign at the Battle of Largs. It is interesting to note the presence of clergy with the Norse fleet at this time. A Saga which describes the expedition, says:

King Hakon has a very select company aboard his ship; there were amidships; Thorleif, abbot of [Nidar] Holmr; Sir Askatin; four priests and the chaplains of the king.

After the defeat at Largs, during the retreat northwards:

there (at Gigha) died friar Simon; and his body was taken ashore in Kintyre and buried at the Greyfriars monastery, with a pall over him.[22]

Hakon himself was taken mortally ill on the journey and lay dying in the Bishop's Palace in Orkney. According to the Saga he had the Bible read to him and some Norse books.[23] An expanded version of the incident says that

to recreate his mind, he cauſed his chaplains to read latin books to him which not ſufficiently comprehending by reaſon of the application they required, and he was unable to give, he ordered the hiſtory of the kings of Norway his predeſſors done in the Norwegian tongue by Halfdane the black, to be brought and read to him.[24]

At the last, however, the old warrior received extreme unction in the presence of Bishop Thorgils, Abbot Thorleif and many others and so made a good end.[25]

This Golden Age in Scotland's history came to an end with the sudden death of Alexander, in 1286. One of the oldest scraps of Scottish literature laments the event:

> quhen Alysandyr oure Kyng wes dede,
>
> . . . .
>
> Oure gold wes changyd in to lede,
> Chryst, borne into Vyrgynte,
> Succoure Scotland and remede,
> That stad is in pirplexyte.[26]

Scotland was indeed perplexed, and the interference of the King of England, during and after the short reign of the little Princess from Norway, proved to be the beginning of a long struggle for the independence of Scotland.

Edward I, of England, was able to fill the Scottish throne with a puppet-king, John Balliol, but even a puppet had to resent his exactions. Scottish raiders crossed the Borders in force and harried the northern counties of England. The chronicler of Lanercost tells a tale for edification concerning these raiders, which shows that they had some regard for the rites of the Church. He says that

perfidious persons desire under the cloak of Christianity to be esteemed like righteous ones, not in reality, but in appearance. This may be easily proved about these [Scots]; for whereas they knew that they had acted most wickedly towards the aforesaid nuns, at the last they sought out a priest who should celebrate mass for them. He, indeed, as I suppose, more by fear than any other motive, performed the sacred office as far as the Confectie, but when he was about to handle and consecrate the bread, suddenly it

vanished, wishing to conceal his shame, he took another
host intending to consecrate it but it disappeared between
the fingers that held it. All those present... fled from
the place.[27]

King Edward replied to these raids by marching into Scotland
in force. At the head of his army the Standard of St John of
Beverley was borne by Gilbert de Grymmesby, who had the
promise of the first vacant benefice of twenty pounds for this
service. Other clerks had charge of the banner[28] of St Cuthbert,
the Cross of St Neot, and the captured Black Rood of Scotland.[29]

One of the strongholds taken by this force was the Castle of
Dunbar, and among the garrison appears the name of John de
Somerville, clerk, who may have been chaplain to the castle.[30]
The English occupation which followed this invasion provoked
the fiercest resistance, and the clergy of Scotland were among its
leaders from the outset.

For example, Thomas, Chaplain of Edinburgh, was charged
before an English tribunal

> with publicly excommunicating the King [Edward] with
> bell and candle, confesses in the Marshall's presence he did so
> in the King's despite.[31]

A second illustration from such legal records is in a lighter vein,
and suggests an unsung Friar Tuck in Scottish history. At Perth,
on the 8th of August 1296, Matthew of York was accused by
Christiana of St John of robbery, in that he

> on Thursday next before St Botulph's day, came to her
> house in company with a thief, one William le Waleys, [and
> took] goods and chattels, viz. beer to the value of 3s.[32]

Matthew declared himself a Clerk and therefore not bound to
answer, and was adjudged to penitence. His companion in this
foray may not have been the future champion of Scottish freedom, but if he were, then Matthew might claim to have been
his chaplain.

Returning to the sober affairs of national history, it is easy to
show that Sir William Wallace did have chaplains with his patriot

B

army, indeed, he had the support of the greater part of the clergy of Scotland. A modern historian firmly declares that

> it was beyond all question the Church of Scotland which, more than any class or community in the Kingdom, inspired and kept alive the spirit of resistance to England throughout the long and bitter years of the war of Independence, and she it was who, in season and out of season, preached the sacred duty of war against the English yoke, and in the person of her bishops and her priests, often led the way on the field of battle itself.[33]

The Church Militant does appear again, in such as the Abbot of Arbroath, who dared to deliver to King Edward the instrument of Renunciation; in David, Bishop of Moray, who roused and raised the north-east; and in the Bishop of Glasgow, who used the new oak beams for his cathedral roof as military battering-rams.[34] But, of more importance for our purpose, the clergy appear again as chaplains to the army.

The existence and activity of such clergy with the men who followed the fortunes of Wallace is vouched for by Blind Harry, who wrote the life of that hero. He declares that his own writings were based upon a 'latyne buk', which had been compiled by two of the chaplains of Wallace's army. The passage in which he mentions his source book and its authors is worth repeating.

> Maiſter Johne Blair was ane of that meſſage,
> Ane worthy Clerk baith wiſe and richt ſauage.
> Leivit he was befoir in Pareis toun,
> Amang Maisteris in ſcience of gude Renoun.
> Wallace and he at hame in ſchule had bene,
> Sone efterwart as veritie was ſene;
> He was the man that principall undertuke,
> That firſt compylit in dyte the latine buke,
> Of Wallace lyfe richt famous of Renoun,
> And Thomas Gray perſoun of Libertoun.
> With him thay war, and put in History all
> Oft ane or baith mekill of his trauaill,
> And thairfoir heir I mak of thame mentioun.[35]

The book he says they made has never been found, but Blind Harry is so guileless in giving to them all credit that it seems but right to accept his statement for the existence of the book and of its chaplain-authors, Messrs John Blair and Thomas Gray. Another quotation from the minstrel gives us a glimpse of the chaplain on duty in the Scottish camp.

> Than Wallace thocht it was na tyme to ly,
> He blissit him, ſyne ſuddenly up he rais
> To tak the air, out of his Tent he gais.
> Maiſter Johne Blair was reddy haiſtelie,
> To Goddis ſeruice bownit richt reuerentlie.
> Quhen that was done Wallace couth him array
> In his armour, quhilk was baith gude and gay.[36]

Blind Harry's testimony to the presence of chaplains with Wallace receives valuable support from the hostile Chronicle of Lanercost. The monkish historian writes:

> many ordained priests are known to have taken part in the war, not only by exhortation but also by weilding arms.[37]

Of another occasion he declares that

> in this manner was slain not less than a thousand rebels, and several tonsured were found among the dead.[38]

The Chronicler is not surprised that clergy are on the battle-field, but by their attendance upon the rebel, or Scottish, army. The clergy of England, in fact, continued to follow the armies of their king, and were employed in diverse capacities. It was fitting that two friars were employed to offer terms of peace to the Scottish army before the battle of Stirling Bridge, but it is more surprising to find them employed as army engineers.

The Wardrobe Accounts of Edward I, for the year 1300, show that one cleric, at least, was so employed. They record a payment to Brother Thomas of Bamburgh, a monk of Durham, for the timber and for the construction of two large engines:

> for the defence of the town of Berwick on Tweed in the time of Dom. Phil. de Vernaco, then keeper of the said town, ...   6s. 8d.[39]

The name 'Master Thomas the Engineer' appears on a roll of the English garrison of Edinburgh Castle, in the same year, and may refer to the same Brother Thomas.[40]

It is scarcely relevant but may be noted that Edward not only used churchmen as engineers but also used church roofs to provide munitions of war. He caused the lead to be stripped from the cathedral roofs of Brechin, St Andrews and Dunfermline, for use at the siege of Stirling, giving orders that the altars should be protected from the elements.[41] In 1305 he directed that compensation be paid to these churches for five, twenty-two, and fifty-three cart-loads of lead, respectively, at the rate of five marks per load.[42]

In spite of his unorthodox use of churchmen and church roofs, Edward was not unmindful of religious usages. He carried with him to the Scottish wars a portable chapel, that he might worship wherever his camp should be set up. An illustrative item from his accounts, is:

> For a wagon and ten oxen and two grooms to carry the chapel from Dunfermline to St Andrews .   .   .   10s.[43]

There were, indeed, a great many clergy with the English army, and, during a fray between the Welsh and English contingents, no less than eighteen of them were slain. One division of the invading army escaped the fate of others, who had fallen into a Scottish ambush, because they had delayed to hear Mass.[44]

The task which Wallace had begun was now passed on to another champion, Robert the Bruce. He might well have lost the whole-hearted support of the Scottish clergy by the sacrilegious slaying of John Comyn. Other motives prevailed, however, and the Church continued its great part in the resistance to England. Sir Walter Scott states the case poetically, when he makes the Abbot of Iona say:

> De Bruce, thy sacrilegious blow
> Hath at God's altar slain thy foe;
> O'ermastered yet by high behest,
> I bless thee, and thou shalt be blessed.[45]

What Scott romantically suggests was practically expressed by the presence of the leading clergy of Scotland at the Coronation of Bruce, in 1306. These men quickly showed themselves such warriors as the times demanded, but the Church Militant received a heavy blow when most of them were captured by the English in Cupar, Fife. Wishart of Glasgow was taken in armour, and was barely saved from death by his sacred office. Lamberton of St Andrews was for long a prisoner, on a daily allowance of sixpence for himself, threepence for a servant, and three halfpence each for his footboy and his chaplain. Lamberton and Wishart wore fetters or some part of their detention.[46] The Abbot of Cupar had to subsist on the smaller allowance of fourpence for himself, and threepence to provide for a groom and a chaplain.

The Bishop of Moray, however, remained at liberty and was able to do so much for the cause of freedom in the north-east that the English commander at Falkirk reported, in 1307[47]:

> that Sir Robert de Brus never had the goodwill of his own followers or the people at large, or even half of them, so much with him as now ... and they firmly believe, by the encouragement of the false preachers who come from the host, that Sir Robert de Brus will now have his will.[48]

A hostile source thus bears witness to the presence of preachers with the Scottish army, and also makes it clear that these had added to their normal duties that of publicists for the cause among the people at large. The King of England also witnesses to this clerical activity. He complained bitterly to the Pope that the Bishop of Moray

> told them they were not less deserving of merit who rebelled with Sir Robert and his men, than if they should fight in the Holy Land against pagans and Saracens.[49]

It has been suggested that Walter Heroc, Dean of the Bishopric of Moray, and William de Crewsel, precentor to that diocese, were among the preachers of this Crusade against England.[50] But speculation whether this or that prelate supported the cause of Bruce is of little importance, for it is evident that the majority

of the clergy of every degree were firm in their sworn allegiance
to him.[51]

The years between his coronation and final victory saw many
changes in his fortunes. His army, for instance, was taken by
surprise and routed at Methven. Among the Scottish prisoners
was Hugh, chaplain to the Bruce. It is said that many of the
prisoners were put to death by the English and that the chaplain
was first to fall.[52] The long years of struggle reached the point
of decision in 1314, on the field of Bannockburn, and there is
ample evidence that the chaplains of the victors were not unworthy of their office or of the day.

The oldest and simplest account of the battle is that of 'Master
Johne Barbour', and he had no doubt of the presence and activity
of the Scottish priests. He tells how, in the period of preliminary
skirmishing,

> On [sonday than] in the mornying,
> Weill soyn eftir the sonne-Rising,
> Thai herd the meſs full reuerently,
> And mony schraf thaime deuotly,
> That thocht till de in that melle,
> Or than to mak thar cuntre fre,
> To god for thair richt prayit thai
> Thair dynit nane of thame that day,
> [Bot for] the vigill of sanct Johne,
> Thai fastit bred and water ilkone.[53]

Thus prepared, they came to the day of battle, and the tale
continues:

> The scottis men full deuotly
> Knelyt [all] doune, till god to pray,
> And a schort prayer thair maid thai
> To God, till help thame in that ficht
> And quhen the yngliſh king had sicht
> Of thame kneland, he said in hy—
> 'Zon folk knelis till ask mercy'
> Schir yngerame ſaid, 'Ze ſay ſuth now
> Thai ask mercy, bot nocht at zow.

For thair trefpafs to god thai cry.
I tell zow a thing sekirly,
That zon men will wyn all or de,
For dout of ded thar sall nane fle.'
'Now be it swa', than said the kyng,
We sall it se. ...'[54]

Another account of the battle, in *Scotichronicon*, tells how Maurice, Abbot of Inchaffray, celebrated Mass at an altar set up in the midst of the Scottish camp, and spoke words of encouragement to the soldiers. He then bore a Cross through the ranks and encouraged all to pray.[55] The presence of sacred relics at the field of Bannockburn may be presumed, but nothing is known for certain. The Brecbennoch may have been with the army, and the Quigrich, or Crozier of St Fillan, is said by Boece to have come there by miraculous means. Boece is not too reliable, even when he does not deal in miracles, so the matter of the relics must remain an open question.

Barbour's tale of the kneeling Scots is confirmed by the Chronicle of Lanercost, which says:

when the two armies had approached very near each other, all the Scots fell on their knees to repeat *Pater Noster*, commending themselves to God and seeking help from heaven after which they advanced boldly against the English.[56]

A modern historian holds that this evidence for the incident makes it a sober fact of history, and he reads into it:

the influence of those bishops and priests of the Church of Scotland who had made of the war a Holy War and had preached so untiringly, so ardently and so boldly, the sacred duty of resistance to England.[57]

None of the historians of this battle has suggested that the kneeling Scots 'kissed the ground', as a token partaking of the Sacrament, but it is possible that this was done. Such a custom was established before 1314, and is mentioned by several ancient chroniclers. It is discussed at some length by James Anson Farrer, in his *Military Manners and Customs*. According to this authority,

the custom of falling down and kissing the earth before starting
on a charge or a battle is mentioned several times in Montluc's
commentaries. He continues:

> but so little was it understood by a modern French editor
> that in one place he suggests the reading: *baissèrent la tête* (they
> lowered their heads) for *baisèrent la terre* (they kissed the
> earth). . . .

This kissing of the earth was an abbreviated form of taking
a particle of it in the mouth, as both Elham and Livius
mention to have been done by the English at Agincourt
before attacking the French; and this again was an abbreviated form of receiving the sacrament, for Villani says of the
Flemish at Cambray (1302) that they made a priest go all
over the field with the sacred elements, and that, instead of
communicating, each man took a little earth and put it in
his mouth.[58]

In the absence of definite evidence that the Scots did observe
this practice, it would be rash to suggest that the English at
Agincourt adopted it from their teachers at Bannockburn, along
with certain lessons in the tactical use of men and weapons.

The story of the army chaplains at this battle must include
some mention of Friar Baston. He was a Carmelite, who accompanied the English army with the specific task of producing a
poem in honour of the anticipated victory. By the fortunes of
war, Baston was among the captives brought before Bruce, to
have their ransoms assessed. He was valued at a poem, but it
must be written to exalt the Scottish triumph. The poem was
made, and it begins with a lament that such must be its theme.

> De planetu cudo metrum cum carmine nudo,
> Risum retrudo, dum tali themate ludo.

Lord Hailes is of the opinion that

> the unhappy poet had great part of the description of the
> battle ready made when he was taken prisoner. His poem is
> a most extraordinary performance, and must have cost him
> infinite labour.[59]

If Baston did compile his description of the battle before the event, it might account for his unsupported statements that calthorps and sharp stakes were used by the Scots. The struggle for Scottish freedom did not end with this victory, and the years that followed are full of fighting. The Church Militant is prominent again in such as the Bishop of Dunkeld who rallied the Scottish defenders at Inverkeithing, in 1317.[60] On the other side too, the Church provided military leaders, although the Archbishop of York was not successful in this role at the 'Chapter of Mytton'.[61, 62]

The successes and failures of the clergy as army commanders must give place to such facts as are known of their work as army chaplains. The scarcity of Scottish records compels reliance upon those of her neighbour and enemy, in the belief that they contain at least an indication of the conditions in the northern country. There is a Wardrobe Account of Roger de Waltham, which gives the rates of pay in the English army raised for the Scottish war by Edward II.

This begins:

> with the roll of the Welsh foot, who have divers officers not found in the Englifh corps, thefe are leaders, fub-leaders, chaplains, phyficians and cryers. The pay of the leader was 2s. per diem; the fub-leader, every efquire, centenary or commander of a hundred men and chaplain had 1s. per diem each. Phyficians 6d.[63]

Before the year 1348, however, some changes had been made in this list. The chaplain still had his shilling, in company with 'butlers, furgions, minftrellis', but the 'chaplines of welchmen', were valued at the lesser price of sixpence.[64] There were thus gradations of pay among the clergy with the army, the highest rate being paid to the Bishop of Durham, for he received six shillings and eightpence per day when present at the siege of Calais.[65]

It may have been one of the humble shilling-a-day chaplains who shared in the defence of Edward III, when the Scots raided his camp in 1327. The raiders achieved complete surprise, and had cut the ropes of the royal tent before the resistance of the king's attendants, including the chaplain, enabled their master to escape death or captivity. The chaplain, whom Hemmingford calls 'vir audax et armatus', was killed.[66]

Such bands of Scottish raiders had their own chaplains, and one of these was less worthy than this unknown hero. He seems to have done his best to delay and discourage his own army before the battle of Halidon Hill in 1333. The Chronicle of Lanercost describes the incident thus:

> Before the Scots army arrived at Berwick a certain monk who was in their company and had listened to their deliberations exclaimed in a loud voice—'Go ye no further but let us all turn back, for I behold in the air the crucified Christ coming against you from Berwick brandishing a spear.' But they, like proud and stubborn men, trusting in their numbers, which were double as many as the English, hardened their hearts and would not turn back.[67]

That his words were prophetic of defeat may have been a consequence, but scarcely a justification, of their utterance. Among those who fell in this battle was Hugh, Earl of Ross, although he was wearing that sacred relic, 'the shirt of St Duthac'. The English most honourably returned the relic to his family, influenced, perhaps, by its proved inefficacy.[68]

The Scots were again defeated at the battle of Neville's Cross, in 1346, by an army raised by the Archbishop of York, which included many ecclesiastics. The English clergy had, indeed, little chance of escaping service in the feudal armies. Three times in the reign of Edward III did a royal command declare that

> all men of our ſaid kingdom of England, as well clergy as laity, to wit, every man of them according to their ſtate, poſſeſſions and abilities, ſhould be armed and arrayed, to go forth, for the ſafety of the holy church and the ſaid kingdom, againſt our enemies, if any ſhall preſume to enter the ſaid kingdom.[69]

It is a little unkind of Grose to suggest that these reiterated commands were made necessary:

by ſome new contrivance of the clergy, to avoid the performance of their military ſervices by calling a convocation.[70]

Whether they came willingly or not, the clergy continue to
attend upon the armies of Scotland and England throughout the
troubled years of the fourteenth and fifteenth centuries. The
dress and deportment of these ecclesiastics must have varied
greatly, if we may judge by the repeated injunctions of the
Councils of the Church. These ordained that the rectors and
vicars of churches

> be marked by decency both in mind and outward attire, that
> they wear not garments of red, green or striped colours, nor
> garments that would attract attention by their excessive
> shortness . . . that no priest under pain of half a mark, carry
> the long knife known as a hangar [longum cultellum, qui
> vocatur hangar] except he be equipped for a journey.[71]

The level of spiritual teaching which they gave was surprisingly
high, and should not be judged by the prayer used by Scottish
raiders in plague-swept England:

> Gode and Sant Mungo, Saint Romayn and St Andrew,
> ſchield us this day fro Goddis grace [wrath?] and the foule
> death that Engliſhmen dien upon.[72]

Against such a prayer with its patriotic limitation of God's mercy,
not unknown in later days, must be set such a sermon as this:

> Ffor we bid and praye ishe day in holy churche—all maner
> of prestis and other men also—for to have pees. But the
> more harme is, we have evermore strives and debates, ishe
> man wel uye with other, that ther is no pees in herte. For
> no man loveth other. And outwardly we may knowe all
> that we ben in warre azeyns many londes on iche syde, and
> thai azeyns us.[73]

Such preachers of peace were given the protection of such
Articles for War as those made in 1385 to govern the Franco-
Scottish army of that year, or those made in 1390 by Richard II
of England. Such Articles declared

that none be ſo hardy as to rob and pillage the church nor
deſtroy any man belonging to the holy church, religious or
otherwiſe, nor any woman, nor to take them priſoners, if
not bearing arms, nor to force any woman on pain of being
hanged.[74]

The exception made of a cleric bearing arms would justify the
slaughter of the chaplain of Douglas at the battle of Otterburn in
1388. John Major, writing about 1521, tells the story in some
detail, and he adds a valuable comment on the military chaplain
of his own day.

Major says that Douglas fought his way deep into the ranks
of his enemies, and:

he was attended at the last by two of his company only,
that is, his squire, sir Robert Hert and a priest—sir William
who came from North Berwick, and who was accustomed
throughout the whole course of any war to stay by the side
of his lord, so that nought could move him from that place.
...Now that presbyter who...received himself three
mortal wounds, was archdeacon of Aberdeen. This priest
received the highest praise as a warrior. You must not
marvel that I have to relate such things of priests; for Britain
can show forty thousand priests who could be matched as
fighting men against a like number of men from any nation.
For every small laird has one chaplain, who is no despicable
soldier, and the great nobles have as many as five or six who
will gird on their sword and shield and go with their lords
to the field. Yet this is a fashion that I no way approve.
For inasmuch as their clerical office is of the Lord, they
should spend their time in divine worship and not in warfare.
Yet I do not deny that for their country, or to defend their
own lives, they may take up arms.[75]

There are two Statutes of Henry VIII which endorse this statement of the large number of chaplains attached to the gentry of
England in the sixteenth century. Section ii of 21 Henry VIII,
c. 13 (1529), authorises every archbishop and duke to have six
chaplains; every marquis and earl to have five; every viscount

and bishop to have four; the Chancellor of England and every baron and Knight of the Garter to have three; the Master of the Rolls to have two chaplains, and the Chief Justice of the King's Bench one chaplain. By a later statute, 25 Henry VIII, c. 16 (1533-4), the Judges of the King's Bench and Common Pleas, with the Chancellor and the Chief Baron of the Exchequer, the Attorney and the Solicitor General, may each have one chaplain.

Scotland could furnish many instances of such warrior-chaplains and one of these is sufficiently unusual to be deserving of mention.

In the year 1399, walter Danielſton, parſon of Kincardine O'Neil in Aberdeenshire, by ſome means took poſſeſſion of the caſtle of Dumbarton. Three years after, on the death of Trail, biſhop of St Andrews, ... Danielſton offered to ſurrender Dumbarton, if the ſee were aſſigned to him. The terms were accepted by Albany; but Danielſton only ſurvived this ſtrange tranſaction half a year.[76]

Such militant churchmen were, indeed, so common and so notorious that they were one of the objects of attack by the Reformer Wycliffe. He declared that

Friars now say that bishops can fight best of all men, and that it falleth most properly to them since they are lords of all this world. They say, Christ bade his disciples sell their coats, and buy them swords; but whereto, if not to fight?[77]

The storm of the Reformation was not to change the Church of Scotland for many a year to come, but there were signs of a change in the Army of Scotland. The feudal levies had obvious defects in a prolonged campaign, and a statute of James III, in 1482, hints at the beginnings of a 'Standing Army'. It called for garrisons to be raised for a chain of forts along the English Border, who were to be paid, 'two shillings and sixpence for every spear'.[78]

This tentative approach to a mercenary force may reflect something of the tension between the central government and the nobles of Scotland, which culminated in open war in 1488. James III, fleeing from the battle which ensued, was thrown from his horse. He was picked up and recognised by those who kindly sought a priest for the injured King.

It ſo chanced that ſome of the rebels were in the neighbour-hood, engaged in a diſorderly purſuit; and a prieſt, one of Lord Gray's followers as is ſaid, riding up, exclaimed, 'I am a prieſt, where is the king?' Being conducted to the place, he knew his ſovereign ... the prieſt, it is averred, heard his confeſſion; and then ſtabbed the unfortunate monarch, whoſe weakneſs deſerved a better fate than to fall a victim of a lawleſs ariſtocracy.[79]

With this deplorable instance of a chaplain-regicide, a point is reached in Scottish history of which some official record has survived. The earliest extant accounts of the Lord High Treasurer of Scotland deal with the period in which the revolt against the monarchy was crushed, and the authority of James IV established. For our purpose these Accounts show to what extent the clergy were called upon for assistance against the rebels. The latter had seized upon the Castle of Dumbarton, and, in April 1489, preparations were made by the central government to lay siege to this stronghold.

The Accounts for that month include:

Item to Mussche [the Royal messenger] to pass for the Bisschoppes of Sancttandros, Breyching, Dunblane, the Abot of Arbroytht, Dunfermeling, Lundoris and Scwne to cum to Dumbarton . . . . x s.[80]

On 4th December of that year another entry shows payments made to clergy and others for their attendance at the siege.

Item giffin the Chanchler for xvij dais wagis in Dumbartane for xxiiij personys	. .	xx li. viij s.
Item to the Master of Houshald	. . .	xx li. viij s.
Item to the Chamerlane	. . . .	xvij li.
Item to Lord Holefant	. . . .	viij li. x s.
Item to the Bischop of Glesgu	. .	x li. iiij s.

Item to the Priour of Sanctandros   .   .   x li. iiij s.
Item to the Bischop of Galway   .   .   .   v li. ij s.

A reasonable deduction from these items would suggest that
the Bishop of Glasgow and the Prior of St Andrews each provided twelve men, and the Bishop of Galway found six men, for
seventeen days' service at the siege of Dumbarton.[81]
This is a contribution to the very scanty information available
concerning the feudal duty due by the Prelates of Scotland to the
King, but it does not discover whether these dignitaries rendered
any spiritual service to the royal army. The Acts of the Lords in
Council of a later date imply that they had other than spiritual
tasks to perform. In the month of May 1523 the Lords commanded that

> lettres be writtin to requir the sprituale lordis quhiklis war
> requirit befor be lettres to cum her and come nocht nor send
> thai excus that thai cum to this toun of Edinburgh with thar
> houshaldis as mony as duellis on this syde Northesk the xxv
> day of May instant thar to remane for the spaice of xx days
> efter thar cuming thaim self to geif consall in the commoun
> materis and thar houshaldis bodin in fere of weir redy to
> defend the realm, under the pane of regognicioun of thar
> temporalitie that thai hold of the King.[82]

The Spiritual Lords, therefore, were expected to attend the
muster in person to give of their advice, while their attendants
augmented the ranks of the army.
    Some of the churchmen with the army at this time did much
more than give advice. One clerk, for example, received a
payment from the Royal Accounts, in 1494, for his work in
'making of the Kingis cartis for his gunnis'.[83] From the Accounts
we also learn of the portable Chapel belonging to James IV. It
is mentioned from time to time in connection with the 'tursing
of the gear'. It seems to have been complete even to an organ, or
what was then called a 'pair of organs', a small instrument sometimes known as 'regals' or 'portatives'.[84]
    The reign of James IV came to an end in the gallantry and folly

of the Battle of Flodden. The story has no place here except in regard to the presence of the Scottish clergy in the field. Pinkerton's list of the noble dead shows that the hierarchy were well represented. It begins:

> Le Roy d'Ecoſſe
> L'archeveque de ſainct Andrew
> L'eveque des Isles
> L'eveque de Katnes
> L'abbe d'Ynchaffraye
> L'abbe de Kilwenny
>
> . . . .
>
> . . . .
>
> . . . .
>
> Le Doyen de Glaſco.[85]

From other sources, however, we learn that the Bishop of Caithness did not fall at Flodden, he died in 1518.

The presence of the lesser clergy with the Scottish army is shown by Buchanan, in an attack upon the mendicant friars.

He declares that

the mendicant friars, then the most strictly religious species of monks, who had the money which those who fell in battle had deposited for security in their hands but having received it withour witnesses, they retained it, and becoming greatly enriched by this plunder, relaxed the severity of their ancient discipline.[86]

While the justness of this charge is open to some doubt, the fact that it could be made is a strong indication of the presence of the friars on the eve of the battle.

The minority which followed upon the death of the King at Flodden repeats the familiar pattern of baronial strife and intrigue, as the great lords, Albany, Angus and Arran, struggled for the possession of the young King and for power. The clergy played their part in such struggles, but there is little scope in these ignoble bickerings for the army chaplain. In this period the Abbot of Kelso is called upon to provision the 'fortalice of

Blacadir' by the Lords in Council.[87] Another prelate's 'clattering conscience' betrayed the armour beneath his peaceful garb.[88] The only clerk who might claim to have resembled an army chaplain was Johanes Cantaley, who travelled to and fro as an envoy between the camp of Albany and that of Dacre, the English general.[89]

But the duty of praying for the army was not neglected. The Lords in Council, in 1523, gave instructions that

> generall processioun to be maid and lettres to be direct therupon to all ordinaris that all kirkmen pas daly and the commone pepill that remanis at hame fra the host to pas and follow the saidis processiouns prayand for the stait and prosperite of my lord governour and the army and their returning with honour to this realm again.[90]

The common people may not have joined in these processions with much enthusiasm, for the repute of the clergy was low, and the call for reform in the Church was beginning to be heard.

The commencement of the Reformation struggles obviously confuses the question of army chaplaincy, and this seems a suitable point to consider and to summarise what has been uncovered of the work of the clergy with the feudal armies of Scotland.

One is tempted to take the easy line of division, and to say roundly that the activities of the clergy fell into two departments, the spiritual and the temporal. In the first would be all that pertains to the office of the priest, whether in peace or in war. The second category would comprise all the military service that the prelates owed to the crown, and all such service, as 'engineers' and 'ordnance officers', which the clerk was able to render. Such a division would be more simple than accurate, for the line between must needs be blurred by the prelates who did not forget to pray, and by those priests who came to pray and remained to fight.

Any generalisation on these early chaplains must also include the conception that so many of them were attached to the retinue of a particular superior, and that their duty to him came before any obedience to the King. This last was so notorious that there

c

was a proverb of the sixteenth century which said, 'Lyke Lorde, lyke chaplayne'.

Out of all this confusion of purpose and function the chaplain of the feudal army bequeathed certain things, good or bad, to his successors. First the traditional and unquestioned right to attend the army in the field.

Second, a limited loyalty to a territorial section of the army, from which sprang the regimental chaplaincy of a later day.

Third, a limited period of military duty, which was to yield slowly and reluctantly to a more efficient system of commissioned and professional service.

REFERENCES

1. *The Letters and Journals of Robert Baillie* (1841), Bannatyne Club, vol. i, p. 245.
2. J. A. Farrer, *Military Manners and Customs* (1885), p. 195.
3. Caesar, *De Bello Gallico*, vi.14.
4. John Dowden, *The Celtic Church in Scotland* (1894), p. 104.
5. Adamnan, *Life of St Columba*, Book 1, ch. i.
6. Bede, ii.2.
7. Joseph Anderson, *Scotland in Early Christian Times* (1881), pp. 240f.
8. Joannis de Fordun, *Scotichronicon*, cura Walteri Goodall (Edinburgh, 1859), vol. i, p. 203.
9. *Anglo Saxon Chronicle*, under date 1056.
10. A. O. Anderson, *Scottish Annals from English Chroniclers* (London, 1908), p. 82 n.
11. *Carmen de Morte Sumerledi*, Rolls Series, No. 75, vol. ii, pp. 386-8.
12. William Dodsworth, *An Historical Account of the Episcopal See and Cathedral Church of Salisbury* (1814), p. 20.
13. Sir David Dalrymple, Lord Hailes, *Annals of Scotland, 1057-1370* (1819), vol. i, pp. 84ff.
14. Cosmo Innes, *Sketches of Early Scotch History* (1861), p. 94.
15. *Concilia Scotiae* (Bannatyne Club), vol. i, pp. cciiif.
16. Fordun, *Scotichronicon*.
17. ibid.
18. *Calendar of Documents relating to Scotland*, vol. i, p. 668.
19. Matthew Paris, *Chronica Majora*, ed. H. R. Luard (1877), pp. 379f.:
     'qui omnis unanimis, confessi, et praedicantium consolatione, quis pro patris sua juste dimicaturi forent, animati, mori minime formidabant.'

20. Anderson, *Scotland in Early Christian Times*, p. 242.
21. *Proceedings of the Society of Antiquaries of Scotland*, vol. xii, pp. 134f.
22. Frisbok, *Hakon Hakon's son's Saga*, c. 327.
23. ibid., c. 328.
24. Patrick Abercromby, *The Martial Achievements of the Scottish Nation* (1762), vol. i, p. 400.
25. Frisbok, c. 337.
26. Andrew of Wyntoun, *The Orygynale Chronykil of Scotland*, ed. D. Laing (1872), the end of Bk. vii.
27. *The Chronicle of Lanercost*, ed. Sir Herbert Maxwell (1913), pp. 136f.
28. Hailes, *Annals*, vol. i, p. 297.
29. *Cal. Docs. relating to Scotland*, vol. iv, p. 448.
30. ibid. vol. ii, No. 742.
31. ibid., vol. ii, No. 822.
32. ibid., vol. ii, No. 825.
33. E. M. Barron, *The Scottish War of Independence* (1934), p. 27.
34. George Grub, *Ecclesiastical History* (1861), vol. i, p. 345.
    Francis Palgrave, *Documents and Records illustrating the History of Scotland* (1837), vol. i, p. 348.
35. *The Actis and Deidis of Schir William Wallace*, ed. by Wm. A. Craigie (1940), Fifth Book, p. 42.
36. ibid., Eighth Book, p. 105.
37. *Chronicle of Lanercost*, p. 139.
38. ibid., p. 140.
39. Francis Grose, *Military Antiquities* (1786/8), vol. i, pp. 274f.
40. *Cal. Docs. relating to Scotland*, vol. ii, No. 1132.
41. Hailes, *Annals*, vol. i, p. 380.
42. *Cal. Docs. relating to Scotland*, vol. ii, No. 1687.
43. ibid., vol. ii, No. 1580.
44. Hailes, *Annals*, vol. i, pp. 331f.
45. Sir Walter Scott, *The Lord of the Isles*, ii.31.
46. Hailes, *Annals*, vol. ii, p. 323.
47. *Cal. Docs. relating to Scotland*, vol. ii, No. 1814.
48. Barron, *War of Independence*, p. 265.
49. ibid., p. 378.
50. ibid., p. 269.
51. Hailes, *Annals*, vol. ii, p. 40.
52. Robert Kerr, *History of Scotland during the reign of Robert I* (1811), vol. i, p. 222.
53. *The Bruce compiled by Master John Barbour*, ed. by W. W. Skeat (1870, 1889), Book xi, lines 374ff.
54. ibid., Book xii, lines 476ff.
55. Fordun, *Scotichronicon*, vol. ii, p. 250.
56. *The Chronicle of Lanercost*, p. 207.

57. Barron, *War of Independence*, pp. 461f.
58. Farrer, *Military Customs*, pp. 201f.
59. Hailes, *Annals*, vol. ii, p. 67.
60. Barbour, *The Brus*, c. cxx.
61. ibid., c. cxxix.
62. *Chronicle of Lanercost*, pp. 226f.
63. Grose, *Military Antiquities*, vol. i, pp. 277f.
64. ibid., p. 279.
65. ibid., p. 278.
66. Hailes, *Annals*, vol. ii, pp. 280f.
67. *Chronicle of Lanercost*, pp. 280f.
68. John Major, *History of Greater Britain* (1892), Scottish History Society, p. 273.
69. Grose, *Military Antiquities*, vol. i, p. 67.
70. ibid., vol. i, p. 5.
71. Hume Brown, *Scotland before 1700* (1893), p. 1.
72. John Pinkerton, *History of Scotland* (1797), vol. i, p. 20 n.
73. G. R. Owst, *Literature and Pulpit in Medieval England* (1933), pp. 563f.
74. Grose, *Military Antiquities*, pp. 64f.
75. Major, *History*, pp. 321f
76. Pinkerton, *History*, vol. i, p. 174.
77. Robert Vaughan, *Life of Wycliffe* (1831), vol. ii, pp. 212f.
78. Pinkerton, *History*, vol. i, p. 301.
79. ibid., vol. i, pp. 334f.
80. *Accounts of the Lord High Treasurer for Scotland*, Record Series, Edinburgh, 1877-1907, vol. i.
81. ibid., vol. i, p. 125.
82. *Acts of the Lords in Council*, May 1523.
83. *Treasurer's Accounts*, passim.
84. ibid., p. ccxxxii.
85. Pinkerton, *History*, Appendix.
86. G. Buchanan, *Rerum Scoticarum Historis*, trans. J. Aikman (1827), vol. ii, p. 257.
87. *Acts of the Lords in Council*, March 1517/18.
88. Pinkerton, *History*, vol. ii, p. 182.
89. ibid., vol. ii, p. 208.
90. *Acts of the Lords in Council*, 15 October 1523.

II

DURING THE REFORMATION

D URING the reign of James V the prelates of Scotland
grew more fiercely militant as the Reformation gained
ground in England. They endeavoured to secure the
willing service, even on the battlefield, of all churchmen, and, to
this end, they caused the re-enactment of an old law. This
secured to the next of kin of any incumbent the disposal of the
benefice, if the incumbent

> beis slane or hurt to deid in defence of the realme in resisting
> or persute of our auld inymys of Ingland or deis be seknes
> taikin be thame in the army during the tyme of this present
> weire.[1]

With this guarantee, which showed more consideration for the
heir than for the benefice, the clergy joined that expedition which
ended ingloriously at Solway Moss. This debacle was followed
by the death of James V, and Scotland entered upon yet another
period of minority rule, complicated by foreign intervention and
by religious schism.

The ancient enmity of England and France, now intensified by
religious difference, made the help of Scotland not merely desirable but essential for both of these powers.

Scotland was divided as between England and France, but the
majority of the clergy were united in opposition to heretical
England. Meeting in a Convention, in 1543, they bound themselves to raise large sums for the prosecution of the war, and
declared themselves willing, if need be, to take the field in person.

The English found that this was no mere form of words when they attacked Kelso Abbey, for it was held against them for a long time by a garrison which included a number of monks.[1] The great Scottish castles were also garrisoned at this time, and the Treasurer's Accounts show that payments were made to the chaplains of Edinburgh and Hamilton.[3]

The growing danger that a divided Scotland might fall a prey to the English army induced France to send troops to reinforce her sympathisers. A proportion of these were themselves Scots, including Archers of the 'Garde du Roy de Franche'.[4]

A period of ascendancy for the French party, and the clergy, followed upon this reinforcement, and Cardinal Beaton thought the time ripe to burn out the disease of heresy, in such plague spots as Perth and Dundee. The heretics retaliated vigorously and not less brutally, by murdering the Cardinal at his Castle at St Andrews

These conspirators, for their own safety, retained possession of that castle, and were joined by many well-wishers as they prepared to stand siege. This regiment, or garrison, has been held up to execration by Bishop Keith, who declared that

> the besieged, notwithstanding their pretences to a more pure worship, have during the siege lived in such debauchery within the castle, so now, after they have got this respite, and were out of all fear of an enemy, they did not only make frequent excursions into the neighbouring parts, and commit depredations with fire and sword; but, as if the liberty got by their arms were to be spent in whoredoms, adulteries and such like vices, they ran into all the wickedness which idle persons are subject to, and they measured *right* and *Wrong* by no other rule than their own lust.[5]

But this black picture is not, and could not be, the whole truth, for John Rough and Henry Balnaves were preachers to this garrison, and they would not condone such conduct by their silence. It may be claimed that these two were the first Scottish Protestant army chaplains, and that they set a very high standard for those who came after. Rough was destined to glorify God in the flames at Smithfield, and Balnaves withstood every attempt upon his fidelity in France.

There was another chaplain to the castle and his fame is world wide, the great leader of the Scottish Reformation, John Knox. He has himself told how

> thei of the place, but especiallie Maister Henry Balnaves and Johne Rowght, preacher, perceaving the manner of his doctrin, begane earnestlie to travaill with him, that he wold tack the preaching place upoun him. But he utterlie re-fuissed. . . .[6]

Then, at the close of a sermon on the election of ministers, Rough turned upon Knox, and cried, 'I charge yow, that ye refuise not this holy vocationn.' John Knox fled from the kirk in tears, but was eventually persuaded to accept the call to office. He continued of the company and shared their fate of imprisonment when the Castle fell.[7] The clerical party had crushed this rising against their authority, but they were faced with a greater danger when an English army moved against them and their French allies.

The clergy came into the field once more with the Scottish levies, and James Grant describes a regiment of more than one thousand monks, who were

> drawn forth to battle in fear of the English Reformation spreading into Scotland more than it had done. Save their armour, which was generally black, they wore white, grey or red surcouts, with crosses, to distinguish them as Black, Grey or Red Friars.[8]

The attendance of the clergy in such very large numbers may have been due to zeal for the cause, but those who ordered the levy did not trust entirely to such a motive. They made assurance doubly sure by sending forth letters

> charging all kirkmen to cum fordward to the army and be in Edinburgh ultimo Augusti under the panys of tynsale of their benefices.[9]

This warning, coupled with the renewal of the Act which secured to the next of kin the disposal of the benefice of any that should die in the campaign, helped to speed the laggards and to confirm the waverers to battle for the faith.[10] In spite of the help of the clerical regiment the Scots were beaten at the battle of Pinkie Cleugh.

One of the best accounts of this campaign and battle is that of W. Patten, a Londoner. He does not seem[11] to have served as a chaplain to the English army although he dates his book from the Parsonage of St Mary Hill. This book is so revealing of its period that no apology seems to be required for quoting from a discussion in a humorous vein, upon a Saint's Day.

> This dai is markt in y' kalendar with the name of ſaincte Gorgon, no famous ſaint ſure, but eyther ſo obſcure that no man knowes him, or els ſo aunciente as every man forgettes him.

Patten feels that, out of his knowledge of the classics, he might do something to lighten this darkness, were it not that he has some doubt whether this saint is masculine, feminine or neuter. The neuter saints, it would seem, are such as St Christmas, St Candlemas, and, 'ſwete ſainct Sunday y' comes ones a weke'. If this saint is the lady with the serpentine locks, she musts needs be feminine, but if the object of veneration be the shield of the sequel, then the saint must be neuter.[12]

The humorist appears less pleasantly on another occasion in his tale. He describes the building of a great fire at the mouth of a cave in which some Scots were hiding. The smoke poured into the cave

> with ſo great a force & for ſo long a while that we could not but thinke they must nedes get them out or ſmoother within, and forasmuch as we found not that they did the tone, we thought it for certain thei wear ſure of the tother.[13]

His diary gives only one glimpse of a chaplain in action, and that is more militant than spiritual in context. He tells us that the Scots made one attack that was almost successful, but had they kept on, they wear prouided for accordingly, for one parſon Keble, a chaplain of his graces, and two or three oother, by and by diſcharged foure or fyve of the cartes of municion and thearwith beſtowed pykes, billes, bowes and arrowes to as many as came, ſoo that of carters and other thear wear ſoon weaponed thear about a thousand, whoom parſon Keble and the oother dyd very handſomly diſpoſe in array, and made a prety mouſter.[14]

Patten also confiems the presence of Scottish clergy at the battle, and that numbers of them were slain. He says:

a banner of whyte ſarcenet was found under whiche it was ſayd theſe kirkmen cam, whearupon was paynted a wooman with her hair about her ſhoulders, knelynge before a crucifix, and on her right hande a church, after that written a long upon the baner in greate Romane letters, 'Afflictae ſpouſae ne obliuiſcaris', whiche wordes declared that they would haue this wooman to ſignifie, the Churche Christes ſpouſe. ... It was ſayd it was the abbot of Donformling's Banner, but whuther yt wear his or the Biſſhop of Dunkels, y' goovernours broothers (who I understood wear both in the felde). And what the number of theſe kirkmen was, I could not certainly learne.[15]

This defeat left the Scots without an effective army, though sporadic fighting continued. Moreover there was an increasingly strong party within Scotland who would rather see England victorious than that the party of the Queen Mother, the French and the reactionaries should continue to dominate the land. The Queen Mother was warned by Methven that

part of the legis has tayn new apoynsionis of the scriptour and has don agen the law and ordinance of holy kirk.[16]

These new opinions were spreading fast, preached by many mouths, including that of Knox, returned from his French imprisonment. He was, for a time, employed in the ministry at Berwick on Tweed, and had the garrison there as part of his charge. In 1561 he told the Queen of Scots about his sojourn in that town, and said:

> God so blissed my waik laubouris, that in Berwick (whair commonlie befoir their used to be slauchter be reasone of quarielis that used to aryse amongis soldartis) thair was as great quyetnes, all the tyme that I remaned thair, as thair is this day in Edinburgh.[17]

This was not the only service of John Knox as a military chaplain, for he was one of the preachers to that army which was organised in Scotland to further the cause of the Reformed religion. One of the Frenchmen then in the country confirms the presence of preachers in this 'rebel' army which followed the Lords of the Congregation:

> Ilz disent que c'est pour la réligion, et de faict ilz ont des prédicateurs avec eulz.[18]

Many years later, in the course of a sermon to the Lords, Knox spoke with pride of his services in the field.

> In your most extreame dangearis I have bein with you: Sanct Johnestoun, Cowper Mure, and the Craiggis of Edinburgh, ar yitt recent in my heart; yea, that dark and dolorouse nyght whairin all ye, my lordis, with schame and feare left this toune, is yitt in my mynd; and God forbid that ever I forgett it.[19]

That the conditions under which this service was rendered was sufficiently arduous can be shown from his own description of the skirmishing in Fife.

> For twentie and ane dayis thei lay in thair clothes; thair buttis never come of; thei had skarmissing almost everie day; yea, some dayis from morne to evin.[20]

The Regent's troops continued to be well supplied with clergy, and, on one occasion, their reinforcements from France were predominantly ecclesiastical. For,

> on the 19th September [1559], there arrived in Scotland, Nicolas de Pelue, Bishop of Amiens, together with three

French Doctors of Divinity, and Monsieur la Brosse, a
military person.[21]

These clergymen were expected to win back the Scots into the
fold of the mother Church by learned argument, but, finding
this task beyond their powers, they contented themselves with
the less onerous duty of instructing the Scots clergy in the better
performance of the ritual, in churches ceremonially purged of
the taint of heresy.

It might be said that the church of St Giles required to be
purged of more than heresy, for it had been used as a workshop
for the manufacture of scaling ladders, by the order of the Lords
of the Congregation. This was done

> to the great displeasure of the preachers, who affirmed that
> they dreaded the success of that enterprise, which began by
> such irreverence put upon the places where people ought to
> convene to common prayers and preaching, and that God
> could not suffer such contempt to go long unpunished.[22]

The chaplains to this Protestant army had also to deplore the
attitude of some of the rank and file, who were not paid regularly
and were inclined to transfer their service to any better paymaster.
Knox complains that

> The men of warr (for the maist parte wer men without God
> or honestie) made a mutiney, becaus thai lacked a parte of
> thair waiges; Thei had done the same in Lynlythqu befoir,
> quhair thei maid a proclamatioun, 'That thei wald serve any
> man to suppress the Congregatioun, and sett up the Messe
> agane.[23]

The chaplains of this army had, therefore, enough to do. They
had to rebuke the shortcomings of both high and low, and had
to inspire and encourage the whole force to continue the long
struggle. John Knox performed the latter task when he preached
at Stirling, in November 1559. He took for his text some verses
of the 'Fourscoir Psalme', beginning:

> O thow the Eternall, the God of hostis, how long shall thow
> be angree against the prayer of thy people?

From this text he preached the discipline of Providence, declaring, however, that in their early days of weakness they had trusted in God, but that latterly they had begun to reckon the number of spears their noble recruits could bring to their aid, and had not called on God as formerly. By such sermons were 'the myndis of men wounderouslye to be erected'.[24]

The numbers of those who preached to this army were increasing, for they now included John Willock, later to be Superintendent of the West, and, indeed, all of the clergy who were to become the Protestant ministers of Scotland. There was possibly one exception, 'Christopher Gudman, quha the maist pairt of the trubillis had remanit in Ayre'.[25]

The arrival of strong reinforcements from England compelled the French party to retire to the Castle of Edinburgh and the town of Leith, in both of which they had the services of their own clergy. In the words of the 'Diurnal of Occurrents':

> Vpoun the firſt day of Apryle the zeir of God abonementionet, Marie quene regent paſt from Halyrudhous to the caſtell of Edinburgh, thair to remayne induring the ſeige following, accumpanyit with Johne archbiſchope of Sanctandros, the biſchopes of Dunkell and Dumblane. The commendatare of Halyrudhous, the archbiſchope of Glaſgow and George lord Seytoun, paſt to Leith with monſoieur Doſſell Labroſche, the compt Marlis and the biſchope of Amiance, and thair remanit the haill tyme of the ſeige thairof.[26]

This campaign ended, at last, in peace and in the withdrawal of both French and English troops. Peace endured for the opening years of personal rule of Mary, Queen of Scots, but, in 1565, some of the nobles rose in rebellion against her. John Knox was careful on this occasion to avoid any commitment with them, and the 'Runabout Raid' as it was called came to nothing. The Raiders had the support of one clergyman, at least, for Robert Hamilton, who held the Rectory of Torrens, was accused of

> being a follower of the Duke of Chattelherault and concerned with him in the Earl of Moray's rebellion.[27]

The Queen had dealt with this attempt with skill and success, but her continued follies built up an opposition which compelled her surrender at Carberry Hill, and her entry into virtual imprisonment for life.

The one brief period of liberty she enjoyed, after her escape from Lochleven Castle, brought armies into the field in Scotland once more. The majority of the ministers were ranged against her, and would have echoed the words of Knox:

> We see a wicked woman, whose iniquity known and lawfully convict, deserved more than ten deaths, escaped from prison ... if she had suffered, according as God's law commandeth, 'murtheris and adulterers to die the death' ... the plague would have ceased.[28]

There was a minority among the ministers, however, composed of those who, from motives of affection or interest, still maintained that Mary was the Queen of Scots, and some of them were active on her behalf. One of these was Thomas Hepburn, parson of Oldhamstocks, who was not content to act as a chaplain to her army, but attempted a *coup de main*. A letter to Sir William Cecil declares:

> Upon Monday, Dunbar was like to have been surprised; for at one instant there arrived into the town the Parson of Auld Hamstock with a xx, and as many sent from Lord Hume; but the town more affected to the Lord Hume increased his strength so much, that the Parson desisted from his enterprise and so returned.[29]

Hepburn had been active in arranging for the marriage of Mary and Bothwell, and he was one of the three 'servants of Bothwell' for whom search was being made in Edinburgh, when the Casket of letters was found. The Parson was forfeited for 'certayne crymes of treason', and was later discharged from the ministry for heresy.[30]

Others of the clergy also took the Queen's part in the civil war, though in a less combatant manner. Nine titular bishops were among those who signed her bond after her escape, although these may not have performed any duty as chaplains to her army. Claude Nau implies that there were Protestant preachers present with her army before the battle of Langside. He says that when the force was assembling near Hamilton Castle:

> some of the 'sectarian' lords who were on her side tried to persuade her that since the external profession and worship of the Catholic religion was not permitted to her, she should choose one of the ministers of 'the sect' (as the expression is), and should be present at the sermons and prayers which he recited according to the custom. They assured her that this would be good policy; for not only would it show that she followed some definite form of religion, but would also draw to her side many from the opposite faction, who were opposed to her on no other grounds than religion.[31]

He goes on to say that the Queen rejected this suggestion, so that it is unlikely that she attended the services of such as Archibald Hamilton, vicar of Kilbirnie, who was forfeited 'for joining his kinsmen in defence of Queen Mary'.[32]

The utter defeat of the Queen's army at Langside drove her to flight and to life-long imprisonment in England, but the peace of Scotland was still to be troubled by the rivalries of Kingsmen and Queensmen for years to come.

The powerful family of Hamilton were partisans of the Queen and several clergymen of that name were involved in the struggle on her behalf. For example, John Hamilton, parson of Dunbar, appears in the guise of a 'gun-runner', bringing munitions of war from Spain to the Earl of Huntly.[33]

Another Hamilton, the Archbishop of St Andrews, was one of those taken prisoner when Dumbarton Castle was taken for the King. He was executed for complicity in the murder of Darnley. These, and their kinsfolk, may have been chaplains to the party of the Queen, in addition to their concern for affairs military and political. They are, however, of less importance here than those clergy of the Reformed church who refused to serve the Regent Lennox as chaplains to his army. They gave him their reasons for this refusal in 1571:

We doubt not but your grace and honourable counsall, has found and findis fault with us, that we have bene absent fra the kingis service in our awin persones, at thir appointit quarteris at Leith, whair intill our awin conscience vald accuse us, onles we had a sufficient defence afoir God and man: which is that we dare not ioyne our selves in hasarde with the professed enemies of Christis Evangle. We call not onlie such as by oppin hostilitie makis warre against the frie preaching of the same, (as now a dayis the traytoris that occupie the castle and towne of Edinburgh), but enemies to Christ Jesus, we call all such as directlie or indirectlie, goe about to deface the ministrie of his blissed evangle, of which cryme, in our conscience, we neather can nor dare excuse your grace, nor yet your counsall.

The letter continues with specific charges against the Regent, of his efforts to bridle the pulpit, of his literal starvation of the ministers, and of his presentations to benefices, by which

courteor's babes, and persones vnable to guyde them selves, are promoted be you to sic benefices as requyre learned preachoris.[34]

The death of Lennox and the succession of Mar to the regency did something to heal this breach, and some ministers were on active service with the army in its long assault upon the town and castle of Edinburgh. When a truce was arranged in 1572 many of the citizens were able to return in triumphal procession to their homes within the walls:

As they come into the toun, Jhone Brand, minister, and ane that feared God and the kingis actions, being in the formest ranke as they enterit the portes, heaving on his govne, and a byble vnder his oxster, and Jhone Durie, exhortare in Leyth, and a good suddart of God and the kingis, cuming behind with his armour and callevere vpon his shulder; one of Edinburgh sayes to Jhone Brand, what meanis this? ye cum with your govne, and a buke vnder your oxster, and Jhone Durie with his callever, and two dagis at his belt;

Jhone Brand answeris, it meanes we cum to offer peax, whilk gif ye refuse, ye shall have weir.[35]

John Durie and his 'callever' could be matched in the other party by equally militant clergy. Thus:

> about this time a Frenchman called Sorbie arrived with ſome money from the Duke of Alva, which Mr Andrew Douglas, Parſon of Dunglas, conveyed ſafely in a Freare of Figs to the Caſtle of Edinburgh. This Prieſt for meddling in State Affairs, and dipping his fingers in the Civil Diſh, came but very foul off; for being taken by the Aſſociators, his name-ſake Morton handled him pretty roughly.[36]

When the Castle fell at length to the King's army, some 3,000 cannon shot were found among its ruins, and the Prior of Cold-ingham and the Bishop of Dunkeld were made prisoners among the garrison. These clerics must have taken part in the services held during the siege in the church of the Castle, which stood on the north side of the Grand Parade, and which continued in use until the middle of the eighteenth century.

The fall of the Castle brought to an end any real hope of success for the Queen's party, but under the grasping rule of the Regent Morton strife broke out again. This was aimed at the overthrow of the Regent, and the rebel leaders appealed to the ministers for their countenance.

On 12th August 1578:

> The quhilk day, the Brethren of the Exercyiss of Edinburgh beand convenit with the Commissioner of Lowthiane, hering the ernist suitt of the Lordis laitlie departit out of this Toun to haif ane minister, has appointit their brethren, Johne Brand and Mr Thomas McGye, or ony ane of thame, to pass unto the saidis Lordis, according to thair desyir; willing thame to travell nocht onlie in preiching of the word, but also in persauding, alsweill thame as the parttie in Striviling, to concord and unitie, seing thai aught to be preichers of peace to all parteis.[37]

The letter which commissions these chaplains to the army is surely of some historic importance. It shows the Reformed church accepting a responsibility for the spiritual oversight of the Army, and it created a precedent for the supplying of such chaplains through the Courts of the Church.

The occasion for the service of these chaplains was soon over, but the intriguing for power in the land continued, until it culminated in the Ruthven Raid which wrecked the pro-France schemes of D'Aubigny. The Raid was cautiously approved by the ministers of the Church, and the new government did something to redress their grievances in return for this support. In 1583 the young King escaped from the Raiders and the leaders of the Church had to flee the country and his royal vengeance.

Many of the nobility of Scotland also had to make their escape into England, where they gathered in the northern counties. The fugitive clergy joined them there and an unusual field for the service of chaplains was seen and developed. James Melvill, nephew of the great Andrew Melvill, leader of the Church and also in exile, tells in his diary of his work in the north of England at this time.

He had escaped from Scotland, 'in an open little bott', and had rowed, himself, 'till the hyd cam aff my fingers'.[38]

When he reached Newcastle, he had the intention of continuing his journey southward,

> but Mr Jhone Davidsone, being ther with the Lords informes me sa in all maters . . . that I sould abyd with the Noblemen exerceising tham in the Word of God, till that ather they all, or sum of tham at least sould returne back againe.[39]

Melvill consented to undertake this duty, and he at once drew up for them an Order of Instruction, of which the strictness may be judged from the first clause.

> First, Ther shalbe four Sermones in the ouk; twa on Sonday, and twa on the ouk-dayes: one before noone, and an uther efter, on the Sabothe: and, on the ouk-dayes, an on Wednisday and an uther on Fredday.[40]

D

To make certain that this spiritual discipline was enforced, he arranged for the appointment of Elders and Deacons, and for the noting of any who should absent themselves from these diets of worship. Melvill was later relieved from this duty by another exiled minister, Mr Patrick Galloway, when he removed to Berwick and then to London. In 1585 it suited the policy of Queen Elizabeth of England to permit these exiles to march into their own land once more, and the invading force carried its chaplains home in its ranks. James Melvill was not with the army but he says that they were accompanied by:

> my uncle Mr Andro, Mr Patrick Galloway, and Mr Walter Balcanqual.

And:

> marching fordwart with diligence cam to St Ninian's Kirk, a myll from Sterling, upon the first day of November, and ther camped to the number of ten thousand horsemen.[41]

This display of strength was sufficient and another new government was set up. The jockeyings for power continued but rarely developed into open warfare, but when armies did assemble the clergy companied with them. This was true of the battle of Balrinnes or Glenlivet, in 1594, where the Earl of Argyll opposed the Catholic lords, Errol and Huntly. Argyll had with him 'Neill Campbell, Bishope of Argyle, and two preachers', and his opponents took, for their signal to charge, the cry 'The Virgin Mary'.

It is said too, that the latter

> went to their deuotion, in confessing and receauing the Sacrament, and according to the custom of that profession they hallowed theyr arms and enseiyns.

Argyll suffered a sharp defeat, and the victors

> all with theyr priest gaue God thanks in that solemn song Te Deum Laudamus, offring in one and the same place, as upon ane altar, double sacrifice of blood and thanksgiving.[42]

The King was reluctant to march against the northern Earls, but his hand was forced by this battle and he had to show some measure of activity. James Melvill tells how and why some ministers were included in the royal army.

The King, with companies of horsemen and futtmen under wages, by [forbye] the comoun forces gathered be pro- clamation, past Northe against these rebelles, whom my uncle Mr Andro and I, with uthers of the ministerie accom- panied also at his Majestie's desyre, to bear witness of his peanes and sevear proceidings against these, because the peiple war yit gealous over the King for his knawin and kythet [manifest] favour to the Erle of Hontlie.[43]

From this expedition James Melvill was sent back to Edinburgh by the King, to raise more money to pay the troops, and carried with him a letter to the ministers of that city from those who accompanied the army, which was signed by:

A. Meluile
Mr. P. Gallouay
Ja. Nicolson.[44]

The royal demonstration in force achieved its object and the rebel earls fled the country without a trial of strength.

A more persistent troubler of the peace of this reign was Francis, Earl Bothwell, and he had the assistance of at least one chaplain.

This was Andrew Hunter, minister of Newburn, in the Pres- bytery of St Andrews. In 1594 the King demanded that the General Assembly excommunicate him, for deserting his flock to become a chaplain to the rebel Earl of Bothwell.

The General Assembly replied cautiously that as Mr Hunter

was declarit the Kings rebell, and according to the costume was put to the horne, they thought necessar to depose him of his functioun, till he had bayth satisfeit the Kings Majestie and the Kirk for that fault; and found, be thair generall reasoning and common vottis, that they could not decerne him to be excommunicat.[45]

It was suggested that the ministers secretly approved of Hunter's rebellious exploits, and a contemporary account goes even further. This anonymous History declared that the English ambassador

> tampers for Bothwell, (the immediate end of his errand), deals with the *Ministers*, the most especial among them to countenance his fresh Insurrection with numbers of loose persons; and, which troubled the King, they commend *Andrew Hunter*, one of their own, to be Bothwell's Chaplain in Ordinary. And being thus emboldened they go to raise Moneys themselves, levy Souldiers, to assist his Treasons.[46]

It may be that others should share responsibility for Hunter's treason, but he had to bear the punishment of life-long exile. He became chaplain to a regiment of Scots in the service of Holland, and will be noticed again in that capacity.

Another minister was involved with Bothwell, whose parish is not known. This was John Ross, who preached before the Synod of Perth a sermon in which he attacked the King for his too great friendliness toward the wicked. He was summoned to appear before King James, and attempted to escape, and was caught

> north of Burntisland disguised with a plaid, a bonnet and two dags, without breeches, as one suspected of going to join Bothwell.[47]

Gradually the King's peace was established throughout the whole of Scotland, even the Highlands, Islands and the Borders, the 'peccant parts' of the kingdom, being brought to some degree of order. The chaplain with one expedition to the Western Isles, in 1608, played an astute but unworthy part in its success. Some of the chiefs would not give the pledges of good conduct that the King required of them. Lord Stewart of Ochiltree, who was in command

> be the awyſs of the Biſchop of the Yllis, callit Mr Andro Knox, callis thame into ane ſermond in the Kingis ſchip

callit the Mone, quhair efter the ſame, he mowit thame to dyne. Bot in end, he ſayes to thame, that thay moſt ſtay, becaus the ſame was his Maieſties will; and taking up ſaill, bringis thame with him . . . to Edinburgh.[48]

One is tempted to cap this story of a treacherous Scottish chaplain with that of the English cleric who was the chaplain of a pirate ship captured in the Orkneys in 1610.

His duty included the saying of prayers to them twice a day, but both his nationality and the naval nature of his service rule him out.[49]

Scotland and England being now under the rule of the same king, the little-known Articles for War which were published in 1627 may be taken as applying in general to the northern kingdom. These Articles do not seem to have been known to Grose, having been found by Captain Bullock filed among the Naval Papers of the reign of Queen Elizabeth. The First and Second of these Articles are as follows:

1. He that ſhall take God's name in vain or blaſpheme God ſhall for the Firſt offence in that kind, be kept three days in Priſon with Bread and water, and for the ſecond time of offending ſo, ſhall have a hot iron thruſt through his tongue and be ſtripped to his ſhirt and ſo Baniſht the Army.

2. The like penalty ſhall be inflicted upon thoſe who ſhall either ſay or do aught in diſpite or deriſion of God's word or the Miniſters of God.[50]

In spite of the care shown here for the 'Ministers of God', there does not seem to have been any serious attempt to provide the royal army of that day with chaplains. This is implied by Richard Bernard, Rector of Batcombe, Somersetshire, in his book *The Bible-Battels or the Sacred Art Military*, published in 1629. It is his avowed intention to give guidance 'for the rightly wageing of warre according to Holy Writ', and he regards as essential the providing of the army with ministers.

It is no queſtion but Miniſters may go into the wars, its neceſſary to have men of good gifts to preach to ſouldiers,

but they muſt be good and conſcionable to give example,
zealous in reproving and gratious in prayer, that as *Moſes* did,
while the other fight, they may pray, and help forward the
victory. If ſuch were in a Campe and reverenced, the Armie
would proſper the better.

He continues by giving instances from biblical and European
history of the presence of priests with the army, and continues:

> The *Spaniards* have their Prieſts with them and doe punish
> thoſe that in word or deed doe offer them iniury. Why
> ſhould our Armies goe forth without good Teachers?[51]

This would seem to indicate that, in the transition from the feudal
levy to the standing army, the office and function of the army
chaplain was in danger of disappearance. The rival armies of the
Civil War, calling for every 'fencible man' in the land, reversed
this tendency and established the chaplain as an accepted part of
the army thereafter.

Before entering upon the turmoils of that period, however,
the contribution of the Reformation struggle to our study must
be summarised.

First, the Reformed Church of Scotland accepted the necessity
for the attendance of ministers upon the army, at least as early as
1578, and established a precedent that such ministers should be
appointed by the Courts of the Church.

Second, the appointment by James Melvill, in 1584, of Elders
to manage the Kirk discipline of the exiled Scots in England
suggests the beginnings of the practice of having a Kirk Session
in every Scottish regiment, at home or overseas. It is to the
Scottish regiments abroad that we must now turn, for they
maintained the tradition of Presbyterian chaplains during the
early years of the seventeenth century.

REFERENCES

1. *Acts of the Lords in Council*, January 1532/3.
2. *Concilia Scotiae* (Bannatyne Club, 1866), vol. i, p. cxliii.
3. *Treasurer's Accounts*, vol. viii, pp. 240 and 290.

4. *The Scottish Correspondence of Mary of Lorraine*, Scottish History Society, pp. 70 n. and 81.

5. Robert Keith, *History of the Affairs of Church and State in Scotland* (1845), vol. i, p. 127.

6. John Knox, *The History of the Reformation in Scotland*, ed. David Laing (Edinburgh, 1846), vol. i, p. 186.

7. ibid., vol. i, p. 187.

8. James Grant, *British Battles*, vol. i, p. 138.

9. *Treasurer's Accounts*, vol. ix, p. 110.

10. Keith, *Affairs*, vol. i, p. 131.

11. W. Patten, Londoner, *The Expedicion into Scotlande of the most worthely fortunate prince Edward, Duke of Somerset* etc. (1548), not numbered.

12. ibid.

13. ibid.

14. ibid.

15. ibid.

16. *Correspondence of Mary of Lorraine*, p. 241.

17. Knox, *History*, vol. ii, p. 280 and n.

18. Quoted in Agnes M. Mackenzie, *The Scotland of Queen Mary* (1936), p. 100.

19. Knox, History, vol. ii, p. 384.

20. ibid., vol. ii, p. 9.

21. Keith, *Affairs*, vol. i, pp. 227f.

22. ibid., vol. i, p. 241.

23. Knox, *History*, vol. i, p. 453.

24. ibid., vol. i, pp. 465f.

25. ibid., vol. ii, p. 87.

26. *Diurnal of Occurrents* (Bannatyne Club, 1833), vol. ii, pp. 729f.

27. Hew Scott, *Fasti Ecclesiae Scoticanae* (1869), vol. ii, p. 291.

28. Keith, *Affairs*, vol. iii, p. 199, and Calderwood, *History*, vol. ii, pp. 481f.

29. Keith, *Affairs*, vol. ii, p. 803.

30. *Fasti*, vol. i, p. 376.
T. F. Henderson, *The Casket Letters* (1889), pp. 113f.
British Museum, fol. 216, Add. MSS. 32,091.

31. Claude Nau, *The History of Mary Stewart*, ed. James Stevenson (1883), p. 168.

32. *Fasti*, vol. ii, p. 170.

33. *Diurnal of Occurrents*, pp. 184f.

34. Richard Bannatyne, *Transactions in Scotland* (1806), pp. 250f.

35. ibid., p. 359.
John Durie, cf. *Fasti*, vol. i, pp. 5, 103, 147.

36. David Crawford, *Memoirs of the Affairs of Scotland* (1753), pp. 218f.

37. *Balcarras Papers*, vol. vi, No. 88, in the *Miscellany of the Wodrow Society* (1844), pp. 407f.

38. *The Autobiography and Diary of Mr James Melvill* (Wodrow Society, 1842), p. 169.

39. Melvill, *Diary*, p. 172.

40. ibid., pp. 183f.

41. ibid., pp. 222f.

42. *Spottiswoode Miscellany* (1844), vol. i, p. 257.

43. Melvill, *Diary*, p. 318.

44. ibid., p. 322.

45. *The Historie of King James the Sext* (Bannatyne Club), pp. 815f; cf. *Calendar Papers Scot.*, vol. xi, p. 617.

46. *A Compleat History of the Lives and Reigns of Mary, Queen of Scotland and her Son, etc.* (1656), p. 176.

47. *Fasti*, vol. ii, p. 829.

48. *Ane Cronikill of the Kingis of Scotland* (Maitland Club), pp. 176f.

49. ibid., p. 180.
     Letters and State Papers during the reign of King James VI, chiefly from the collection of Sir James Balfour (1838), p. 195.

50. *Journal of the Society for Army Historical Research*, vol. v, p. 112.

51. Richard Bernard, *The Bible-Battels or the Sacred Art Military* (1629), pp. 159f.

III

EMPLOYED BY OTHER NATIONS

FRANCE

IF Hector Boece were in higher repute, his account of an alliance, between the Emperor Charlemagne and a Scots king called Achaius would establish an early date for the arrival of Scottish mercenary troops, and their chaplains, upon the Continent of Europe. The relevant passage in his Chronicle is as follows:

> and that the said band be the mair strengthy roborat, we have ordanit oure brothir, guilliam, with iv men of singylare erudition and prudence to pas with you in France, to make the said band; and hes sent iv.M. armit men. to pas with King Charles in quhat region he plesis, aganis the ennimies of Christian faith.[1]

Lord Hailes is sceptical of this alliance, and A. O. Anderson dismisses Fordun's version of it as baseless:

> because Alcuin's Scots were the Irish . . . Irish also were the 'two priests from Scotland, namely John and Clement, most learned men' who, at the instigation of Charles the Great, founded the Paris University, according to Fordun, in this reign.[2]

There is, on the other hand, the opinion of the historian of the Scots in France, Francisque-Michel, that

> les anciens historiens sont unanimes pour dire que l'alliance entre la France et l'Écosse remonte au règne de Charlemagne,

opinion accréditée, que les nouveaux, depuis la réunion de
ce pays à l'Angleterre, traitent de fable. Quelques historiens
français ont rapporté le même fait, et il paraissait si indubi-
table en France du temps de Henri II, et même de ses fils,
que dans le contrat de mariage entre le Dauphin François et
Marie Stuart, comme ailleurs, il est dit que l'amitié des deux
royaumes avait duré huit cents ans, ce qui revient au règne
de Charlemagne.[3]

Such a division of opinion among the historians precludes a re-
opening of the controversy, in the absence of fresh evidence.
But it seems possible that the tale had its origin in the recruiting
of fighting Scots, or Irish, with their due proportion of priests,
as chaplains, for the army of Charlemagne.

Leaving speculation for history, it appears that the link between
Scotland and France was strong before the end of the thirteenth
century. There were then some sixty taxpayers in Paris whose
names declared their Scottish forebears. Many of the Scots who
came to France found employment in the army, and were formed
into Scottish regiments as early as the fifteenth century. In
common with the native troops they had their attendant chaplains,
of whom some at least were Scots. One of these Scottish priests
was present at the battle of Verneuil, in 1424.

His story is told by a French historian as follows:

Plus heureux que la pluspart des Écossais qui prirent part à
la bataille de Verneuil, John Carmichael, de la maison des
Carmichael du Douglasdale, échappa au carnage; il était
chapelain du duc de Tourraine, resta en France et devint
évêque d'Orléans où il eut l'occasion de prêter une notable
assistance à Jeanne Darc pendant le siège de cette ville. Rien
de plus naturel que d'attribuer à ce prelat, nommé par nos
historiens, Jean de Saint-Michel, l'institution de la messe qui
se disait encore au siècle dernier pour les âmes des Écossais
mortes dans cette circonstance.[5]

Carmichael was not alone in his service to the Scots in France.
There is, indeed, a suggestion that another Scottish priest followed
the fortunes of Joan, and witnessed her death. He is said to have

become a monk at Dunfermline, and to have written a life of the Maid of Orleans, which has been lost.[6]

The Scots who survived the slaughter at Verneuil were incorporated in the Garde du Corps Écossais, who were the personal guards of the Kings of France. Into this elect corps, who attended the sovereign even at his devotions, heresy crept. One of these Scottish Archers adopted the teachings of the Reformers, and wrote a little book, of which the title is descriptive. It is:

The Meroure of an Chrſtiane, compoſed, and drawn forthe of holy Scriptures; by Robert Noruell, a man of armis, during the tyme of his captiuitie at Paris in the Baſtillie, for the teſtimonie of our Sauior Jeſus Chriſt.

The Prologue gives more detail of his imprisonment:

Foure yeres in priſon, they held me their expreſſe,
Foure monethes, and foure weekes als certaine,
Foure dayes, foure houres, in nombre and no leſſe,
I did into the Baſtillie remaine;
For Goddes word, as it is known plaine
And for no lawes, that I had done Tranſgreſſe
Nether to God, nor to my ſoueraine.[7]

The vast majority of his fellow archers were indifferent or actively hostile, and the author concludes with what he calls his New Year's Gift to the Archers of the Guard.

To all the Archeris of the ſcottis gard,
I wyſhe health, honour and proſperitie,
If that I ſhould ſeke them, trewlie to reward;
Throe Scotland, Englande, france & Italie;
Spayne, Portungaill, Irlande & Almanie,
Turkie, Thrace, Medois, and the Moirs of Inde;
Syne rake hell, and the bodum of the ſie,
I could not find ſo many, ſo unkynde.[8]

The experience of this Scottish soldier suggests that the spiritual oversight of the Corps was not neglected, and that its chaplains were alert to detect and to punish any who followed the new teaching. Among such zealous shepherds there would be a growing number of Scots priests in exile for their faithfulness to the old religion. One such was John Hamilton, who established himself in Paris about 1575. He was an enthusiast for the Catholic league, and an advocate of the extermination of the Protestants. When the city was besieged by Henry IV in 1590, Hamilton organised a regiment of clergy who marched to battle singing hymns. This militant spirit could be matched among the reformed clergy, when they in turn were exiled. John Welch, formerly minister of Ayr, distinguished himself for courage during the siege of St Jean d'Angely, carrying gunpowder in his hat in an emergency.[9]

The large numbers of Scots in the French service grew still greater after the death of Gustavus Adolphus, when many of those who had served with that great leader entered the army of France. This influx led to the setting up of a new unit, Régiment d'Hebron, or Hepburn's Regiment.

This was a very large formation, which included
3 field officers, 45 captains, 1 captain-lieutenant, 45 lieutenants, 48 ensigns, 4 surgeons, 6 adjutants, 2 chaplains, 1 drum-major, 1 piper, etc.[10]

There were in all 8,316 men, mustered in 48 companies, a considerable parish for the two chaplains who make their appearance on the official strength of this professional fighting force.

The following anecdote is told of Colonel Hepburn, who commanded these Scots, and one of the clergy who accompanied the army.

The famous Capuchin, Father Joseph de Tremblay, usually accompanied the French army at this time, and, as he pretended to have great skill in military matters, frequently contrived to thrust himself into councils of war and would there give his opinion with the utmost confidence to the oldest and most distinguished of the French marshalls. As the army approached the Rhine, he was one day during a halt on the march, exhibiting his talents in this manner to Hepburn, and, with a large map spread before him, was pointing out a number of strongly fortified towns, which he

affirmed could be reduced with the greatest of ease. . . .
Hepburn listened for a time to the garrulous capuchin, as he
pointed from fortress to fortress, and then said with a smile,
'Go not so fast, good Father Joseph, for, believe me, towns
are not taken with a finger end.'[11]

The Reformed Church of Scotland was aware of these mercenary soldiers and endeavoured to make certain that they were
provided with suitable chaplains. The General Assembly of 1642
decided

> That the Council be supplicated for an act, that in no regi-
> ment which goes out of the kingdom any papist bear office;
> and that the colonel be required to find caution for this
> effect, before he receive the council's warrant for levying any
> soldiers; and that he find caution for the maintaining of a
> minister, and the keeping of a session in his regiment.[12]

One of the Acts of the Assembly of 1643 was to license the
Earl of Irvine

> to take over to France any two ministers he could persuade
> for his regiment; the one to be provyded in a thousand
> pounds; the other a thousand merk, with intertainment to
> themselves, horse and man.[13]

Another instance of such care in the provision of ministers to
the mercenaries is shown in a letter from the Scottish Commissioners in London to the Commission of the Assembly, dated in
1647. The letter refers to a regiment to be raised for the service
of the Duke of Guelder in his war against Spain, and continues:

> That ye may be cleare in the mater of his petition, so farre
> as may concern the poynt of Religion, his Lordship hath
> desired me to give you notice, that together with his com-
> mission from the Duke of Guelder, hee hath also full liberty
> granted to himself and his whole regiment for the publick
> exercise of the Protestant Religion, for which end his Lord-
> ship intends to desire the Presbyterie of Afoord, with your
> advice and consent, to provyd three preachers for that
> regiment.[14]

Recruiting for the French service continued throughout the period of the Restoration and only came to an end with the accession of William of Orange to the throne of both kingdoms. The spiritual welfare of these latest recruits has been suggested by Sir Walter Scott, in a conversation of Morton and Bothwell, concerning the experiences of the latter while in the French army.

'In other respects you liked the service?' said Morton. 'Par excellence,' said Bothwell, 'women, wine and wassail, all to be had for little but the asking: and if you find it in your conscience to let a fat priest think he had some chance to convert you, gad, he'll help you to these comforts himself, just to gain a little ground in your good affection. Where will you find a crop eared Whig will be so civil?'[15]

The service of the Scots in France was drawing to an end at the period of this conversation. The danger to the throne of England caused the recall of a considerable number of them in 1678; the regiment into which they were formed continues as the Royal Scots, the first regiment of the line of the British Army.

Out of respect for the 'Auld Alliance' the story of the Scottish soldiers of fortune in France has been taken first, but there were other lands of Europe which also made good use of the soldiers of Scotland.

DENMARK

One of the first to do so was Denmark for her war against Sweden, in 1507. Sweden was indignant and a little alarmed at this. Heming Gad, the Bishop of Linkoping, wrote, 'the King of Denmark expects a powerfully efficient force from Scotland'. He mentions the Scots again, four years later, when he calls them 'ocristelige' or 'unchristian'.[16] If the hasty word of an enemy is to be relied upon, these Scots may have lacked chaplains. There is evidence that the moral tone of these auxiliaries was not very high, for an Act of the Lords in Council, in 1519, ordains

that respittes suld be given to all maner of persons, fugitives, banist men, rebellis and uthris under ony accusation of cryme within the realm of Scotland . . . frelie to cum to Alexander

Kingorne, doctour in medecyne, ambassatour [to the King of Denmark].[17]

The use of such a supply for recruits for service abroad was no temporary expedient, for more than one hundred years later, in 1627, it was still accepted. In that year Lord Speynie was authorised by the Privy Council to press into his regiment all 'strong, able and counterfeit limmers, callit Gypsies', and all sturdy beggars, vagabonds, masterless men and idle loiterers. Thus many of the Scottish mercenaries left their country for their country's good.[18]

These bands of undesirables who served in the army of Denmark may not have had chaplains of their own, but one of their fellow countrymen, John McAlpine, was a leader of the Reformation in that country. He had been Prior of the Dominican monastery of Perth and adopted the new ideas of reform. He became Professor of Divinity at Copenhagen and one of the advisors of the Danish king in his establishment of the Reformed church. It seems possible that such a Joseph would have a care for the spiritual needs of his brethren in the ranks of the Danish army.[19]

SWEDEN

The example of Denmark was followed by Sweden, and Scots were early recruited for the army of the latter country. They were found to be rather mutinous if their pay was too long delayed, and Russov, a Lutheran cleric, is critical of their want of courage. He also says that they belonged to that dangerous creed of Calvinism, which suggests prejudice on the part of the critic, and some form of religious observance on the part of the criticised.[20]

The rate of recruitment of Scots for the Swedish army was greatly increased in the reign of Gustavus Adolphus, in spite of the opposition of James VI of Scotland, who had ties of marriage with the Danish court. This opposition led to an attempt to smuggle certain ship loads of men from a northern Scottish port in the summer of 1612. This expedition landed in Norway and endeavoured to reach Sweden overland. They were ambushed

on the way and almost every man was slain in battle or as
prisoners.

There are suggestions that they were accompanied by a chaplain. One hint comes from an imaginary painting of

> the arrival of 'Colonel Sinclair' on the coast of Romsdalen
> with five or six vessels, and the plundering of the inhabitants
> by his followers, one of whom in the garb of a Calvinistic
> priest, is engaged in abducting a fair Norwegian maiden,
> whilst the rest are engaged in looting.[21]

A second suggestion of the presence of a minister is in the account
of the wanderings of the doomed band, where it is said that

> they here held a day of prayer, on account of the proximity
> of Rosten, Baegels-Kleven, and the 'highbridge', in order that
> they might safely pass these dangerous places.[22]

The 'day of prayer' and 'the Calvinistic priest' surely suggest the
presence of a minister, and it is but fair to add that the official
Danish investigation of the affair reported that

> we have also ascertained that those Scots who were defeated
> and captured on their march through this country have
> absolutely neither burned, murdered nor destroyed anything
> on their march.[23]

In spite of the disastrous failure of this expedition, many Scots
made their way to Sweden, until, in 1624, they filled eight
regiments ready for battle, and one more for garrison duty. In
common with the whole of Gustavus's army these regiments had
their chaplains, whose position and duties were laid down in the
Articles for War which governed that army. These regulations
were to have a considerable influence upon those drawn up for
the spiritual welfare of the Scottish regiments during the Civil
War, and are, therefore, given here in some detail.

In 1639 Robert Ward published *Animadversions of Warre*, in
the second part of which he prints his version of the rules which
were laid down by Gustavus, as follows:

Inprimis, No Commander, nor private Souldier whatſo-ever, ſhall uſe any kind of Idolatry, Witchcraft, or Inchant-ing of Armes, whereby God is diſhonoured, upon pain of death.

2. If any ſhall blaſpheme the name of God, either drunk or ſober, the thing being proved by two or three witneſſes, he ſhall ſuffer death without mercy.

3. If any ſhall ſeem to deride or scorne God's word or Sacraments, and bee taken in the fact, hee ſhall forthwith bee convented before the Commiſſioners Eccleſiaſtical, to be examined, and being proved guilty, he ſhall be condemned by the Court of Warre to loſe his head; but if they were ſpoken through haſte or unadviſedly, for the firſt offence hee ſhall bee in yrons fourteen dayes, and for the ſecond, be ſhot to death.

4. If any ſhall ſwear in his anger by the name of God, being convicted, ſhall pay half a moneths pay unto the poor; or if any be found drinking or at any other evill exerciſe, he ſhall forfeit half a months pay, and at the next aſſembly of prayer or preaching, he ſhall be brought upon his knees before the whole aſſembly, and there crave pardon of Almighty God.

5. To the end that God's word be not neglected, Our Will is, that publike prayers bee ſaid every morning and evening throughout the whole Camp, at one time in every ſeveral Regiment, they being called thereunto by the ſound of the Generals or Marshals Trumpets and the Drums of every private Company and Regiment.

6. Whatſoever miniſter ſhall neglect his time of prayer, except a lawful occaſion hinders him, he ſhall for every time being abſent, pay half a moneths pay.

7. Whatſoever Souldier ſhall neglect the time of prayer, and is thereof adviſed by his Captain, he ſhall lie in priſon 24 hours, except a lawfull occaſion hindered.

8. If any Miniſter be found drunk or drinking at ſuch time as he ſhould preach, or read prayer, for the firſt offence he ſhall be gravely admoniſht by the Commiſſioners

E

Ecclefiafticall, and for the fecond fault be banifht the Leaguer.

9. Every Holy Day and every Sabbath-day at leaft, fhall be kept folemn with preaching, in a place convenent, before and after noon; this alfo to be done twice every week, if the time permit.

Sections 10, 11, and 12 are concerned to prohibit markets in the camp during the hours of prayer and preaching, and then follows an important section governing the appointment of chaplains and the establishment of an ecclesiastical court or consistory for the whole army.

13. All priefts or Minifters that are to be in our Camp or Leaguer, fhall be appointed by the Bifhop of the fame Dioceffe or Land from whence the Souldiers come whom he is to be among; no Colonell nor Captain fhall take what minifter he fhall think good, but fhall be content with whom the Bifhop fhall appoint him.

14. To the intent that all Church bufineffe, as well in the field as otherwhere, may have an orderly proceeding, Wee ordain, that there be one Ecclefiafticall Confiftory or Commiffion in our Leaguer, the Prefident or chiefe perfon whereof fhall be Our own Minifter, when We Ourfelves are perfonally prefent in the field. In Our abfence fhall the chief minifter to the Generall be the man; his fellow Commiffioners or ordinary Affeffors fhall be the chiefe Minifters to every Regiment of Horfe and Foot; unto whom We give full power and authority to be Judges in all Church offences, according to the Law of God and holy Church; what fhall by them be decreed, fhall be of as great force and ftrength, as if it were determined in any other Confiftorie whatfoever.[24]

Rules 15 and 16 declare that no chaplain may be dismissed from office without the assent of this Consistory, and that all cases of scandal affecting the clergy must come before that Court; then, and only then, do these Laws of War pass on to the matters more military.

It will be shown in its place that these rules were adopted almost literally by the Scots army at the outbreak of the Civil Wars, especially those relating to the Ecclesiastical Consistory, which the Scots preferred to term a Presbytery, for the management of affairs spiritual within the army.

These religious regulations of the King of Sweden were observed in practice, as is shown in a letter from a German general, dated August 1631. He wrote:

> As for my King's camp, all is in good order. We receive but little money (commonly in twelve weeks a month's pay) but for meat and drink we have enough, thanked be God. . . . The King is very Godly and prays diligently, and causeth both morning and evening prayers to be said in each regiment.[25]

Under such a leader the chaplains held a privileged position and they would be expected to give good service in return for opportunity and encouragement. It is not likely that they were paid more regularly than the other officers, but the rate of pay which should have been received by the chaplains of Lord Reay's regiment, in 1631, was 42 rix-dollars per month. Few of the chaplains of the Scottish regiments of Gustavus are named in the history of the corps, but that of a chaplain of Colonel James Spen's regiment, in 1624, was 'A. Bedie'. But there was one among them who attained a measure of fame in later years, Robert Douglas, many times Moderator of the General Assembly. According to Wodrow, Douglas was ordained for service as a Chaplain with the Scots under Gustavus. He says that that leader said of his Scots chaplain:

> 'Mr Douglasse might be a counselour to any Prince in Europe. For prudence and knowledge he might be Moderatour to a Generall Councill; and even for military skill,' said he, 'I could very freely trust my army to his conduct.'[26]

Douglas's experiences with the army in Germany were to stand him in good stead at home during the Civil War, and his abilities as a Moderator were freely called upon by the Church of Scotland during difficult days. His further career as an army chaplain will appear in its place.

In addition to their sharing in the hardships of a camp in which the best entertainment 'was bread and water, abundance of the last but not so of the first',[27] the chaplains of Gustavus were called upon for arduous duties.

For example, when plague broke out among the soldiers of Alexander Leslie in 1628, he hastily improvised a quarantine station, and staffed it with an officer, some non-commissioned officers, a surgeon and a chaplain; the fate of this little band is not known.[28]

A more cheerful note is struck by the description of a Thanksgiving Service held in the Swedish camp after the victory of Witstock.

> The Swedish general spent three days partly in piety partly in polity, yet piety preceded and polity followed as the handmaid. First hee assembled his companies to give thankes to him who had covered their heads in the day of battel, and blessed the enterprise with so good and great successe, singing Te Deum after their manner, and supplying the want of organs and other church musicke with drums, fifes, trumpets, cannonadoes and musquetadoes intermingled, not to the disturbing of the souldiers devotion, but the raysing of their spirits, who rejoysed that they had now opportunity to spend their powder in triumph not in an uncertaine fight against the enemy.[29]

A footnote to such a noisy Thanksgiving is provided by an account of the Swedish camp after the victory of Breitenfeld in 1631, when it was said of Gustavus that

> he could not sleep for the deafening clatter that his men were making with the sacred bells they had looted from the priests in the defeated army.[30]

All the victories and the rejoicings came to an end with the death of Gustavus at Lutzen. On the morning of that day Gustavus had prayers read to himself by his chaplain, Fabricius. The rest of the army sang Luther's hymn, 'our God is a strong tower', and Gustavus himself led another hymn, 'Jesus Christ, our Saviour, he overcame death'.[31]

The death of the King broke the link which bound so many Scots to the service of Sweden, and, as we have seen, some joined the army of France, while others reappear in the armies of the Civil Wars at home.

DANZIG

Among the continental powers which made use of Scottish mercenaries in their frequent wars was the city of Danzig.

As early as 1577 this community raised a regiment of 700 Scots, who had permission

> as being of the reformed faith, to bring with them a preacher of their own persuasion.

This preacher was Patrick Griech or Grieg, who received a salary of two hundred gulden.[32] He is said to have

> held services after the manner of the Presbyterians, in the church of St Nicolas, also called the Church of the Black Friars, while the Pastor of St Elisabeth also celebrated the Holy Communion in the same way for the benefit of the levied Dutch and Scottish troops.[33]

Around the nucleus of this regiment there grew up a Reformed congregation in Danzig, which ten years later received a friendly letter from the Moderator of the General Assembly.[34]

They continued for many years under Scots and English pastors, of whom a list may be found in Steven's *History of the Scottish Church, Rotterdam*.[35]

POLAND

The chief enemy of Danzig was Poland, where a great many Scots had found homes. So notorious was the influx of Scots, indeed, that it was used as an argument against the early proposals to unite the peoples of Scotland and England.[36]

Most of the Scots in Poland seem to have been engaged in trade and commerce but some were undoubtedly employed as soldiers. Sigismund III, King of Poland, in 1604 appointed

> Abraham Young, commander of our Scottish Foot, to act as Conservator, Director and Informer

over the large number of his fellow countrymen in the land, who declared themselves independent of the local laws.[37]

Very few records of these Scots have been discovered, with the exception of the 'Green Book of the Lublin Brotherhood'.

This gives the rules under which the community lived, and includes a large section devoted to the management of their Church. In the absence of other evidence, it may be assumed that these laws applied to the preacher to the Scottish troops. If they did do so, the chaplain was bound by that section of the laws which applied to the Minister, of which two examples will suffice:

He shall do nothing without the consent of the Elders, and:

He shall make no jokes during the sermon.[38]

NETHERLANDS

If the military association of Scotland with Poland is vague and fleeting, that between Scotland and Holland is definite and documented for at least two hundred years.

It began with the enlistment of various independent companies of Scots about the middle of the sixteenth century.

In 1586 these were formed into two Scottish regiments, to which a third was added in 1628. This trio formed the real Scots Brigade, though this might expand to six regiments, as in 1697, or even to seven in the wars of Marlborough.[39]

An early indication that these regiments had chaplains is the payment of 30 guilders in 1597 to

> Andreas Hunter, minister of the Scottish regiment.[40]

This is the same Andrew Hunter who was driven into exile on the charge of having acted as a chaplain to Francis Bothwell. He continued to serve with the Scots in Holland for many years.

The end of his long service is shown by the following letter to the Government of the United Provinces in 1630:

> We, the undersigned colonels of the three Scottish regiments, hereby declare that we have no objection to the United Provinces granting and assigning one hundred guilders more to the widow of the late Rev. Andreas Hunterus, in his life-time minister of our nation; declaring also that during the lifetime of his widow, we shall provide for the support of our minister or ministers without assistance or grant from their High Mightinesses or the Council of State, and that thus we would gladly see that this widow during the short time that apparently she still has to live, be provided with necessary support.
>
> William Brog
Daniel Balfour
G. Couttis.[41]

There may be some who will find in this letter the mixture of caution and kindliness which are said to be typical of the nation to which Hunter belonged.

Another of the early chaplains of the Scots Brigade was John Douglas. He was ordained in the Kirk of Stirling in 1606, as minister of the 'Auld North British Regiment' in the service of the Low Countries.[42]

Mr Douglas became minister of the second charge of St Andrews in 1621 and was made a D.D. in the following year.

While he was a chaplain in Holland he presided at the admission of John Paget to be minister of the church at Amsterdam. He was assisted on this occasion by three members of the Dutch Classis, or ecclesiastical court of that city.[43] This close co-operation of the clergy, civil and military, whether Scots, English or Dutch, was a marked feature of the religious life of the Netherlands.

As early as 1586 the States gave four thousand guilders toward the cost of building a chapel at Flushing, for the English troops sent there by Queen Elizabeth. The pastor of this church in 1610 was a Presbyterian, Mr Thomas Potts, who continued to serve

the civil congregation when the garrison was removed in 1616.[44]
The British residents at Dort were dependent similarly upon the
chaplains to the garrison at Gorcum.[45] This garrison was also
called upon by the British congregation at Utrecht in 1622, when

> the captains joyned with the burgers, and desirous to have an
> English preacher, they wrote their letters and sent express
> messengers to one Mr Thomas Scot, then preacher of the
> English garrisone at Gorcum (who was newly called out of
> England for writeing a book called *Vox Populi* . . .), to call
> him to this place. And they promised to make his stipend
> 600 gulds. by the short month of every single company and
> rateably of the rest.

He was thus expected to serve both the soldiers and the civilian
population and his induction was fittingly performed by a group
of pastors representative of both of these spheres.

> Mr John Forbes, preacher to the Company of English
> Merchant Adventurers, then resident at Delft, who presided
> at his Induction, Mr Thomas Barkeley, preacher to the English
> Church at Rotterdam, Mr Andrew Hunter, preacher to the
> Scottish regiments & Mr Walter Whitestone, preacher to
> the regiment of Viscount Leslie.[46]

Thomas Scot's ministry in Utrecht was brief for he was slain four
years later by a soldier of Viscount Wimbleston's regiment. His
successors in the charge included several chaplains to the army.

Before leaving the subject of Thomas Scot, it might be mentioned that he was the author of some complimentary verses,
which were prefixed to Samuel Bachiler's book, *Campe Royal*.
This was a volume of Meditations or Sermons 'preached in the
Army at the Leaguer'. Scot's poem is a rather laboured panegyric
of an armed camp, in which he argues that a camp is at one and
the same time a school, a court, a theatre, a city, a world, and

> A Church, where God is truly served
> And where the faithful are in death preserved
> From lasting danger; for his numerous host
> Of war-like angels pitch where dangers most.

The whole effort is relieved, and a glimpse of real feeling is shown, in the closing lines:

> And if thou thinkst, I praise the Campe too much
> Know, but for thee, it is or would be such.

Bachiler's Meditations are not unworthy of the passage from Deuteronomy which is their text, 'When the host goeth forth against thine enemies, then keep thee from every wicked thing.'[47]

The ministers who had to serve two masters, military and civil, must have found it difficult to reconcile their conflicting claims, and they did find it difficult to collect their salary from their taskmasters. A letter from the civic authority of Bergen-op-Zoom in 1626, supports one chaplain's claim for overdue salary.

> Dominus Georgius Clerus, a minister of God's word, with churches and congregations of the English and Scottish nations at Bergen-op-Zoom, has intimated and declared to us that he intends to address himself to your lordships to make a request of you not only for subsidy and augmentation of his yearly stipend; but at the same time to complain about some English captains, here in garrison, to the effect, that they withhold from him [and] refuse to pay and supply him monthly with such sums as they ought and are bound to pay to him, and that he is not so well used or paid by them as the ministers of other towns and places where men of the same nation are in garrison, and also seeing that his predecessors, in whose place he was appointed, had been recompensed differently, and consequently he being (under correction) of no inferior condition, ought to be treated the same; and with that end in view he has requested from us writings and letters of recommendation dealing with the matter.[48]

They wrote again five or six months later, regretting that nothing had been done to adjust this matter, and they add that the English captains, without ground or reason, now declare that 'they have not been rightly served by the said Dominus Georgio Clero'. The issue of all this is not clear, but some settlement must have been made, for Mr George Clerk continued in 1643, drawing salary as 'Predikant van di Schotten'.

He was happier in this than was James Forme, 'an Englishman or a Scotsman, minister of the Holy Gospel to the regiments of one of the said nations', who died in debt at Nymegen in 1624, his pay being heavily in arrears.[49]

These chaplains shared in the battles, sieges and other adventures of their militant parishioners. In 1627, for example, four companies of Mackay's regiment were left as a garrison for the weak fortress of Bredenburg. They held this against an overwhelming force for six days before the walls were breached and stormed. Every one of those who survived the siege was brutally massacred, including their preacher.[50]

Another chaplain of this regiment is described by Robert Monro, in terms which leave no doubt of his active sharing in the life of the Corps.

A Preacher for Souldiers, yea and a Captaine in neede, to lead Souldiers on a good occaſion, being full of courage and diſcretion and good conduct beyond ſome Captaines I have knowne, who were not ſo capable as he. At this time he not onely prayed for us, but went on with us, to remarke, as I thinke, men's carriage; and having found a Sergeant neglecting his dutie and his honour at ſuch a time (whoſe name I will not expreſſe), having chidden him, did promiſe to reveale him unto me, as he did after their ſervice. The Sergeant being called before me and accuſed, did deny his accuſation, alleaging that if he were no paſtour that had alleaged it, he would not lie under the injury. The preacher offered to fight with him, that it was the truth he had ſpoken of him . . . the Sergeant, being caſhiered, never call'd Maſter William to account for which he was evill thought of, ſo that he retired home and quit the warres.[51]

Monro has a word of praise for another Scots chaplain in connection with an incident involving some of the Scots, in 1630. A party of soldiers and camp followers was being conveyed by sea when one of the ships was cast away on Rugen, and

in the very moment when our ſhip did breake on ground, there was a ſergeant's wife a shipboard, who without the help of any women was delivered of a Boy, which all the time of the tempeſt ſhe carefully did preſerve, and being come aſhore, the next day ſhe marched neere foure Engliſh mile, with that in her Armes which was in her Belly the night before, and was Chriſtened the next Sunday after Sermon, being the day of our thankeſgiving for our Deliverance; our Preacher, Mr Murdow Mac-Kenyee, a worthy and Religious young man, having diſcharged his part that day, after with much regret did ſever from us, and followed my Lord of Rhee our Colonell unto Britaine.[52]

Murdo Mackenzie became minister of Suddie, in Ross-shire, and will appear below as chaplain to a rebel army.

The long service of the Scots Brigade in Holland was interrupted in 1685, when they were called home to prop the tottering throne of the Stewarts. They had then one chaplain, at least, John Gordon, who appears in the Army Lists as chaplain to three Scots regiments 'lately come over from Holland'.[53] Gordon should have been familiar with the camp which John Evelyn described:

they were all excellently clad and well disciplin'd and were encamped on Blackheath with their tents; the King and Queen came to see them exercise, and the manner of their incampment, which was very neat and magnificent.[54]

We can place the chaplain's tent in this encampment with some confidence, for, according to an ancient publication on the quartering of the Dutch forces, the chaplain had his in the centre of the officers' lines, and he was entitled to the use of a baggage wagon on the march.[55]

The Scots Brigade soon returned to the Dutch service, where they continued to be very highly valued as fighting men. An English observer remarked upon this in 1622, and said that the Dutch

mingle and blend the Scottish among them, which are like Beans and Peas among chaff. These [Scots] are sure men, hardy and resolute, and their example holds up the Dutch.[56]

The Scots and English regiments returned home once more as part of the invasion force of William of Orange, and served in Ireland before they returned to their own proper sphere in the Netherlands. Before we follow them and their chaplains into the wars with France, some attention must be given to the ecclesiastical framework in which these chaplains worked.

The historian of the Scottish Church at Rotterdam is convinced that the regimental chaplains and the clergy who served the other Britons throughout the Low Countries speedily formed themselves into a Synod. This Court is mentioned in Consistorial registers and by Dutch authors as the Synod of British clergy in the United Provinces.

The Minutes of their meetings have not been discovered, but Steven offers the strong evidence of a State document in proof of the existence of this Church Court.

It reads as follows:

To the Synod of the English and Scottish clergy in the Netherlands, the annexed articles were exhibited and delivered, this nineteenth day of May 1628, in the name of King Charles the First, by the Right Hon. Dudley Carleton, Baron of Imbercourt, H.M. Ambassador Extraordinary to the States General of the United Provinces.[57]

The purpose of this communication, to forbid the Synod to make a liturgy, is of no importance here, but it does seem reasonable to accept that this body did exist.

While the army chaplain would have his place in this Court, he would be more intimately concerned with the lesser Church court, the Kirk Session of his Regiment.

As we shall show, such Kirk Sessions were the rule in the Scottish regiments of the Civil War and we have noted that the General Assembly was anxious that no regiment go out of Scotland until the Colonel had 'found caution for the maintaining of a minister and the keeping of a session in his regiment' (page 53). The existence of such courts in the Scots Brigade might, therefore, be presumed. There is solid evidence for the existence of one of the Kirk Sessions of the Scots Brigade, for the Minutes of its meetings for the years 1761-5 are preserved. This Kirk Session belonged to the regiment commanded by Colonel James Gordon, and the Minutes begin with the ordination, by the chaplain, Alexander Pitcairn, of three senior officers to be Elders and of two of lesser rank to be Deacons. From this entry it would appear that Pitcairn founded or, perhaps, revived the Kirk Session in this regiment. The first meeting entrusted the operation of the Poor Fund to the minister. Thereafter the Minutes merely record the disbursements of this Fund until, in August 1764, the Kirk Session receive a new Elder, a Captain James Cunningham. The seemingly harmless Minute which notes his inclusion in the Court was deleted by order of the Commander in Chief, the Duke of Brunswick, in November of that year.

The reason for this extraordinary interference of the secular arm is to be found in the Minutes of the meetings held between these dates. From these we learn that the chaplain, instigated or encouraged by his new Elder, got the approval of the Session for the new method of singing the psalms, without 'giving out the line'. The innovation did not meet with the approval of Colonel Gordon and there was such a clash as must arise from an attempt to operate the rules of democratic government within the framework of army discipline. The chaplain replied to the colonel mildly and quite correctly

> that the new way of singing the psalms hath been earnestly recommended these many years past by the General Assembly, and is now practised by the greatest part of the congregations in Scotland, and indeed in all Protestant churches.
>
> We did not imagine that you would have disapproved of our proceedings, and hope that upon this representation, after seriously considering the matter, you will see no reason to doe so; and it will give us great pleasure to be informed that you are satisfied with our conduct, tho' as a session we conceived that we are only accountable to a superior Church Court.

The case is now fairly stated and battle is joined, not so much on the original issue of the Psalms, but as a test of conflicting authorities. The Colonel now includes the resignation of Cunningham from the Session in the terms of surrender, and the Session, while they see their way to concede the method of singing, which was only on trial, are of the opinion that only a Church Court can reverse the ordination of an Elder. The Colonel now makes use of the power of the Purse, and threatens to withdraw the Chaplain's salary; the Commander in Chief is called in, and the military Elders find that discretion compels them to resign, and victory falls to the big battalions.[58]

One author, commenting on this episode, declares that the difficulty was overcome by transferring the Chaplain to another regiment.[59] But the registers of marriages and baptisms show that Pitcairn continued as minister to the regiment for some eighteen years after this storm, that he became Dr Pitcairn about 1781, and that the last marriage he performed before the regiment was disbanded was that of his son to the daughter of a Dutch colonel.[60]

In contrast to the colonel who had such conservative views on the singing of the Psalms should be set such as Colonel Robert Monro. We have seen that he was ready to praise the work of the chaplains, but, in addition, he was himself of a deeply religious turn of mind. He wrote a series of Meditations for the 'Chriſtian Soldier going on Service', of which the first reveals the topical note he tries to strike in them all.

> When thou ſeeſt thy Camirade going to Muſter with a faire ſhow outwardly; deckt with brave clothes, and delighting in his plumes, think with thyſelfe, ſuch an outward ſhow is nothing without the inward gifts of the minde; for if thou deſireſt to be a Souldier of Chriſt, thou muſt be adorned with all vertues; that inwardly thou mayeſt be ſuch as outwardly thou doſt appear unto the World.[61]

Under such a commanding officer the minister to the regiment would have all support if he were worthy and would be suitably rebuked for failure in his duty.

It is often most difficult to obtain the private soldier's opinion and we are fortunate in having the views of one such, of the chaplain of his regiment in Holland. It forms part of a long poem by John Scott, who served in the ranks in the early years of the eighteenth century.

He describes one church parade and sermon, thus:

> And some regiments who were protestants,
> Had sermon upon the Lords day.
> Beside the main guard that kirk was prepaired,
> For regiments in toun that did stay,
> Our regiments minister all along the winter,
> In Holland his time he did spend.
> And about the Beltan he came up again,
> To instruct us our lives for to mend.
> Some Saboth dayes in the moneth of May,
> In Leil citydaille he did preach.
> His text he did chusse in the first of the Romans,
> As Paul the Apostel did teach.

The sermon is given at considerable length. It begins with the greatness of the Roman Empire, continues through a consideration of Idolatry, Lust, Gossip and Scandal, to stern denunciation of Roman Catholics, particularly such as dwell in the city of 'Leil'. The soldier-poet concludes this account of the sermon:

> Matters of religion doth little concerne
> Men in a militarie liffe
> To clergie men who do better ken,
> We leave to debaite the striffe.[62]

The chaplain who figures in this poem was George Anderson, who was attached to Hepburn's regiment at this time. He is associated with Mr Donald Bane in an interesting petition to the financial department of the Dutch government in 1709. In this document they declare that they are

ministers of the Gospel of the British regiments of Major General Murray and Colonel Hepburn, in the service of this country, showing, in effect, that they, the petitioners, during the last campaign acted in the said capacity in the regiments aforesaid, and yet act as such in the garrison; and requesting,

accordingly, that their Noble Mightinesses may be pleased
to authorise the clerks of the Union's Financial Department
to make up the accounts of the petitioners salary and expenses
during the last campaign in the way in which other ministers
have enjoyed.[63]

After some discussion the prayer of the petition was granted.
Anderson seems to have been commissioned as chaplain to the
Royal Scots Greys and to have been appointed chaplain at Fort
William, in Scotland, in 1733.

Bane or Bayne continued with the army in 1743. From other
petitions of Scottish chaplains we learn that while their office was
recognised by the United Provinces for purposes of pay, they
did not hold commissions and were not required to take the
oath of loyalty. The case of Angus Macauley, in 1780, proves
they had no commission.

He petitioned that he was appointed

chaplain of Regiment Stuart, March 16th 1778, and as such,
during the lifetime of chaplain Patrick Cunningham only to
receive what salary the regiment might pay him, now petitions, said Cunningham having died 13th instant, for his
commission and for authority to draw his pay on Holland.
Resolved: the latter granted, the former refused. The
Council never issue commissions to chaplains of Scottish
regiments.[64]

The matter of the oath of loyalty is made clear in the case of
another chaplain, when it was laid down that:

chaplains of Scottish regiments receive no commission, and,
therefore, are not allowed to make oath before the Council
of State.[65]

A few years later, however, the insistence of the Dutch government on all the officers of the Brigade taking an oath of loyalty
which would have cut them off from their homeland, brought
about so many resignations that the Scots Brigade virtually
ceased to exist.

To conclude this survey of the chaplains attached to the

Scottish mercenary regiments, we would quote at some length from an eighteenth-century book on military discipline.

There is not a character in any ſphere of life, that requires more circumſpection and ſtrictneſs of behaviour than does that of a regimental chaplain, eſpecially to a regiment abroad, or in foreign ſervice, ſuch as the Scotch Brigade in Holland. As they are the only perſons in the miniſterial way that the bulk of the regiment can converſs with, or whoſe advice and admonitions they can have acceſs to in any of their ſpiritual concerns, they ought to be very cautious that their behaviour in publick and domeſtick life be irreproachable. A chaplain ought to be ſtrict in his morals, regular and exemplary in all his actions, and at the ſame time that in his converſation he keeps up to the dignity of his character, it ought to be familiar, cheerful and condeſcending to the capacities and circumſtances of the people he has charge of; he ought to be a kind of father and oracle to them, both in ſecular and ſpiritual concerns; the ſick ſhould be his particular care, as he may improve the happy moments of diſtreſs to diſengage them from the world, and raiſe their views to a better; the poor, the widow, and the orphan, claim his ſtricteſt attention and care; and that his publick miniſtry, his preaching, prayers, catechiſing and other means of inſtruction, may have their due weight and influence in the regiment, his hearers ſhould be able to trace in his life every feature of virtue which he delineates in his ſermons; and thus the harmony between his doctrine and manners muſt give double weight to all he ſays. . . . His converſation when in company ſhould as much as poſſible take a religious or at leaſt an edifying turn, without moroſeneſs, ſpleen or ill-nature; avoid bigotry and enthuſiaſm, and let univerſal charity and benevolence, a love to mankind, a ſincere deſire to reclaim the bad from vice, and to improve the good in virtue, be the buſineſs, the pride and glory of a regimental chaplain. . . . Such were the chaplains in the army of Guſtavus, and ſuch men of real worth and merit ought all regimental chaplains to be.[66]

F

Whether the chaplains to the mercenary soldiers of Scotland reached this very high standard or not, it is clear that they shared in the making of a tradition of good and devoted service. With all due allowance for the growth of a legend, the army chaplain of a later day owed much to the gallant band who marched with Gustavus and to the long years of faithful service given by his brethren to the armies of Holland.

REFERENCES

1. Hector Boece, *The History and Chronicles of Scotland*, ed. Bellenden (1821), vol. ii, p. 135.
2. A. O. Anderson, *Early Sources of Scottish History* (1922), vol. i, p. 251 n.
3. Francisque-Michel, *Les Écossais en France* (1862), vol. i, pp. 27f.
4. ibid., vol. i, pp. 27f.
5. ibid., vol. i, pp. 153f.
6. J. H. Burton, *The Scot Abroad* (1898), pp. 441f.
7. Robert Noruell, *The Meroure of an Chriſtiane*, etc. (1561), p. 3.
8. ibid., The end.
9. John Howie, *Scots Worthies* (1816), 'John Welch', passim.
10. James Grant, *Memoirs and Adventures of Sir John Hepburn* (1851), p. 231.
11. ibid., pp. 227f.
12. *A Compendium of the Laws of the Church of Scotland* (1840), Part ii, p. 208.
13. Robert Baillie, *Letters and Journals* (Bannatyne Club, 1841), vol. ii, p. 52.
14. *Records of the Commissions of the General Assembly*, Scottish History Society, vol. i, pp. 223f.
15. Sir Walter Scott, *Old Mortality*, chapter ix.
16. Th. A. Fischer, *The Scots in Sweden* (1907), p. 46.
17. *Acts of the Lords in Council*, 30th March 1519.
18. *Privy Council Register*, 8th March 1627.
19. Henry Cowan, *The Influence of the Scottish Church in Christendom* (1896), pp. 114f.
20. Fischer, *Scots in Sweden*, pp. 63f.
21. Thomas Michell, *History of the Scottish Expedition to Norway in 1612* (1886), p. 11 and frontispiece.
22. ibid., p. 91.
23. ibid., p. 95.
24. Robert Ward, *Animadversions of Warre* (1639), Part ii, pp. 42ff.
25. Benjamin Chapman, *The History of Gustavus Adolphus and of the Thirty Years War* (1856), p. 251.

26. R. Wodrow, *Analecta*, vol. ii, p. 136 (1842).
27. Sir Jas. Turner, *Memoirs of his own Life and Times* (1829).
28. Fischer, *Scots in Sweden*, p. 100.
29. *The Principal Passages of Germany* (1636–9), p. 35.
30. C. V. Wedgewood, *The Thirty Years War* (1938), p. 301.
31. Chapman, *History of Gustavus*, pp. 368f.
32. Th. A. Fischer, *The Scots in Germany* (1902), pp. 188f.
33. Th. A. Fischer, *The Scots in Prussia* (1903), pp. 125f.
34. Fischer, *Scots in Germany*, pp. 188f.
35. Wm. Steven, *The History of the Scottish Church, Rotterdam* (1833), p. 109 n.
36. Arthur Wilson, *The History of Greater Britain* (1653), p. 24.
37. *Papers Relating to the Scots in Poland*, Scottish History Society, p. 5.
38. ibid., p. 244.
39. *The Scots Brigade in Holland*, Scottish History Society, vol. i, pp. xif.
40. ibid., vol. i, p. 57.
41. ibid., vol. i, pp. 438f.
42. *Fasti*, vol. ii, pp. 394 and 417.
43. *Scottish Church Rotterdam*, p. 273.
44. ibid., p. 301.
45. ibid., p. 298.
46. ibid., p. 338.
47. Samuel Bachiler, *The Campe Royal, set forth in brief Meditations . . . preached in the Army at the Leaguer* (Amsterdam, 1628, or London, 1629).
48. *The Scots Brigade*, vol. i, pp. 350f.
49. ibid., vol. i, p. 243.
50. *Monro His Expedition with the Worthy Scots Regiment (called Mac-Keyes Regiment) etc.* (1637), Part I, p. 39.
51. ibid., Part I, p. 52.
52. ibid., Part II, p. 6.
53. Charles Dalton, *English Army Lists and Commission Registers, 1661–1714* (1896), vol. ii, p. 48.
54. John Evelyn, *Diary*, 18th July 1685.
55. *Castrametation, or the Measvring out of the Qvarters for the Encamping of an Army*, by Jo. Crvso (1642), pp. 8 and 32.
56. *Account of the Siege and Relief of Bergen-op-Zoom 1622, by an English Eye-witness*, Royal MSS.
57. *Scottish Church Rotterdam*, p. 262.
58. *The Scots Brigade*, vol. iii, pp. 294–306.
59. A. Mackay, *The Book of Mackay*, p. 196.
60. *The Scots Brigade*, vol. iii, p. 249 and passim.
61. *Monro, His Expedition*, Part ii, p. 217.
62. *The Scots Brigade*, vol. iii, pp. 468–71.
63. ibid., vol. ii, p. 95.

64. ibid., vol. ii, p. 492.
65. ibid., vol. ii, p. 493.
66. *Strictures on Military Discipline*, by an Officer (J. Cunningham) (1774), pp. 161f.

IV

THE CIVIL WARS (1)

IN 1638 the General Assembly of the Church of Scotland
deliberately carried out a second reformation of the Church.
They established an uncompromising Presbyterianism, in
defiance of the King's Commissioner and of King Charles himself. The wrath of the latter was such that he prepared an army
to punish his northern kingdom. The Scots, aware of this
probable reaction, also prepared for war, and mustered a large,
if amateur, army.

They entrusted this, with a very wide commission, into the
hands of a veteran of the German wars, Alexander Leslie.

This first measuring of strength passed into an uneasy truce,
and is known as the First Bishops' War.

The main danger to Scotland had been in the north where
Huntly and his friends took up arms for the King. This danger
was met by a force under Montrose, then a good soldier of the
Covenant, which patrolled the north-east until the truce was
made. The evidence of John Spalding, who did not love the
Covenanters, shows that even these early movements of armed
men were accompanied by ministers.

He says that on the 30th March 1639 Montrose

cam not to Abirdene as the toune expectit; but fra the Lynkis,
about 4 efternone, marchit touardis Kintor, with his army in
brave ordour, whair that nicht thay incampit, and Sonday
all day also, haveing thair awin minister and heiring
preiching.[1]

He has a different story to tell of a visit to Aberdeen by the same force in the month of May. Montrose and his chief officers attended the Kirk, but

> the renegate soldiouris, in tyme of both preichinges, is abuseing and plundering New Abirdein pitifullie, without regard to God or man.[2]

On the occasion of their next visit, however, he admits that the soldiers attended 'the Greyfriar churche', and that the ministers of their own army preached to them.[3]

The Minutes of the Synod of Argyll show how some of the ministers of the Covenant army were appointed, for that Court, in 1639, is careful to provide one of its number to go with the army to the Borders, while others must take it in turn to attend upon those men of 'Auchinbreck's company' who remain on guard in Kintyre.[4]

There is, indeed, ample evidence that all parts of this first of the Covenant armies were well supplied with ministers. For example, the appearance of a Royal squadron in the Firth of Forth, after the Scottish army had marched to the Borders, occasioned a hasty mustering of the reserve forces. Robert Baillie describes this in his Journal.

> My Lord Eglinton, who had been appointed with Caſſilis to wait at home to attend any invaſion might be from Ireland, came away with the whole countrey at his back, and I as their preacher.[5]

This naval demonstration came to nothing, and Eglinton and his men joined the main Scottish force at Duns Law. Baillie continued with them and gives a description of his preparations for the expedition.

> For I (quoth the wren) was there among the reſt, being choſen preacher by the gentlemen of our ſhyre who ceme late with my Lord Eglintoun. I furniſhed to half a dozen of good fellows, muſquets and picks, and to my boy [i.e. body servant] a broadſword. I carryed myſelf, as the

faſhion was, a ſword and a couple of Dutch piſtols at my ſadle; bot I promiſe for the offence of no man, except a robber in the way; for it was our part alone to pray and preach for the incouragement of our countreymen, which I did to my power moſt cheerfully.[6]

He also gives a picture of the Scottish camp during the days of waiting at Duns Law.

Had ye lent your eare in the morning or eſpeciallie at even, and heard in the tents the ſound of ſome ſinging pſalms, ſome praying, and ſome reading ſcripture, ye would have been refreſhed: true, there was ſwearing, and curſeing and brawling in ſome quarters, whereat we were grieved; bot we hoped, if our camp had been a little ſettled, to have gotten ſome way for theſe miſorders.[7]

An appreciation of the Scottish chaplains in this camp comes from an English source. It is to be found in a letter from Edward Norgate, who wrote:

To pass by the common people who have frequented the Scottish camp during this treaty, the Earl of Stamford with one servant went thither on Saturday last and dined with General Leslie. Last night he came to Mr Secretary's and told us the manner of his reception ... and that their presbyters, Hindersheim [Henderson] and others defamed among us for so many incendiaries and 'boute-feus' are, every mother's son (their carbines at their backs, swords and pair of pistols at their girdles laid aside), holy and blessed men, of admirable, transcendent, and seraphical learning, and say grace longer and better than our campestrial chaplains that ride before our regiments taking tobacco. My Lord, intending not to be known, was first met by two of their ministers in this evangelical posture, with one Bible for both, these courteously entertained him, and attended him to their camp, ... at dinner a long and excellent grace or short prayer was made by one of these carbine chaplains in 'cuerpo', wherin the King and England was devoutly remembered.[8]

Lest our composite portrait of these Scottish chaplains seem
to be one sided, we give the sarcastic advice of William
Drummond of Hawthornden, who suggested

> that Preachers be Choſen, the fitteſt in the Preſbyteries for
> the Army; not too learned, but Men who have greater
> Fancy than Judgement, vehement and Zealous, and who
> dare play the Souldiers to keep the Army in the Fear of God
> and exhort them to Service, comforting them in Extremities.[9]

Perhaps some of the ministers with the army had more of Fancy
than Judgement, but few of them can have been so naive as James
Gordon, Parson of Rothiemay. He describes how the collapse
of a bank of earth revealed a providential supply of stones:

> rownde for the most part in shape and perfect sphericall,
> some of them oval shapne. They wer of a dark-gray colour,
> some of them yellowish, and for quantitie they looked like
> ball of all syzes, from pistoll to field pieces, such as sakers
> and robinettes . . . but lighter than leade by many degrees
> so that they were only for show and not for use.[10]

The truce which ended the campaign in 1639 did not endure,
and in the following year a Scottish army marched south once
more, and once more the ministers marched with the regiments.
John Livingstone was one of them and he comments upon the
singing of psalms and the reading of Scripture in this new army.
He says, however, 'I was informed that there was much more
the year before.'[11]   Against this must be set the opinion of Robert
Blair, that

> in the army of 1640, was Captain Ellis's company, who were
> all come from Ireland. They were all water lappers, Judges
> vii, 5-7, and bible bearers, I believe since the days of the
> reforming kings of Judah there was never such two armies.[12]

If, however, the piety of the Scots had declined in some measure
from the heights of 1639, that of their opponents could scarcely
be said to exist. Conway, the Royalist General at Newcastle,
declared:

I am teaching cart-horses to manage, and making men that
are fit for bedlam and Bridewell to keep the Ten Command-
ments, so that General Leslie and I keep two schools; he has
scholars that profess to serve God, and he is instructing them
how they may safely do injury and all impiety; mine to the
utmost of their power never kept any law of God or the
King, and they have to be made fit to make others keep
them.[13]

To quote once more from John Livingstone; he gives an honest
account of his own experiences with the army of 1640, which
covers the bones of history with flesh, and with some of the pains
that flesh is heir to.

I was ſent out by the Preſbytery in the year 1640, to go with
the earl of Caſſilis's regiment when our army went to
Newcaſtle. Our army lay a while at Chuſely-wood, a mile
or two from Dunſe, till the reſt of the army came up. I had
a little trench tent, and a bed hung between two leager
cheſts, and having lain ſeveral nights with my cloaths on, I
being wearied with want of ſleep, did ly one night with my
cloaths off; that night was very cold, and while I ſlept all
the cloaths went off me; ſo that in the morning I was not
able to ſtir any part of my body, and I had much ado, with
the help of my man and a baggage man to get on my cloaths.
I cauſed them to put me on my horſe, and went to Dunſe,
and lay down in a bed, and cauſed them to give me into the
bed, a big tin-ſtoup full of water, whereby a ſweat was
procured, ſo that before night I was able to riſe and put on
my cloaths.[14]

Livingstone, who served with the army again and again in later
years, may have been rather innocent of the arts of campaigning,
but in this respect, he was not much worse than the leaders under
whom he served. He himself illustrates their ineptitude. The
Scottish army found itself short of many things, but notably of
gunpowder.

One day when the committee of eſtates and general officers,
and ſome miniſters, were met in the caſtle of Dunſe, and

were at prayer and conſultation what to do, an officer of the guard comes and knocks rudely at the door of the room where we were and told there was treachery diſcovered; for he, going to a big cellar in the bottom of the houſe, ſeeking for ſome other thing, had found a great many barrels of gun-powder, which he apprehended was intended to blow us up. After ſearch it was found that the powder had been laid in there the year before, when the army had departed from Dunſe Law, . . . and had been forgotten.[15]

A somewhat similar incident which took place in August of that year ended less happily, for, by some mischance, the Castle of Dunglas was blown up. Among the large number of the garrison who were killed was their chaplain, John Gaittis, minister of the parish of Bonkle.[16]

The method by which the ministers were appointed to the regiments of 1639 and 1640 requires a little explanation.

We have seen that Baillie was invited to be their chaplain by the gentlemen of his Shire; that Livingstone was sent out by his Presbytery and that the Synod of Argyll also appointed chaplains. The official method seems to have combined the invitation by the laity with appointment by the church court. There is a Minute of the *War Committee of the Covenants in the Stewartry of Kirkcudbright* which endorses this view.

The Committee of the Stewartrie foirsaid, halden at the foir— said Cullenoch callit Clauchanepluk, xiij Julij, 1640.

Act for the Minister of the raigement

Ordaines Bargaltoun and Collin to supplicate the Presbyterie that either Mr Johne McClellane or Mr Samuel Bell may be appoynted by thame as minister to the regaiment.[17]

The Minutes of the Presbytery of Lanark bear this out, while throwing some light upon the rather impromptu arrangements of these early years of the war. In June 1640 that Presbytery chose from a leet of two that Alexander Livingstone should attend upon Colonel Fleming's regiment.

They ordained that he was to be relieved by George Bennet,

the other member of the leet, 'efter twentie dayes or a moneth'. Their Minute for July 1640 is as follows:

Alſo ordaines Mr George Bennet, as was agreed vpon before to goe furth to the camp to Collonell Flemyng his regement, to ſupplie Mr Alexander Livingſtone his place, that he may return home to his charge at Carmichall: and if the ſaid Mr George get not ſatisfactione off the common charges, he ſhall have at his returne, off the brethren of the presbetrie, xxx ſhillings every day, and efter twentie dayes or a moneth on[e] to releive him.[18]

The campaign of 1640 involved the Scottish army in a skirmish at Newburn, which was celebrated by Zachary Boyd, minister at Glasgow, in a 'heroic' poem, of which one verse proclaimed that the pistol balls

In Squadrons came like fire and thunder,
Mens hearts and heads both for to pierce and plunder;
Their errand was, (when it was understood)
To bathe men's bosoms in a scarlet flood.[19]

The same author, in 1641, published a little book which he called The Sword of the Lord and of Gideon, which offers, in more dignified prose, an address and prayers for use before battle, which could, with slight alteration, be used today.

The official account of the fight at Newburn was, apparently the work of John Livingstone. It was laid upon him by

the Preſbytery of the Army, to draw up a narration of what happened in that ſkirmish at New burn, which I did in a paper out of that I ſaw or heard from others, by the help of the Lieutenant-General.[20]

Passing over for the moment the reference to the 'Presbytery of the Army', we find that the town of Newcastle surrendered to the Scots. A service of Thanksgiving was held there in St Nicholas' Church, at which Alexander Henderson preached. One critical auditor says of the sermon that the preacher

so much forgot his text and the duty of his calling, that he fell into a strange extravagant way of applauding their success and depraving the English, making that the whole subject of his discourse.[21]

The honour of preaching on that first Sunday in Newcastle was shared by Andrew Cant, another of the leaders of the Church who were then with the army. He may serve as an illustration of the problem of a divided duty, to the army and to the home church, which perplexed chaplains then and in more recent times. Cant had been invited to become one of the ministers of Aberdeen and he wrote in reply from the camp at Newcastle:

> The generall and prime commanders and nobles will not yield to my removing as yet, and, I feare, verie hardlie this long time; yet I have a mind to be in Scotland against the beginning of March . . . I dare not prescribe; but a letter from you, bearing the appointment of the forsaid dyet and urging my presence sent hither in haist, me thinks, sold be a readie meane of my liberation from hence.[22]

If the giants of the Covenant were growing weary of war's delays, it is little cause for wonder that already there were signs of a disquieting shortage of ministers with the regiments. This shortage was brought to the notice of the General Assembly of 1641 by a letter from the Presbytery of Newcastle, which complained

> that there was a great neglect in many presbyteries to supply the armies with ministers.[23]

According to Baillie, the Assembly provided for a better supply, but their plan was not then put into effect as the Second Bishops' War now came to an end.

The Scots army was again disbanded with the exception of a few regiments and these were soon sent to Ireland to counter the rebellion which had broken out there. These regiments took chaplains with them as shall be shown later.

The cessation of hostilities provides an opportunity to discuss the *Presbytery of the Army*, mentioned above in connection with

Livingstone's account of Newburn. This appears under another name as the Presbytery of Newcastle which wrote to the Assembly asking for more ministers.

There is no doubt possible concerning this Court and its subsidiary Regimental Kirk Sessions. The first section of the *Articles of Militarie Discipline*, printed in Edinburgh in 1639, establishes the ecclesiastical judicature of the army, with a strong resemblance to that ascribed to Gustavus Adolphus, given above.

These 'Articles' declare:

That in every Regiment under a Colonell, there bee an ecclesiasticall Eldership or Kirke Session, consisting of the Minister or Ministers of the Regiment, and of Elders to be chosen to that effect; who shall sit at their appointed times, and judge in all Kirke affaires, according to the word of God, and the rules and order of Discipline used in the Kirke of Scotland for censuring of delinquents, as fornicatours, whoore-mongerers, adulterers, swearers, cursers, drunkards, profaners of the Sabbath, and all scandalous persons, that they may be brought to repentance; or being found obstinat and incorrigible, that the extreame censures of the Kirke passe against them. And that all things bee done herein, as in every parosh in time of peace. Also, that tender care may be had of the poore and needie, and of all such as are not able, or may be disabled to help themselves; there be some Deacons appointed in everie Regiment according to the order used in particular paroshes, and that in matter of greatest weight, there be a generall Eldership, or common ecclesiastick judicatorie, made up of all the Ministers of the Camp, and of an Elder direct from every particular Regiment, who shall choose their own Moderatour and Clerk, have power to set down order in matters ecclesiasticall for the whole Armie; that there may be an uniformitie of worship and Discipline. To whom appellation may be made from the inferiour Sessions and elderships.

Articles II, III and IV deal with such matters military as Courts Martial and Oaths of Loyalty, but in Article V there is a return to matters spiritual, with a strong suggestion of the Swedish discipline.

> For doing of ſervice and worſhip to God Almightie, the Lord of Hoſts, for whoſe Covenant this War is undertaken, from whom we look for aſſiſtance and on whom the ſucceſſe of warre depends; it is thought neceſſary that there be publick prayers, every day morning and evening throughout the whole Leaguer, for which purpoſe, ſome token or warning ſhall be given by ſound of trumpet or drum.* That on the Lord's Day there bee publick preaching, both before and afternoone, and if the time permit, two dayes in the week alſo. If any Miniſter ſhall neglect his time of prayer, or preaching, he ſhall for every abſence forfault an halfe-moneths pay, or as much as may be accounted an halfe-moneths pay, to be taken up by the Deacons, & at the direction of the Elderſhip to be diſtributed to the poore. And whatſoever ſouldier ſhall neglect the time of prayer or preaching, ſhall forfault a dayes wage for every abſence, and if after admonition by his Captaine, he ſhall be found guiltie of neglect or contempt, he ſhall lie in priſon for the ſpace of twentie foure houres, and ſhall be further puniſhed, as his fault deſerveth.

Article VI is concerned to forbid all buying and selling in the camp during the various hours of worship.[24]

Thus the Covenant army was provided from its first beginnings with Ministers, Elders, Deacons, Regimental Kirk Sessions and a Presbytery of its own. We have already noted the Presbytery take action in the Bishops' War, and confirmatory evidence of its existence and activities in this affair comes from the MS. records of the General Assembly of 1642. It is there written that:

> The Moderator having remembered the Aſſembly that the brethren that went to England with the Armie had their

* The use of a Drum Call for Church continued in the British Army to the close of the nineteenth century. In the official *Drum and Flute Duty for the Infantry* (1887), p. 21, it is distinguished from the Recruiting Beat by the addition of the 'Salute'.

Preſbyteriall meetings; the proceedings whereof were collected in Bookes by the Clerk, wherin were very many remarkable paſſages, which bookes the Moderator was informed were left in the hands of Mr George Halyburton, and therefore deſired the ſaid Mr Geoɪge to deliver the ſamine. Mr George having ſhowen that the booke was loſt by the negligence of his boy, and that he had ſundrie minuts beſyd him, Therefore the Aſſemblie deſires the ſaid Mr George Halyburton, Mr George Gilleſpie, Mr John Levingſtoun, Mr Robert Ker and Mr John Neave who were all clerks to the ſaid Preſbyterie to ſeeke out all their papers, minuts, ſcrolls and to ſend the ſame to the Moderator or Clerk that a book may be made up to be a perfect Regiſter.[25]

If such a book was ever made up it has also been lost, possibly sharing the fate of so many of the records of the Church in the later years of the Civil War.

The rapidly mounting tension between the King and the Parliament of England made the outbreak of war inevitable. Both sides to the quarrel mustered their strength, and both were provided with chaplains. The Royal Articles for War direct:

> that there be a Chaplain appointed for every Regiment, who shall read prayers orderly, and duly every day whilst they are in leaguer, and shall preach or expound some place of Scripture or Catechisme once at least on every Sunday, and Holiday, in some such convenient place as the Colonell of the Regiment shall appoint, and by the sound of a Trumpet or a Drumme notice shall be given of the time, in such manner as the whole Regiment may take notice thereof.[26]

The Parliamentary army was also supplied with chaplains, their presence being implied in Essex's Articles of War, in which all commanders are strictly charged

> to see Almighty God reverently served, and sermons and prayers duly frequented.[27]

The attendance of the clergy upon the latter army met with some criticism, and one of their number replied sharply that he had not only enjoyed good health during his fourteen weeks service, but did not see

> any cauſe of ſorrow for my adhering to the Parliament's cauſe, but eſteem it a great honour and mercy from God, that he ſhould move his Excellency my Lord, to require my ſervice in this great expedition.[28]

The first great test of battle took place at Edgehill, in October 1642. The King commanded that

> the sevint psalme (much to his purpois) to be publictlie sung, to the gryte joy of his people, who threw there capis in the air, saying and crying out, 'God save the King, forduard, forduard.[29]

On the other side, the chaplains were active, and

> rode up and down the army through the thickest dangers, and in much personal hazard, most faithfully and courageously exhorting and encouraging the soldiers to fight valiantly and not to fly.[30]

We have shown that the spiritual level of the Royal army was low, and it would appear that that of the Parliament was not remarkably high. George Wither, who led one of their troops of horse, had no illusions in the matter. He wrote:

> Now in myself I notice take
> What life we soldiers lead,
> My hair stands up, my heart doth ache
> My soul is full of dread.
>
> .   .   .   .   .
>
> Defend me Lord, from these misdeeds
> Which my profession shame,
> And from the vengeance that succeeds
> When we are so to blame.[31]

In their anxiety to secure the help of the Scottish army the English Parliament agreed to sign a solemn promise to establish Presbyterianism, and Scotland mobilised once more.

As a part of this mobilisation the ministers of Scotland were expected to provide a list of the 'Fencible Men' of their parishes, and, in addition,

> it was also orderit be the committee of Estaites, that ilk minister should furneish out ane man to this seruice, quhilk wald draw to ane thousand men, because there is 1000 ministeres, quhilk sum heir did furnishe, otheris was over-sein.[32]

Nor was this the end of their usefulness to the cause, for they were expected to come forth themselves as chaplains to the regiments in this Crusade for Presbytery.

The new army of Scotland had its *Articles for War* which commence by setting up the Kirk Discipline of the Army.

> Kirk discipline shall be exercised, and the sick cared for in every Regiment, by the particular Eldership, or Kirk Session to be appointed, even as useth to be done in every Parish in time of Peace; and that there may be uniformitie thorowout the whole Army in matters Ecclesiasticall, there shall be a generall Eldership, or common Ecclesiastick Judicatory, made up of all the Ministers of the Camp, and one Elder direct from every particular Regiment, who shall also judge of Appellations made unto them from the particular Sessions or Elderships.[33]

The second Article makes it clear that these Army Sessions and Presbytery are subject to the General Assembly in the normal manner. The third makes provision for daily prayers and for Sunday diets of worship with penalties for wilful absence, and it forbids all marketing during such periods, after the warning of Trumpet and Drum is given.[34]

The necessity for Kirk Discipline within the army was soon confirmed, for the Scots were accompanied upon their march by a huge crowd of women and children, estimated by one critic at 4,000, and their presence gave rise to the inevitable troubles. The Presbytery brought this scandal in its military flock to the attention of the General Assembly, and that body, through its Commissioners, asked the Scottish Estates to

ordaine the restraint of transporting women to the Armie
in respect of very great scandals arising thereupon.

The Assembly also passed on to the Presbyteries and Ministers
at home the duty of preventing this abuse.[35]

The machinery for the spiritual control of the Scottish army
was thus established and striving to fulfil its task, but it was
prevented from doing so by the bitter fact that there was a
serious shortage of ministers with the regiments. Robert Douglas,
as Moderator of the Army Presbytery, wrote to the General
Assembly on 17th May 1644:

> The necessitie for provyding this Army with able Ministers
> and the equity of releasing them after three months atten-
> dance least some congregations suffer to much by their
> minister's longer absence, is not unknowne to your Wis-
> domes. And it is too well knowne to us. That it was long
> ere some Ministers came up to the Armie. That some regi-
> ments are not to this day provided with Ministers, and that
> some whose reliefe hath been designed and called for, are
> not yet relieved though the time of their attendance be ex-
> pired. Therefore we humbly petition this venerable Assembly
> ... that the cause of these defects may be found out and
> redressed.[36]

This appeal was sympathetically received and a plan was made
for the more orderly filling of the posts of ministers to the
regiments. This plan was as follows:

> That a list be made of three Ministers by the Colonels, or in
> their absence the chief officers of every Regiment, with
> advice or consent of the Presbyterie at the Army, and sent
> to the Presbyteries here, or if the list be of Ministers in divers
> Presbyteries, to the Commissioners of the General Assembly,
> that they may appoint one out of that list to be sent to the
> Regiment to attend them for the performing of Ministeriall
> duties for three moneths. And that the relief of Ministers
> already sent or to be sent hereafter shall be in the same
> manner. And the Assembly ordains Ministers who shall be

thus appointed by Presbyteries or Commissioners of the
Assembly, respective, to repair to the Armie with all diligence,
under paine of suspension; and humbly recommends to the
Honourable Estates of Parliament, to provide some way
whereby these Ministers may have due and ready payment
of their allowance from the time of their going from their
charges here. And it is declared that this order shall be also
keeped for sending forth of Ministers to the Regiments in
the second Expedition.[37]

This plan regularises the practice which we noted in the Stewartry
of Kirkcudbright in 1639. The appeal of the Assembly to the
Estates induced that body to instruct their Committee to consider the provision of an

> allowance to ministeres sent to the Armie in England. And
> for the advance of some proportione thereof for their better
> outreiking.[38]

The Accounts of the Covenant Army show what was decided in
the matter of the payment of the ministers to the regiments.
These show that a minister normally received £5 as 'transport
money', and £7 10s. per month as salary. There are many
instances of payments for one month, or for half a month at this
rate, but not one single instance of the payment of £22 10s. for
three months' service. There are, however, a number of payments
of half of that sum, as 'in full of his three months attendance'.
This was possibly due to a cut in pay similar to that imposed
upon the Royal army, the balance being held in an early instance
of 'post-war credits'. It is also possible that the fine of half a
month's pay for neglect of duty, as laid down in the Articles, may
account for some of the reductions. This latter possibility becomes more attractive when it is known that the ministers who
were attached to the Staff of the Army each received their full
salary of £10 for every month of duty.[39]

The Roll of these Staff Chaplains contains the names of most
of the prominent ministers of the day, including, Robert Douglas,
Frederick Carmichael, Robert Kerr, John Moncrieff, Patrick

Gillespie, James Guthrie, Mungo Law, John Cruikshank, James Simpson, Andrew Cant, Robert Blair, and Robert Bennet.

The new plan of supply and the settlement of the matter of payment did do something to improve the number of ministers with the army, but the very short period of service and the large number of regiments embodied, combined to place an intolerable strain upon the man-power of the Kirk, and the shortage of chaplains continued. Baillie laments this in 1645, declaring that 'in two and twenty regiments there was not one minister'.[40] This is substantiated by the Army Accounts, for these show that almost every regiment had the assistance of a minister at some time during the years 1644-6, but that few of them were properly and continuously supplied.

The Assembly did what it could to mend matters, taking action in such cases as were brought before it. For instance, the Presbytery of Ersiltoun appealed to them from a decision of the Provincial Assembly in 1644.

> The Assembly having at length heard the report of the Committee of Appeals togidder with the letter from the Master of Cranstoun for Mr Thomas Donaldsone, Minister of Smelholme, unto the said Presbytery of Ersiltoun to his regiment. Do therefore Ordaine the said Presbyterie of Ersiltoun to furnish Ministers to the said Master of Cranstoun's regiment, and the said Mr Thomas go forth presently to the said Regiment.[41]

The mills of ecclesiastical democracy ground slowly, but they did induce the attendance of Mr Donaldson for he received one month's pay in November and a further sum of £5 a year later for his service with the said regiment.[42]

A consideration of the shortages and the shortcomings of chaplains with the Scots army must not hide the welcome fact that during the campaign which culminated in the victory at Marston Moor some of the ministers were faithful in their attendance. The Diary of the veteran Robert Douglas tells us little of the opening stages of the march into England, save the texts of his sermons, and curt notes of the weather, such as:

> January 24, snow and drift.
> February 8, it snowes.[43]

When at length the armies formed for the decisive battle, the chaplains were active on both sides before, during and after the action. John Vicars tells us that the Royalist leader, Prince Rupert, heard a sermon before the battle from the Book of Joshua, xxii, 22, and similar exhortations and appeals to the decision of God were made by the preachers of his opponents. The victorious army of the Parliament had not shown a uniformly high standard of steadiness under fire and Simeon Ashe, one of their chaplains, says that,

> as for them of each nation who went away, they have by their ministers and others been so sharply reproved, and their fault in such sort aggravated, that there is a hope they will regain their credit by good service on the next occasion.[44]

From the Scottish point of view, the account of the battle in Douglas's Diary is of the greatest interest. He has no doubt that the Scots did their full share, under God, in defeating the enemy. He dismisses Cromwell's effort in a classical piece of faint praise:

> Then Cromwell charged verie weel, but at the first charge was lightlie hurt, went off, and came not again, as was managed by David Leslie.[45]

Douglas continues his tale:

> God would not give the victorie to so great a multitude, we were then 24 thousand, the enemy 20, therefore he dismayed more than the halfe; they that fled ran fast away; they that stood, God made stand to it indeed. God would not have a generall in the army, he himself was Generall. Leslie went to Bredford, Fairfax to Carwood, my Lord Manchester was fleeing with a number of Scots officers. God used me as ane instrument to move him to come back againe; for I was gathering men a mile from the place, and having some there, he drew that way, and having a purpose to goe away, . . . I exhorted him before many witnesses to goe back to the field.

... That night we stayed on the fieldes all night; on the morrow I viewed the dead; we keeped the fieldes all that day.[46]

The immediate result of this narrowly gained victory was the capitulation of the city of York. On entering the city, according to Douglas,

the 3 Generalls marched with a great traine to the Minster; they desired me to pray and intimat the thanksgiving for the great victory to be upon the 18 day, I went to pulpit, and first exhorted out of the 60 Psalm, 9 verse ... then an exhortation to the souldiers to abstain from sin and injuring the inhabitants; after all the blessing.[47]

The official Thanksgiving was held on the 19th, when Douglas preached in the forenoon and 'Mr Someone [Simeon?], Mancher's minister', in the afternoon.[48]

The Scottish army now concentrated upon the siege of Newcastle, with the help of their second army under Callender. There is no need here to retell the story of the siege, but, during its progress, a shot from the wall killed one of the Scottish chaplains, William Hume, minister of Kirkinner. He had become minister of that parish in 1643, and had married Barbara Meine, the daughter of an Edinburgh merchant. The widow in her petition to Parliament, tells their little tragedy. She says her late husband

having borrowed money to furnish him for his charge in the army, and being cut off after four months service, she desired payment of the arrears due to him and consideration to his posthumous child and herself, he being their only means of subsistence.[49]

The General Assembly supported her appeal, and the Presbytery allowed her a year's stipend, which was not paid.

Parliament ordered that she be given two thousand merks, 'out of the readiest moneys available'. The Army Accounts show that in July 1646 she received £1,333 6s. 8d. Scots, the equivalent of the promised merks.[50]

These Accounts yield other items of interest here, in connection with the concentration of the Scottish army at Newcastle; these are the details of the expenditure on the great Communion feasts dear to the Presbyterian church. The items are as follows[51]:

1645

Mar.	17	Payed for clothis to the communion tables at Newcastle	0003. 10. 0.
Apr.	10	Payed to Thomas Storie carpenter for repairing of the communiom tables and washing the table clothis at Newcastle	0001. 16. 4.
Apr.	20	Payed for 48 gallons of clarett wyne to Thomas Seaton for the use of the communion tables at Newcastle	0006. 08. 0.
May	7	Payed for bread for the communion tables at Newcastle	0000. 16. 0.
Jul.	12	Payed to Thomas Seaton and John Broun for elements to the communion	0011. 19. 4.
Nov.	3	Payed to James Suord for 3 quarters of a hundred dealls and 6 double tries for making the communion tables at Newcastle	0004. 05. 0.

The order observed at such feasts may be gathered in part from Spalding's description of such an occasion in Aberdeen, under the one-time Staff Chaplain, Andrew Cant.

Vpone Sonday, 17th of September, the communion was given in New Abirdene for the first, and vpone Sonday the 24th of September for the last, not after the old fashion, kneiling, but sitting; nor the people sufferit to pray when Mr Andrew Cant prayit, as their custom was befoir, bot all to be silent and dum; nor thair comunion braid baikin nor distribute as wes wont, bot efter ane new fashioun of breid, for it wes baikin in ane round loaf lyk ane tryncheour, syne cuttit out in long scheives hanging be ane tak; and, first, the minister takes ane scheive, after the blissing, and braikis ane piece and gives it to him who is neirist, and he gives the

scheive to his neighbour, whill it be spent, and syne ane
elder gives in ane vther scheive whair the first scheive left,
and so furth.[52]

Before leaving the siege of Newcastle, it should be mentioned
that one of the chaplains to its royalist garrison was George
Wishart, formerly minister of St Andrews. He was among the
prisoners taken when the siege ended and he was imprisoned in
the worst possible conditions in Edinburgh until the successes of
Montrose brought his freedom.[53]

After the fall of the town, Douglas was called upon once more
to preach at the service of Thanksgiving, on this occasion he took
for his text the closing verses of the 46th Psalm.[54]

When the news of this success reached London, the English
Parliament ordered that public thanks should be given by all the
ministers of London and Westminster 'and the Lines of Communication'.[55]

The Scots might have been better pleased if the English gratitude had taken the form of wages or even food, for the Scottish
army was so neglected by its English paymasters that

without Pease, Apples and greene Wheat, they gather from
the ground they are not able to subsist.... It is above a
twelvemonth since a moneths pay was ordered by the House
... immediately after the battle of Longmarston, a good
proportion wherof is yet due.[56]

That this was no exaggeration is shown by the Royalist news
sheet, which encouraged its readers by telling the plight of the
starving Scots before Newcastle.[57] The town fell at last and some
of the Scots were able to return home for food and rest. Douglas
wrote in his Diary, 'upon the 5th of November, I came to
Edinburgh after 10 months' pains and travel; blessed be God
for it'.[58]

With the end of the campaigning season, an opportunity offers
to correct the popular notion that the ministers with the army of
the Civil War played the part of the political commissar of modern
times. The parish ministers of Scotland at this period were
accused with some justice of being tyrants who made the greatest

lords in their districts stoop to their authority.[59] In the army, however, although he may have been willing to have wielded such power, the minister to the regiment failed to do so by default in attendance. The records which have survived show that the main Scottish army consisted of twenty-one regiments of foot, nine of horse, one regiment of dragoons and a considerable train of artillery. To these must be added nine regiments of foot, three of horse, and some independent troops of cavalry, belonging to the supplementary army. In all, there were, therefore, forty-three regiments, some troops of horse and the artillery.

To supply this force with chaplains on a basis of a three-month period of service would have required more than 170 chaplains each year. This would have been an almost impossible proportion of the thousand ministers available, and the pay-rolls for 1644 show that there were twenty-seven ministers with the regiments in that year, and a few attached to the Staff. The latter may have had some influence upon the policy of the Commanders, but it is plain that many of the regiments can have seen little or nothing of a minister throughout that year.[60]

To complete the survey of the ministers with the army in the first years of the Civil War, some attention must be given to those who were involved in the Royalist rising led by Montrose in Scotland. Montrose had begun the war on the side of the Covenant, but he now held the King's commission and proved the most successful of all the Royalist commanders. His first attempt to raise the Borders for the King proved unsuccessful, and he withdrew to the Highlands. Here he formed a raiding column on a nucleus of some 1,600 Irishmen, and began a series of marches and victories, having great tactical success, but achieving little of permanent value for the royal cause.

Such a campaign does not offer much scope for the army chaplain, but there is ample evidence that these were present with the army of Montrose on the march and in the battles. It is not surprising that, in a force mainly Irish and Highland, some of the chaplains were Roman Catholic. This is made plain by the proud boasts of the one party and the bitter accusations of the other.

There were in Scotland, at this time, certain priests of the 'Scottish Mission', and these provided in rotation chaplains for Montrose. They included Father James Macbreck, Father William Grant, Father John Smith and Father Andrew Leslie.[61] These have left an interesting record of their experiences as chaplains to this royal army. They give as a reason for attaching themselves to it that

the expeditions it was likely to undertake afforded a hope of reaching some more remote districts which were ordinarily very difficult of access, which a priest of our Society had long but vainly, wanted to explore.[62]

This reason for their attendance would seem to contradict the suggestion of a modern historian, that Montrose's

rapid movement across Scotland to Inverary in winter was facilitated by the priests whose fugitive life familiarised them with every corrie and pass in the country.[63]

The priests say that they were warmly welcomed by the soldiers, who rejoiced at this spiritual reinforcement. They continued in attendance until just before the last battle at Philiphaugh, and their narrative is full of interesting detail of their duties and journeyings. They were called upon to bless the soldier before the battle of Fyvie, and, indeed, at each of the battles which followed. There is a strong suggestion that there were other priests in attendance, for before the campaign in Kintyre

the priest accordingly prepared all that would be required to say Mass, with further supplies intended for the Irish priests.[64]

The expedition itself is described with some feeling, by one who was by no means familiar with the corries and passes of the country.

When the heights were scaled, hills beyond hills rose above them, still to be ascended and almost perpendicular, so that they had to climb up them on their hands and feet. The soldiers as well as they could, administered cold water to the priest in an earthen jar, seeing him out of breath and exhausted with the toil of the ascent.[65]

When they were deep within the territory of Argyle, a camp altar was improvised for the celebration of Mass.

They placed a quantity of sheaves of corn in such a position as to form a kind of table, and breaking down the door posts, put upon it such pieces of wood as were smooth and well fashioned, as a resting place for the portable altar stone which was laid upon them, and hung up their plaids at the back and on both sides to prevent the wind, often very violent in the hollows at the bases of the hills, blowing the fabric away.

Sentries kept watch over the congregation until the service was at an end, and the account concludes, significantly:

they took care to get the priest away as soon as the Mass was finished, before the flames broke out.[66]

The evidence of his enemies confirms the presence of the priests with the army of Montrose. One of the charges made against the Royalist leader was that:

he has now joyned with ane Band of Irish Rebels and Mass Priests.[67]

There is also a letter from the Synod of Argyll to the Commission of the Assembly, dated 21st September 1646, soon after Montrose had to flee the country, which shows the continued activity of the said priests. The letter states that

there ar a number of freiris and seminarie priests, who are going about Kintyre and some of the Iles, using all diligence and endeavour to seduce the people to Poprie; and many, not only in Kintyre but also of the adjacent Iles, even of the better sort, already following their wayes.[68]

In December of that year the minister of Inverness wrote to the Commission, asking their guidance on several points of discipline, of which one was:

Wher men ar married by priests, what course shall be taken with these, and what to be thought of their marriage?[69]

It would appear from these that the Roman Catholic chaplains of Montrose had not laboured in vain, and that they had sown tares among the wheat for the Presbyteries of the North and West.

Forbes Leith declares that there were no Calvinistic clergy with Montrose in 1645, but a considerable number of ministers were later suspended or deposed for various degrees of compliance with the rebel leader.[70] John Buchan is inclined to the view that these sufferers were mostly unlucky time-servers. If there was no real sympathy for the royal cause the clergy of Orkney and Caithness, who signed the bonds of loyalty presented to them by the rebels, were most unworthy of their calling.[71] The Commission of the Assembly, sitting at Aberdeen, found cause to depose ten ministers and to suspend as many more.

The case of one of the accused shows how closely he came to acting as a chaplain to the rebel army. He was Alexander Clerk, minister of Skiralvie, who confessed

> that he preached before George, sometyme Marquis of Huntly, an excommunicat person, in the Kirk of Kingussie, where he also prayed and had all the exercise of publik worship before the said excommunicat person and his associats and followers in the rebellion, and that he also did the same in his own Kirk of Skiralvie, the said sometyme Marquis having come in after he began sermon.[72]

Some of the compliance of the ministers was probably due to fear, and they had good cause to tremble. Andrew Fraser of Abertarf and Robert Brounlie of Kirktown were murdered 'be the cruell Irishes', and many others were despoiled of all that they possessed.[73] Setting aside those who may have been moved by fear or hope of favour, there still remain some who served the King and his lieutenant, Montrose, as loyally and as well as their brethren served the Covenant. One such was James Wood, minister of Kilpatrick. He was deposed and imprisoned in Dumbarton Castle, for

> visiting James, Marquis of Montrose, though excommunicated, reading the papers of the said James in his pulpit, pressing a messenger to read the said papers at the cross of

Dumbarton, accompanying enemies to the Castle and demanding its surrender, using opprobrious speeches, and calling Mr Robert Rollock a loon minister.[74]

Wood appears again as a companion of Montrose when the latter had to leave the country, in September 1646.

Most of the fugitives got on board ship, and then

the ſame Evening Montroſe himſelf, accompanied only with one James Wood, a worthy Preacher, by a ſmall Cockboat got into a Bark which lay at anchor without the Haven of Montroſe; and being clad in a coarſe Suite, the Lord and Patron paſſed for his Chaplain's Servant.[75]

Montrose was not forgetful of this assistance, and he wrote from Gottenburg to the Earl of Seaforth, just before his last attempt to serve the King:

I am so pressed . . . being to set sail tomorrow for Scotland, that I can say little more; only, I must give your Lordship a thousand thanks for your favours and kindness to your servant Mr James Wood, which I humbly entreat you to continue.[76]

The Commission of the Assembly associated with James Wood and George Wishart two other ministers as deserving of excommunication; these were Andrew Sandilands and Alexander Innes. Sandilands acted as a messenger from the King to Montrose shortly after the battle of Kilsyth,[77] and Innes was described as

a deposed minister, who once made profession of repentance, hathe againe made defection, and now become a preacher to excommunicate rebells and a vehement enemy to kirk and State.[78]

William Maitland, who became minister of Montkeggie, was also named by the Commission as 'a constant follower of and a preacher to these excommunicat rebells, full of bitter railing against the cause and people of God'.[79]

Yet another preacher to the rebels was Murdoch Mackenzie, one time chaplain to a Scottish regiment in the Netherlands and later minister of Suddie.[80]

We have already mentioned George Wishart in connection with the defence of Newcastle. He was released from imprisonment in Edinburgh as a messenger from the city to the victorious royal leader, and he continued with Montrose as his chaplain until the defeat of Philiphaugh cancelled forever a sermon he had expected to preach to the rebel army. When in exile in Holland, Wishart became chaplain to a Scottish regiment in the pay of that country, which was stationed at Schiedam, and wrote a eulogy of Montrose which roused the wrath of the Covenanters. Wishart became Bishop of Edinburgh after the Restoration, and is said to have had ever a kindly thought for the prisoners in the dungeons of that city.[81]

Montrose's last desperate bid on behalf of the King came to an ignominious end at the battle of Corbiesdale, and in the list of the rebels made prisoner on that occasion are the names of two ministers, Mr Kiddie and Mr Meldrum. Mr Kiddie may be that Mr James Kid who became minister of Holyroodhouse, Edinburgh, after the Restoration.[82]

Montrose was himself taken prisoner and carried to Edinburgh for execution. It is said that at Keith he had to listen to a most virulent sermon from William Kinamond, the minister of that town.[83] In fairness to Mr Kinamond it must be said that he was not ignorant of war for he had been ordained as minister to Major General Leslie's regiment in 1644 and continued with them apparently until they were disbanded in 1647, when he received an excellent testimonial, and his services were sought once more when the war was renewed.[84]

Mention of Mr Kinamond is a reminder that the armies which endeavoured to withstand Montrose were also served by ministers. The very first of these, destroyed at Tippermuir, had been blessed by Frederick Carmichael and James Robertson. The former of whom, who had been with the army in England, dared to say:

if ever God spoke truth out of his mouth, he promised them, in the name of God, a certain victory that day.

Although proved a vain prophet, Carmichael was with the

Covenant army beaten by Montrose at Kilsyth, when he and Thomas Kirkcaldy, minister of Carnwath, were captured.[85] Mr Carmichael was not the only leader of the Covenant to fall into the hands of the rebels under Montrose.

Shortly after this battle at Kilsyth a party of the rebels captured Andrew Cant and held him and his travelling companions prisoners for some weeks. During their captivity Mr Cant bore himself very well, conducting daily prayers for the prisoners, and even preaching to their guards on the Sabbath. The story ends happily when the prisoners were able to take possession of the building in which they were held and to defend it until they were relieved by their friends.[86]

Returning once more to the battle of Kilsyth, the theme of a sermon preached to the Covenant army before the engagement has been preserved. Robert Blair, who had preached to the members of Parliament in the forenoon of 27th July, went out in the afternoon

> to the army, and preached to Crawford's and Maitland's regiments, to whom he had been minister in England, they being now recalled and joined with other forces at home. In his sermon he told that brigade that he had learned that they were become very dissolute and profane; he assured them that unless they repented, and that very speedily, there was a sore stroke ordained for them, and that though the Lord had honoured them to stand at Long Marston when many fled, and then covered their head in the day of battle, so that though they were often charged, yet very few of them were killed, not above three of Crawford's regiment, yet now they should not be able to stand before their enemy, yea, they should be routed and killed.
>
> He said that he expected that they would like well of his freedom with them because that they knew that he loved them, and that when he was with them in England he had a care both of their souls and bodies.[87]

Robert Blair might be criticised for depressing the troops before battle, but his criticisms were shared by many who knew the

truth of the misconduct of the Covenant army. The author of
Manifest Truths is more explicit than Mr Blair, for he says:

> want of pay is ſome excuſe for Free Quarters or Pillage,
> but for Rapes, murthers, violence, ſwearing, drunkenneſſe,
> I know none, neither do I believe them to be puniſhed
> according to Eccleſiaſticall and military Law, as is pretended.
> And take it not ill, that I ſay, if you love the *Preſbytery*,
> reforme the Army, for it is very ſcandalous.[88]

The Scottish army had fallen far from its beginnings at
Duns Law, and their enemies joyfully reprinted the proclaimed
reasons for a solemn fast held in Scotland. One of the reasons
being

> the great and fearfull ſinnes of our Armies abroad, (as we are
> informed), meeting with our ſins at home, as uncleanneſſe,
> Blaſphemy, ſpoile and rapine indifferently of our friends,
> as well as theſe who are diſaffected, whereas before their
> piety and devotion was admired, and ſo they were the more
> formidable to their enemies, now little difference 'twixt
> ours and the Malignant Armies, ſave in the formality of
> Worſhip.[89]

The blame for this decadence might be divided over many
factors, such as the length of the campaign, which forced a
greater dependence upon those who served for pay or plunder,
and the dilatoriness of the English Parliament as paymasters.
But the factor of importance here must be the serious shortage
of ministers with the Army, a shortage which continued as the
Civil War dragged on into its second phase.

REFERENCES

1. John Spalding, *Memorialls of the Trubles* (Spalding Club), vol. i, p. 156.
2. ibid., vol. i, p. 194.
3. ibid., vol. i, p. 279.
4. *Minutes of the Synod of Argyll*, Scottish History Society (1943), pp. 6f.
5. Baillie, *Journals*, vol. i, p. 201.

6. ibid., vol. i, p. 211.
   Cf. J. K. Hewison, *The Covenanters*, vol. i, p. 327. He calls Baillie, 'a perfect Bombastes Furioso', for his having 'his little son girt with a broadsword'.

7. Baillie, *Journals*, vol. i, p. 214.

8. C. S. Terry, *Life of Alexander Leslie* (1899), p. 73.

9. Wm. Drummond, *The Loadstar or Directory to the New World* (1711).

10. *History of Scots Affairs* (Spalding Club), vol. ii, p. 253.

11. *A Brief Historical Relation of the Life of Mr John Livingstone* (1756), p. 33.

12. *The Life of Mr Robert Blair, minister of St Andrews*, ed. Thos. McCrie (Wodrow Society, 1848), p. 163.

13. *Calendar of State Papers Domestic, 1640*, 268.

14. *Life of Livingstone*, pp. 32f.

15. ibid., p. 33.

16. *Fasti*, vol. i, p. 407.

17. *Minute Book kept by the War Committee*, etc. (1855).

18. *Selections from the Registers of the Presbytery of Lanark* (Abbotsford Club, 1839), p. 21.

19. Zachary Boyd, *The Battel of Newburne*, in *Various Pieces of Fugitive Scots Poetry*, Second Series (1853).

20. *Life of Livingstone*, p. 33.

21. *Calendar of State Papers, Domestic, 1640/41*, p. 29.

22. Spalding, *Memorialls*, vol. ii, p. 484.

23. A. Peterkin, *Records of the Kirk of Scotland, 1638-50* (1837), p. 308.
    Cf. Baillie, *Journals*, pp. 298f.

24. *Articles of Militarie Discipline* (Edinburgh, 1639). Printed by James Bryſon.

25. MSS. *Acts of the General Assembly*, Sess. 5, 1st August 1642. In the Library of the General Assembly, Edinburgh.

26. C. H. Firth, *Cromwell's Army* (1902), p. 313 n.

27. ibid., p. 314.

28. *A Plea for Defensive Armes, or a Copy of a Letter written by Mr Stephen Marshall to a Friend*, etc. (London, 1642), p. 2.

29. Spalding, *Memorialls*, vol. ii, p. 200.

30. John Vicar, in Firth, *Cromwell's Army*, p. 200.

31. George Wither, 'A Soldier thinks of Sin', in *The King and the Commons*, ed. Henry Morley (1868), p. 157.

32. Spalding, *Memorialls*, vol. ii, pp. 298f.

33. C. S. Terry, *Papers Relating to the Army of the Solemn League and Covenant* (1917), vol. i, pp. 3f.

34. ibid.

35. MSS. *Acts of the General Assembly*, Sess. ult., 1644.

36. ibid., Sess. 2, 1644.

37. ibid., 3rd June 1644.

H

38. *Acts of the Parliament of Scotland*, vol. vi, pt. 1, p. 197.

39. Terry, *Army of the Covenant*, vol. i, pp. cf.
    Grose, *Military Antiquities*, vol. i, pp. 291f.

40. Baillie, *Journals*, pp. 298f.

41. MSS. *Acts of the Assembly*, Sess. ult., 1644.

42. Terry, *Army of the Covenant*, vol. i, pp. 189 and 192.

43. 'The Diary of Mr Robert Douglas', in *Historical Fragments Relative to Scottish Affairs* (1833), pp. 52 and 53.

44. Firth, *Cromwell's Army*, pp. 314 and 321 n.

45. Douglas, *Diary*, p. 63.

46. ibid., pp. 63 and 65.
    Manifest Truths . . . containing a narration of the Proceedings of the Scottish Army, etc. (1646), p. 41.

47. Douglas, *Diary*, p. 66.

48. ibid., p. 66.

49. *Fasti*, vol. i, p. 735.

50. Terry, *Army of the Covenant*, vol. ii, p. 394.

51. ibid., vol. i, p. 279, passim.

52. Spalding, *Memorialls*, vol. ii, p. 279.

53. George Wishart, *The Memoirs of James, Marquis of Montrose* (1893), Preface, p. xxii n.

54. Douglas, *Diary*, p. 78.

55. *Journals of the House of Commons*, vol. iii, p. 677.

56. *Divers Papers presented to the Hon. House* (1645), p. 4.

57. *Mercurius Aulicus*, 29th Sept.-5th Oct. 1644.

58. Douglas, *Diary*, p. 79.

59. *Memoirs of Sir Ewen Cameron of Lochiel* (Abbotsford Club, 1842), p. 87.

60. Terry, *Army of the Covenant*, pp. xxiii f, and passim.

61. Wm. Forbes Leith, *Memoir of Scottish Catholics*, etc., (1909), vol. i, p. 313.

62. ibid., vol. i, pp. 295f.

63. Donald Maclean, *The Counter-Reformation in Scotland, 1560–1930* (1931), pp. 123f.

64. Forbes Leith, *Memoir*, vol. i, p. 298.

65. ibid., vol. i, p. 302.

66. ibid., vol. i, p. 310.

67. Mark Napier, *Memorialls of Montrose and his Times* (1848–50), vol. ii, p. 163.

68. *Records of the Commissions of the General Assemblies of the Church of Scotland* (Scottish History Society), vol. i, 21st Sept. 1646.

69. ibid., vol. i, 30th Dec. 1646.

70. Forbes Leith, *Memorial*, vol. i, p. 317.

71. John Buchan, Lord Tweedsmuir, *Montrose* (1928), p. 280 n.

72. *Records of the Commission*, vol. i, 17th May, 1647.

74. ibid., 30th December 1646.
    Fasti, vol. i, p. 504.

74. *Fasti*, vol. ii, p. 361.
75. *A Complete History of the Wars in Scotland* (1720), p. 132.
76. Mark Napier, *Memoirs of the Marquis of Montrose* (1864), p. 734.
77. ibid., p. 565.
78. *Records of the Commission*, vol. i, p. 269.
79. *Fasti*, vol. iii, p. 584; *Records of the Commission*, vol. i, p. 269.
80. *Fasti*, vol. iii, p. 285.
81. Wishart, *Memoirs of Montrose*, Preface passim.
82. *Fasti*, vol. i, p. 85; *A Complete History*, p. 185.
83. Napier, *Memoirs*, p. 775.
84. *Fasti*, vol. iii, p. 205; Terry, *Army of the Covenant*, vol. ii, pp. 525 and 526; *Records of the Commission*, vols. i and ii, 19th Feb. 1647 and 26th Jan. 1649.
85. Terry, *Army of the Covenant*, vol. i, p. 240.
    Napier, *Memoirs*, pp. 429 and 551.
86. Spalding, *Memorialls*, vol. ii, p. 505; Appendix, vi.
87. Thomas McCrie, *Life of Mr Robert Blair* (Wodrow Society, 1848), pp. 174f.
88. *Manifest Truths*, p. 41.
89. *A True Relation of the happy fucceffe of his Maiefties Forces in Scotland under the conduct of Lord James, Marquise of Montrose* (1644).

V

THE CIVIL WARS (2)

IN July 1645, Robert Baillie wrote from England:

> There is great need, that with all the ſpeed may be, those ſix thouſand foot we hear of, be ſent up from Scotland, and with them ſome gracious miniſters.[1]

Another letter from him, written on the same day, repeats and amplifies this plea for ministers. He says:

> Under God the wellfare of Scotland depends on this army. The Chancellor can informe how neceſſar it is to have a ſtrong Committee and Preſbyterie there to keep better diſcipline than hes been; raviſhing and plundering of friends, unpuniſhed, will make God to puniſh all for a few.[2]

The shortage of ministers continued and grew more serious as time passed and enthusiasm waned. The Army of the Parliament of England was likewise poorly supplied, and Baxter declared that the growing power of the Sectaries was to be traced to this neglect. He wrote:

> I ſaw that it was the Miniſters that had loſt all, by forſaking the Army and betaking themſelves to an eaſier and quieter way of Life.[3]

Strenuous efforts were made by the General Assembly and by its Commission to obtain a reasonable supply of ministers to the Army. The Assembly, for example, tried to meet the present and future needs of the Earl of Lanark's regiment, by instructing the Presbyteries of Glasgow, Paisley, Biggar, Lanark, Stranraer and Hamilton, to supply the post by turns. The Presbytery of Glasgow must send Mr Hew McKale 'tymously', and the churches left temporarily vacant are to be cared for by the brethren who remain at home.[4] The Assembly did, sometimes, admit of delay or excuse the services of a minister with the army, as they did of Mr Robert Scott, if his reasons be found good by the Presbytery concerned.[5] They could and did resent undue delay, as in the case of James Nasmyth.

Their Acts contain the following rebuke:

> The General Assembly, understanding that Mr James Nasmyth was appointed by the commissioners of the late Assembly to attend Lord Montgomeries regiment, and having heard the said Mr James, personally present, finds that he has been too slow in repairing to that regiment, therefore ordains him to go unto the said regiment presently without delay.[6]

The Commission of the Assembly endeavoured to supplement the supply of ministers to the regiments by letting it be known that expectants and ministers without charges were eligible to receive a call to a regiment. Thus the Commissioners considered the testimonials of Eleazar Gilbert, and recommended him to be employed in the ministry by any Scottish regiment 'who shall give unto him a calling'.[7]

There is no evidence that Mr Gilbert ever received such a call, but others were admitted to the ministry in the first instance to serve the army. One such was Thomas Thomson, who was admitted by the Presbytery of Glasgow to be minister to the garrison of the Earl of Calendar, on 11th June 1645. The Army Accounts show that this garrison held the town of Hartlepool, in England, which agrees with the statement in Fasti, that Thomson was minister to a congregation in that place.[8]

Despite such innovations, however, the main source of supply of chaplains to the army continued to be by appointment from a list submitted by the regiment concerned. This sytem was clumsy and productive of delay, for it sometimes happened that a list had to be rejected entirely, as in the case of Dunfermline's regiment in July 1646.

> The Commission, finding that they cannot choose any of the list sent from Dunfermling for a minister to his regiment, because of thee inabilitie of Mr James Sibbald and Mr Thomas Melvill, and in respect of ther are so manie alreadie out of the presbytrie quhair Mr Johne Meldrum is, therefor appoints aduertisment to be sent for a new list.[9]

Appointments from the lists submitted were made as speedily as possible, the Commission filling four regimental vacancies by such means in one day in August 1646.[10]

These efforts were so far successful that the number of ministers who received payment for their attendance upon the Army rose from 27 in 1644 to 54 in 1645, but fell in the following year to some 39. To these must be added the chaplains to the Staff, of whom there were considerable numbers in the camp at Newcastle, which held the King in 1646.

The complicated history of this period when the King and the two kingdoms strove all three for the mastery, is not relevant here save as it concerns the chaplains to the army in their proper sphere. During all the intrigues, religious and political, the Presbytery of the Army continued to function and to send and receive letters from the Commission of the Assembly. One such will indicate the involvement of the Presbytery in the affairs of the day. The Commissioners of the Assembly wrote to them in December 1646:

> Reverend and loving brethren, We ar to tak your desire concerning a minister to attend the King's family to our consideration, and according to your other desire have appoynted the Clerk to send yow a printed Covenant, though many printed copies have been sent thither before. ... Mr Robert Traill who was designed for the Levetennent Generall is now coming toward yow. The minister that was appoynted for the Master of Yester's regiment being excused for his infirmity, we attend upon another list from the

Master. Commending all your labours to the Lords gracious direction, we remaine, Your loving brethren.[11]

The gradual withdrawal of the Scottish regiments into their own land, which became possible about this time, called for the appointment of a novel type of army chaplain, one who was 'to keep session only'. This new office is detailed in a letter from the Commission to Mr John McGhie, minister of Direleton, dated 25th December 1646.

Reverend and loving brother, The Lord Ramsayes regiment being now quartered through diverse parts of Lothian they ar necessitat to addresse themselves for hearing the Word on the Sabboth in these places where they quarter. Only it is their desire that some minister be appoynted to keep session with them for discipline, that diverse scandalls may be censured: And this day one of the officers of that regiment having given a list for a minister to that employment, wee have nominat yow out of that list, and hes appoynted Thursday next and weeklie thereafter, or once in the 14 dayes, as yow and the Session of that regiment shall think fitt for the dyet, Tranent to be the place of the meeting of that Session for disciplin. It is their desire also, and we do approve it, that, seing at the meeting of the Session diverse others of that regiment may be easily drawen together, that you make some short exhortation on some passage of the Word before the meeting of the Session, Comending this to your care, etc.[12]

Mr McGhie found this duty tended to expand beyond these instructions, for, within a fortnight, he sought the guidance of the Commission in dealing with the 'scandalous persons in Dalhousies regiment, now lying about Tranent'. The Commission replied:

that the adulterers in the said regiment should be sent to the Presbyteries wher that offence wes committed to satisfie ther; and fornicators to the Sessions in the parishens quhair they faulted.[13]

When the Scots army returned home with a moiety of the
money owed it by the Parliament of England, many of its regiments were disbanded. This disbandment was coupled with the
taking of an oath of loyalty to the Covenant and the surrendering
of weapons of war. It is said that:

> at first they refuſed, but at laſt they were induced to accept
> of them; partly by meanes of their Lieut. General David
> Leſly, and partly by the incitements of their miniſters.[14]

The small force which was retained became known as the 'New
Model', and steps were taken to make certain that it was properly
supplied with ministers. The Commission of the Assembly was
informed by Mr Robert Traill in February 1647 that the army
commander left with them the whole choice of such ministers,
only desiring

> one to be appoynted to attend himself, two to attend the
> trowpe of horse, and one for evrie regiment of foot.[15]

On the same day the Commission proceeded to fill all of these
places and to arrange for their relief. Ministers are named for the
first and second turns, and are told:

> those that ar to serve in the first turne to addresse themselves
> to be at their charges respective aforesaid against the first of
> March preceislie, and to continue therein till the first of
> Junij; and that those that ar to serve in the 2d turne to be at
> their said charges against the 15th of may next, that they may
> be there 15 dayes before the other brethren serving shall
> returne; and from that tyme serve untill the General
> Assembly.[16]

All is now done briskly and there is no talk of lists or of consulting
the presbyteries concerned, but it did not work out so smoothly
in practice. The first alteration concerned Andrew Cant, who
was excused attendance on the score of 'age and infirmitie', but
who was required to find an adequate substitute for whom he
shall be answerable. James Nasmyth also begged to be excused[17]
and had the powerful support of the Duke of Hamilton, who

pleaded that the illness of the Lady Marquesse of Hamilton, made the presence of the minister desirable. This or some other argument secured his exemption and another was appointed.[18] But they did not all with one accord begin to make excuses, for some, like Mungo Law and John Nevey, took up the task willingly, and the Commission and the Presbyteries made elaborate arrangements for the supply of their pulpits during their absence with the army.[19]

The reasons for this urgency in providing chaplains for the New Model army can be gathered from a letter from the Commission to General Major Munro, which was written a few days before the appointments were made. This declared:

> we receive letters from the brethren of the ministrie who do wait on the regiments under your honours command, by which we ar informed of some bad and unreasonable men, small freends to the cause, who do bestirre themselves to hinder the rise and growth of the work of God, and to crosse, so farre as in them lyeth, the setling of honest and able ministers in these quarters by going about to cutt them short, if possiblie they can, off the means of their lyvilihood and maintenance, when they find themselves frustrat of the successe of their other bywayes and designes.[20]

Neither the zeal of the Commission nor the greatness of the need could secure a full supply of ministers for even this small army, and a complaint was made by its commanders to the Commission in March 1647. The Commission reacted by instructing all Synods and Presbyteries to speed the laggards.[21] The answer of the Commission showing their diligence in this was sent under cover to Mungo Law, who seems to have acted as Chaplain General to the army. He was one of the ministers of Edinburgh and he gave frequent and good service to the army throughout the long period of the war. His term of service with the New Model expired about the end of April, and the General pressed that it should be extended, but the Commission refused on the plea that Edinburgh had need of him.[22] In contrast with the willingness of Mr Law we might set the continued reluctance of

James Nasmyth. The latter offered reasons at both the forenoon and afternoon diets of the Commission on 1st July, why he should not be sent to the army, but that body determined that,

> having heard againe Mr James Nasmith, do, notwithstanding anything he has yet said, appoynt him to repare to the army for releef of Mr Johne Nevey.[23]

In spite of such firmness the vacancies were not filled, and in July the Commission had to write apologetically to General Lesley:

> Wee are sorie that, notwithstanding all our endeavours for ministers, yet hithertills it hath come to passe that the army hes not been so well supplied. Wee have of late nominat some for that attendance, and shall studie to make them keep to their dyets.[24]

Leaving for a time the ungrateful task of reporting the short-comings of the ministers of Scotland, we would say a word in defence of one of those who did attend upon the New Model army, and who had for his reward execration and death in exile. This was Mr John Nevey, minister of Loudoun, in the Presbytery of Irvine, and 'a very zealous and honest though somewhat violent man'. He was one of those appointed by the Commission to the New Model army, in February 1647. His specific appointment was for the second turn with Holburn's regiment. He was with the army when it was employed in the west country in stamping out the flames of rebellion kindled by Montrose. The incident which earned notoriety for this chaplain was in connection with the surrender of a rebel garrison at Dunavertie. Bishop Guthry tells the story thus. The Irish part of the garrison having escaped by sea, the remainder

> ſubmitted upon Quarter given them by *David Leſley*. But having ſurrendred their Arms the Marquis and a bloody Preacher (Mr *John Newy*) prevailed with him to break his Word, and ſo the Army was let looſe upon them, and killed them all without Mercy. Whereat *David Leſley* ſeemed to have ſome inward Check: For while the Marquis and he,

with Mr *Newy* were walking over the Ancles in Blood, he turned about and *ſaid, Now Mr John have you not once gotten your Fill of Blood?* This was reported by many that heard it.[25]

Sir James Turner, who was in a position to know the truth, comments on this account of the incident that

three hundred men could not make so great a puddle of blood on so hot a day, and David Leslie never saw these men either dead or alive.

Turner, however, does say that Leslie was wont to blame Nevey, 'put on by Argyle', for urging the slaughter.[26]

On the strength of this evidence, which implicates the Marquis as the instigator and Lesley as the executive, Nevey has been held up to horrify posterity as an example of Covenanting fanaticism by many modern historians.[27]

Is it not possible that he has been judged 'out of the context'? Montrose had left a legacy of hate and fear which had ripened into ruthlessness on both sides; indeed, a very few years later, the Scottish prisoners after Dunbar were so badly used by the Puritan army of England, that within two months sixteen hundred of them were dead.

It is surely less than just to single out for reproach one cleric who was not in advance of his generation.

The Church of Scotland has been made a partner in his guilt by such statements as that in the *Highland Papers*. There we have it said that Nevey was 'one of the leaders of the Kirk' [true], and that he 'had been specially appointed by the Kirk to the Army' [false].[28] Nevey had no special appointment but was merely one of a score of ministers who were to provide the first and second turns of supply with the New Model army.[29]

From the same source comes the statement that 'the difference between an honest fanatic and a criminal lunatic is difficult to define'.[30] Abuse of this kind has been poured out upon this minister who did have the courage to attend upon the army in a campaign where cruelty had begot cruelty. Nevey was driven into exile after the Restoration and wrote to his former parish of Loudoun:

Thanks be to your Lord and mine, I am well provided, and, I truſt, ſhall be ſo ſtill: I deſire you to look to the Repairing of the Manſe; and what you would beſtow on me, beſtow on it; for who knoweth but I may yet live a while, and die in it? However an honeſt Man ſhall bruik it when I am gone.[31]

He never did see Loudoun again and died in exile as the price of his zeal for the Covenant.

The New Model army of Scotland was kept in existence on a half pay basis during the winter of 1647-8.[32] The conduct of the soldiers continued to be scandalous, for the Synod of Dumfries complained in April 1648:

We have thought it very necessary to acquaint yow with the barbarous and savage behaviour of some of the souldiers that ar quartered in our bounds, whose crueltie is broken out to the vtmost in murdering, mutilating and wounding severall of our people, as the inclosed paper will more particularlie informe.[33]

The Commission was aware of such abuses and continued to press for the better supply of ministers to the regiments and the garrisons of Scotland. For example, they urge the Synod of Moray to

supplie the garrisons in Ruthven of Badenoch with a minister from tyme to tyme, and that they be no longer left destitut without preaching and other ordinances, as we ar informed they have been.[34]

The petition of John Middleton, minister of Rayne, was also supported by the Commission before the Estates. He asked for satisfaction for his services with the army for a total of ten months during the years 1646-7, with some reparation for the losses he had sustained from the rebels.

This plea was favourably received and this chaplain was awarded eleven Scots merks.[35]

The comparative peace which Scotland was enjoying was now to be disturbed by the course of events in England.

It was felt by many Scots that the English Parliament was demanding too many concessions from the captive king, and the Scottish Estates presented what was virtually an ultimatum to England demanding that the King be set at liberty. To add weight to this demand the Estates sought to levy a powerful army but found that the Church had no love for the Engagement, as this movement came to be called.

The Commission warned all Presbyteries against any compliance,

> specially that yow neither send any of your number forth to attend their forces, nor yet read, or allow any others to read, any ordours or papers concerning the advancement of their present Engagement.[36]

The efforts of the Commission are now, as it were, reversed, for they are directed to the prevention of any ministers from going forth with this Scottish army. The Estates, also approached the Presbyteries, soliciting their help:

> Wee doe confidentlie expect, That as the Ministers of the kingdome have ever hitherto beene most active and exemplary in furthering the former expeditiones, So now you will continue in the same Zeall to stirr vp the people by your preaching and prayeris and all vtherwayes in your Calling to a cheerfull obedience to our orders and engadgeing in this bussines.[37]

The majority of the ministers were proof against such blandishments, and opposed and denounced the Engagement from their pulpits. Sir James Turner, when attending church in Glasgow with some of the levied troops, found that the preacher 'railed maliciouslie against both King and Parliament', and ordered his men to leave the building.[38] The clerical opposition passed from words to deeds, and, in the western lowlands, verged upon armed revolt against the authority of Parliament. A body of troops under Middleton was sent to restore order, and at Mauchline a skirmish ensued. According to Bishop Guthry

The Chief Commanders of the Weſtern People, were ſome Miniſters, viz. Mr *William Aldair*, Mr *William Guthry*, Mr *Gabriel Maxwell*, and Mr *John Neve* (old *Cant*'s Nephew). They parly'd with *Middleton*, and would needs fight it, and ſo would their miſled people.... The Fight laſted not long; *Middleton* in an Inſtant put them all to the Rout, eighty of them being killed upon the Place, the reſt were taken Priſoners, except a few that eſcaped by Flight.[39]

From other sources some names can be added to this list of the ministers who led the insurgent force at Mauchline in 1648. These include Matthew Mowat, Thomas Wylie, and Alexander Blair.[40] All of these ministers were taken but the charges against them were allowed to drop for reasons of policy.

In spite of this considerable opposition, both active and passive, an army was raised and marched south to free the King. The leadership of the army was poor, for the veteran generals of the earlier wars would take no part in it, and the morale of the troops was low for many reasons, of which one was the threat of excommunication and damnation pronounced by the Church on all who should take part in the Engagement.[41]

To counteract the effect of this clerical opposition, the party of the Engagement had been at considerable pains to recruit some chaplains for their army. The list of those who served in this capacity has been preserved by their opponents, in a Minute of the Commission of the Assembly, dated 26th September 1648. This Minute states that the

deposed ministers and expectants and others pretending to the ministry, afternamed, notwithstanding of the frequent publik declarations of the General Assembly and their Commissioners concerning the unlawfulness of the late Ingagement in warre against the Kingdome of England, have yet served in the said Engagement, and performed dewties of the ministeriall charge to the forces that went to England and now in armes in this Kingdome in prosecution of the said vnlawful Engagement, Therfore in respect of the vncertantie of their ordinary residences, and some of them cannot be

personallie sumonded, being with the forces vnder the co-
mand of the Earle of Lanark and George Monroe. They doe
appoint that Mr William Cherilaw, Mr Robert Schidow,
Mr William Watsone, brother to Mr James Watsone of
Sauchtonhall, Mr William Purdie, Mr Robert Beatoun,
brother to the Laird of Westhall, Mr John Cruikshank, Mr
Thomas Panther, Mr Henry Erskene, Mr Andro Keir and
Mr John Halyburton be warned out of the pulpitts of
Edinburgh, Leith and Cannongate, to appear before this
Commission at Edinburgh the 10 day of October nixt, to
answer for their said offenses and appoints Mr Francis
Cockburne, who is in towne, to be sumonded presently to
the said day to answer for the same offence. The Commission
of assembly vnderstanding that Messrs John Broune, Robert
Broune, Patrik Forbes, Zacharie Wilkie, Patrik Mortimer,
William Herving, Robert Merser who went to England
with the Armie in that Engagement in Warre against that
Kingdome, to doe service in the ministerie to that Armie,
are not yet returned, nor any certainty what is become of
them, Therefore appoynts their names to be marked, that
upon their returne, or as informatioun shall be concerning
their condition, the Commission may accordingly proceed
with them.[42]

In this list of ministers to the Army of the Engagement, two
alone, Andrew Keir and Robert Broune, had been ministers of
parishes in Scotland. Francis Cockburn had been a minister to
a regiment in the Civil War, and Patrick Forbes, may have been
that chaplain to a regiment in Holland, who became Bishop of
Caithness after the Restoration. Many of the others on the list
have no traceable history in the Church of Scotland, it is possible
that some of them, like Henry Erskine, the father of Ebenezer,
may have found clerical employment in England, others may
have gone to Ireland.

The Army of the Engagement was routed in England and its
survivors made the best of their way to Scotland, which they
found more sharply divided than before. An army from the

west lowlands had marched upon Edinburgh, and stood face to face with the levies of the Scottish Parliament, just outside that city. This irregular force did not lack for chaplains, for the Commissioners of the Assembly resolved, on the 9th September 1648,

> for correspondence with the Noblemen and Gentlemen with the forces come from the West and now at Leith, to repair to Leith presently to the South Kirk, and there with these Noblemen and Gentlemen confer vpon the matters.[43]

This they did and the Commission met within the armed Camp and dated its Minutes 'at the Leager vpon the North Craiges neir Edinburgh', and, 'at the Leager near Falkirk'.

One of the matters which were then discussed was the lawfulness of seeking aid from England against the Engagers.

The Commissioners of the Church agreed that this could be done, if the English complied with two conditions:

> 1. That they maintaine the Doctrine, Discipline and Government of the Kirk of Scotland.
>
> 2. That they have Ministers to dispense vnto them the ordinances such as are Presbyterians and approven by the Synod of Divines.[44]

It is surely unique that the fitness of an ally should be determined by the denomination of his military chaplains?

The two armies in Scotland were disbanded without serious hostilities and a treaty was made between the parties they represented. The Commission of the Assembly, however, continued to seek out those 'pretenders to the ministry', who had dared to defy them by acting as chaplains to the Engagers. One or two of the more interesting cases will illustrate this activity. Thus, on 12th October 1648,

> Mr Henry Areskine appearing and declaring that he went out with Duries Regiment as a single sojer, that he never preached, but only prayed to the Regiment, and twice, at the desire of Durie, had a publick exhortation to the said Regiment publicklie from some passage of Scripture, which

being considered, the Commission thinke him worthie of a
sharp publick rebuke, and that the Moderator is accordinglie
to rebuke him for reading and interpreting Scripture publickly, he being only a privat man and not comanded to
exercise publickly, and discharges him to enter vpon any
tryall for the Ministerie.[45]

Mr Erskine's original fault in going with the Engagers was lost
to view in the more grievous breach of Presbyterian orders by
preaching before he had passed his trials and had been licensed.
A different case concerned Mr Robert Brown. He had been
minister of Kirkbean and had lost that charge for refusing to sign
the Covenant in 1638. According to *Fasti*, he did sign eventually
and became chaplain to Middleton's regiment. It is possible that
he did not sign for his chaplaincy was in the Army of the Engagement. His whereabouts were not known to the Commission
when they compiled their list, but, in 1650, he petitioned them,
as minister of 'Washingtoun in England', and acknowledged his
accession to the Engagement. The Commission referred his case
to the Presbytery of Dumfries. He seems to have been chaplain
to the Master of Caithness's regiment in 1651, and to have retired
to Holland after the final defeat of the Scottish army at Worcester.[46]

While the Commission was engaged in seeking out and punish-
ing those who had been chaplains to the wrong army, the drama
of King and Commons in England was played to its tragic end
upon the scaffold, in January 1649.

This event shocked the parties of Scotland into a temporary
truce founded upon a common resentment, and they proclaimed
Charles II as King.[47]

As a result of this we find ministers being appointed once more
to the army. As early as the month of March 1649, the Commission petitioned Parliament to settle some competent maintenance upon ministers when in attendance upon the army.[48] They
also directed Mr Robert Keith and Mr John Young to the forces
in the north engaged in subduing a rebellion under Pluscarden.[49]

The Commission, indeed, were most anxious to attach a

I

goodly number of ministers to the army at this time, as 'a very effectuall meane for purging of the Army', and[50] they appointed a further supply of four ministers on the 11th May. On this occasion they wrote to Mungo Law, once more with the army, to express their joy in the victory gained and to tell him of the new appointments. They continued:

> We know your being there hath been and is verie acceptable to those whom yow attend, and profitable vnto all; and therefore we pray the Lord to blesse your self with health for the attendance, and your travells with good succes.[51]

Apart from dealing with this rebellion, and that of Montrose a year later, this small standing army was mainly occupied with garrison duties. The Commission were anxious that these garrisons be supplied with ministers for other reasons than the spiritual welfare of the men.

The letter sent by the Commission to Mr John Makgill on his appointment to one such garrison makes this very clear.

> Reverend and loving brother,—Being informed that in the garisone of Perth, which yow are appointed to attend, there are many Malignant and vitious persons, Wee have recomendit to the Committee of Estates, and to the General Livetennent that some effectuall and speedy course may be taken for purging that garisone. We doe therefore desire that yow take speciall notice of such persons, whither officers or souldiers, and in your place and calling endeavour the discoverie of them, and that yow will actively assist and concurr with the persons entrusted for their removeall.[52]

The garrison chaplain was thus commissioned as a spy upon his military parish, not to detect and convert the sinner against God's law, but to detect and expel the political heretic. It may have been some suspicion of their motives which made it difficult for the Commission to place chaplains in each garrison. In December 1649, for example, they wrote to the Committee of Estates concerning such an appointment to the Castle of Edinburgh:

The garrisone of the Castle of Edinburgh, and the prisoners there, who are many tymes persons of qualitie, and the importance and considerableness of that place, do all requyre and call for ane able and faithfull Minister to attend there. How beneficiall he will be both to the place and to the publik, and how prejudiciall the want of it may prove to both, your Lordships can better consider nor we need to expresse. It is therefore our humble desire, that in your wisdome yow may be pleased to find out some way for a maintenance to a minister there, and we shall not be wanting to provyde a faithfull and able man for the charge.[53]

While these efforts are being made to secure a Covenanted Army in Scotland, negotiations were in progress to have a Covenanted King. These achieved a nominal success when Charles II submitted to the terms imposed, and came to Scotland with an un-Covenanted Court.

The menace of a restored monarchy brought the English army, under Cromwell, across the Scottish Border, and the Scots levied troops to meet the invaders. The confusing and unhappy tale of the divisions that rent Church and State in Scotland, even in the face of this danger, cannot be told again here; it is sufficient for our purpose that the Commission of the Assembly were active to secure the appointment of ministers to the regiments of the expanding army.[54] The Records of that body for the months of June and July 1650 show that they appointed considerable numbers of their brethren to such duty, with exhortations to use all diligence.

Some of those sent forth carried their diligence on to the field of battle, and they are reported to have been in action during the preliminary skirmishing near Edinburgh, when the attempts of Cromwell upon Leith and Queensferry were checked. A contemporary letter states that on one such occasion, the Scots were accompanied by four ministers, who:

being not known, received the lot of war, three of them killed and one taken. This was the party they most relyed upon, as being specially consecrated by the Kirk to this service.

Their ministers told the people before our army came, that they would not need to strike one stroke, but stand still and see the sectaries destroyed.[55]

The Scots held a very poor opinion of the spiritual condition of their enemies. Johnston of Wariston was told that

the Inglish sayd no grace befor and after meat, had no sermons on Sunday, . . . When I heard that they, instead of sermon wer killing Bacleugh's deer and spoyling the countrey, I thought it God's just judgement upon us for the disorders of our airmy in Ingland upon their people.[56]

It is only fair to quote against this from an English witness, that there was in the English camp:

such Preaching, Praying and heavenly communion with God, that we doubt not to hope that the Lord is with us and will prosper us.[57]

The balance of success in the early encounters and manoeuvres of the campaign lay with the Scots, and might have continued with them even to final victory, had not the dissensions of the country been reflected within the Scottish army. In these dissensions the ministers to the regiments were called to play an important part.

The duty expected of them was stated by the Commission on 1st August, when it appointed

the ministers of the severall regiments to bring in a list of all these who are now officers or volunteers and were formerly in the vnlawfull Engagement; as also to bring a list of all scandalous persones, that course may be taken for their removeall from the army.[58]

Johnston of Wariston tells how seriously and thoroughly this purging of the army was done. He says that on 16th August

wee spent al day in going through al the regiments of horse and foote, and purging out and placing in of officers, wherin I pressed upon their consciences that the guilt and blood and mischeife that may follow on haiving Malignant, profan, scandalous persons and Ingagers in our army, lye at their doors who gives not information.[59]

It is dangerously easy to condemn this purging of old Royalists from the new Royal army, but it was done from a firm conviction that God could win by the worthy few.

Those of the Scottish leaders who might have preferred to trust to big battalions were forced to acquiesce in the purge lest they lose that large part of the army who followed the Kirk and adhered to the Covenant.

So many of the ministers were now with the army, that the Minutes of the Commission for 21st August show that,

> There being few present in respect of ministers attendance vpon the army, the brethren are desyred to meet the morne at tua afternoon.

Another adjournment to the 23rd had no more success, and the meeting was called for 'Tuesday at 10 houres, if the motions of the army doe not impede the ministers coming'. There is no record that this meeting was ever held, for the next entry is dated 'Sterline 11 September, post meridien', when the battle at Dunbar had been lost and won.[60]

The English army, outnumbered and out-manoeuvred, was penned in the peninsula of Dunbar, and was in grave danger when the Scots left their favourable position, an error which Cromwell punished severely. It is customary to place the blame for this defeat upon the ministers with the army, for urging action, and, indeed, history would have been changed had they counselled, as formerly, that there was no need to strike one stroke. But in defence of their conduct and advice it should not be forgotten that Leslie himself put the blame on other shoulders. He wrote to Argyll, a few days after the battle:

> Concerning the misfortunes of our Army I ſhall ſay nothing; but it was the viſible hand of God, with our owen lacines, and not of man, that defeat them, notwithſtanding of orders given to ſtand to theire armes that night. I know I get my

own ſhare of the fault by many for drawing them ſo neer the enemie, and muſt ſuffer in this as many tyms formerly, though I tak God to witneſs wee might haue as eaſily beaten them as wee did James Graham at Philipſhauch, if the officers had ſtayed by their troops and regiments; which is all, etc.[61]

It seems a pity that the Scottish General had not known that it was really all the fault of his chaplains and so have avoided the mistake of sharing the blame with his negligent officers.

It is said that there were several ministers slain in the battle and pursuit, but their names are not discoverable.[62]

According to an English source, Mr Patrick Gillespie and Mr Waugh were among the prisoners.[63] Mr Carstairs, having been wounded and left for dead, was also taken prisoner, and used by Cromwell in his negotiations with the Western Army.[64] The three thousand Scottish prisoners who were herded into the cathedral church of Durham died by hundreds. In October it was said:

> I cannot give you, on this sudden, a more exact accompt of the prisoners; neither can any accompt hold true long, because they still dye daily.[65]

The defeat of the Scottish army at Dunbar did not mark the end of Scottish resistance, but it did so much to inflame the differences and the factions in the Church that it proved impossible to present even an appearance of unity in the face of a common enemy. The difference arose out of the obvious difficulty of raising a new army if the old barriers against Engagers and others were to remain. When the Estates put the question to the Commission they declared that all, with few exceptions could be employed in the national emergency.[66] But this decision was protested and contested by a considerable party within the Church, who argued with some justification that once the old Royalists had the power of the sword, it might prove difficult to take it from them again. The Commission having given its verdict, proceeded to find ministers for the levies of all fencible men, and they called upon all Presbyteries to assist in this. Before the difference could develop into complete separation, the de-

fenders of Scotland received another blow in the rather hasty
capitulation of the Castle of Edinburgh. A number of ministers
were within its walls at the time and these protested strongly
against the surrender. Mungo Law was one of them, and it is
said that he sent to David Leslie a piece of good oatbread, as a
sample of the worst fare the garrison would have had even after
a year's siege.[67]

The Commission continued to supply as many ministers as
possible to the army, with special care for those in authority
within the Camp. In January 1651 they appointed Robert
Douglas to attend upon the Committee of the Estates with
the Army

> for performing ministeriall dueties to them, according to the
> ordinance of the late Assemblie, and with him Messrs James
> Hamiltoune, Mungo Law, John Smyth, Robert Ker and
> James Sharp, two of them at least serving by courses.[68]

But the difficulties in the way of an adequate supply to the
regiments have greatly increased, and in February the Commission once more has to apologise to David Leslie, and suggest
a new scheme for improving the position.

> We are very sorry that the army hath at this time wanted
> [lacked] ministers. As you have done your part, so we were
> not wanting in ours for their provision with ministers. But
> the truth is the Colonells have been negligent to seek them
> from Presbyteries, who would not have refused to have
> provided them.
>
> The next remedy is that the Colonells send to the Presby-
> teries that have interest in the regiments, and if they doe not
> provide them, we shall desire to be acquainted at our next
> meeting with the Presbyteries that refuse or postpone, and
> with all that a list of some ministers be sent to us against that
> time by anie regiment that is not provided by the Presby-
> terie, that we may take course for their supplie; for at this
> present we neither know the regiments nor the Presbyteries
> that have interest in them.[69]

This system, if it can be so called, was clumsy and not necessarily productive of ministers to the regiments.

For example, the Commission replied to a request by the 'Earle Sutherland', that

> for ane minister to your regiment the Presbyterie hath power to appoint and we have written to them to do it with diligence.[70]

When a Colonel did write direct to the Presbytery, he did not always get speedy supply. The presbytery of Dingwall were called to a special meeting by their Moderator on 20th March 1651

> he having received ane lettir from the laird of Tarbat desyring that the pr'ie suld meitt to nominate ane minister for my lord of Kintail his regiment. and the laird of Tarbat compeiring, and giving ane list of two ministers yt were not within their respective bounds, as the letter of the Commission of the Kirk desyred, y'fore the prie ordaines Mr Jon McCra to repare to the Moderator of the province to the end he may be plessit to appoint ane meeting of the province to nominate ministers for the severall regiments and this to be done with diligence.[71]

The outcome of all this 'diligence' was a letter from the Commission in June urging the said Mr McCra to hasten to attend upon Kintail's regiment, he 'being appointed by the Presbyterie of Dingwall already to that imployment'.[72]

In connection with the filling of the vacancy for a minister in one regiment, a pleasanter note is struck, with an indication of a comradely spirit between a chaplain and his Commanding Officer. Massie's regiment asked the Commission for the services of Mr John Knox, and the reply was as follows:

> Mr John Knox is obliged to Sir John Browne for releasing him when he was a prisoner, and is desired to be with his regiment, we could not advise him to be with your honour; but find Mr Harie Knox, his brother to be verie fitt for your regiment. And understanding by the bearer that yourself is verie well content with it, we have appointed the said Mr

Harie to wait upon your regiment, and are hopeful he shall be a comfortable instrument there.[73]

In spite of such happy settlements, the division of opinion in the Church steadily increased the difficulty of obtaining a sufficiency of ministers for the army, and in April 1651 the Commission ordered that

> the ministers that are now putt from their charges by reason of the enemies possessing the other side to attend the Armie, and that each of them be putt with a regiment; . . . Messrs James Robiesone, Charles Lumbsdane, Archibald Newtoun, Patrik Sibbald, and Archibald Turner, personallie present, are desired to go to the Armie and advertise others of their brethren.[74]

This order was clarified in June, when it was stated that such ministers might leave the army and return to their respective parishes, 'so soon as it shall please the Lord to remove the enemy from these parts'.[75]

The Commission also let it be known that certain candidates for the ministry were available for service in any regiment that should call them.[76]

From all of these sources the Commission recruited more than forty ministers for the army during May and June of 1651, and, with this augmentation, the Presbytery of the Army became active once more. That Court wrote to the Commission at the end of June:

> We being an Ecclesiasticall judicatorie, and sittin here at Stirling for the present, could not but take notice of a great scandall given to many under our immediat inspection be Mr David Bennet his publict preaching here today, not onlie contrarie to your orders, but also to all the fair endeavours that the brethren imployed by you for that duetie could use.[77]

The remainder of this letter makes it plain that Mr Bennet had been guilty of preaching against the moderate party of the Kirk, in their stronghold of Stirling and before the troops of their own army. Tragically for Scotland, there were now two Scottish armies who would not unite in face of the common enemy. The more extreme party, or Protestors, as they were called, were strong in the West. They had raised a separate military force and their ministers, meeting in the Tolbooth of Glasgow, called themselves 'the Prefbyterie of the Weftern Armie'.[78]

Such a division of strength made the end inevitable. Cromwell crossed the Firth of Forth and defeated a Scottish force at Inverkeithing, the main part of the army of Scotland marched into England in the forlorn hope of Royalist reinforcement and was routed at Worcester. It is said that there were nine ministers among the prisoners.

The Scots at home could make little more resistance, and the brutal treatment meted out to the town of Dundee induced other places to yield on terms. According to *Mercurius Scoticus*, the minister of the town was among those slain at Dundee, but all three ministers seem to have been alive after the date of the massacre.[79]

Scotland had lost its army at Worcester, and its leaders of Church and State were surprised and captured at Alyth, so that capitulation was rapid and complete, and by February 1652 even the Orkneys had yielded.

There being now no native army the history of Scottish army chaplains is here interrupted, but the interval was filled by those who accompanied the English army of occupation, and mention must be made of these.

Some English zealots for Independency saw in the period of military occupation an opportunity to win converts from the 'pharisaical' priests of presbytery. As early as March 1652, Vane asked Parliament to send into Scotland twelve or more ministers, but this was never carried out.[80] The ministers who accompanied the English army, however, were most zealous in their efforts to set up Independent congregations or 'gathered churches' whereever possible. One such apostle of Independency was Nicholas Lockyer, who, it is said,

was fent for by fome of the Scots to overfee the erecting of new congregations in the North.[81]

Lockyer also published a lecture-sermon, *A Little Stone out of the Mountain*, which was ably refuted by James Wood, Professor of Theology at St Andrews, in 1654.[82]

Mr Wood also appeared as a champion of the Kirk in a debate with Mr Browne, Chaplain to Fairfax's regiment.[83]

Hugh Binning also put to shame one of the sectaries in the presence of Cromwell,[84] and James Guthrie clashed with the English chaplain Hugh Peters.[85]

Scotland was never wholly quiescent under the rule of Cromwell, and many men took to the hill-country, from a variety of motives, and, as Moss Troopers, raided the lowlands as patriots or plunderers. Such armed bands were drawn together into a more formidable rebellion under the Earl of Glencairn, who was replaced by Middleton who had a commission from the King.

Of the part played by the ministers in this rebellion there are as many opinions as there were parties in the land. Robert Baillie, speaking for the Kirk, declared that

> we have been very carefull to give the Engliſh no other offence at all; for in all this Northland ryſeing, to my beſt knowledge, there is no miniſter in Scotland who has had the leiſt hand or any medling.[86]

The English opinion was expressed by Colonel Lilburne in a report to Cromwell:

> I am informed Mr Robert Douglas is the principall man in their plot, and has correspondence with divers presbyters in England.[87]

A Royalist agent with the army of Middleton declares that he did his best to get the support of the ministers:

> but, for your comfort, Mr Presbyter is never like to put his oars in our boate, at least not to sitt at the helme, as formerly he hath done; yet you must not expect that wee should absolutely casheer him at the first dash, so he be not admitted to act you allow him to be a gentle spectator.[88]

The exiled King was emphatic that chaplains should attend upon Middleton's forces. He wrote to this effect to Middleton and also to the Moderator, to whom he said that, his subjects having risen in arms against the rebels,

> assist them in such manner with your praiers, and send such able faythfull and discreet ministers into the army, as may draw downe God's blessing on them and make them fitt instruments for the good work in hand.[89]

A typical Stewart addition to this reasonable appeal was his instruction that a copy of the *Forme of Prayer used heare by the King's commande* should be forwarded for the guidance of the Scots ministers. Sir Edward Hyde, with more tact than his Royal master, suggested to Middleton:

> you are the best judge what use to make of it, since it may be thought ther that his directinge formes of prayer is not agreable to the liberty of the Kingdome of Jesus Christ. Use it as you thinke fit, but give the good secretary a copy of it.[90]

It would appear that the King wanted chaplains with the army, that the Royalists were prepared to make use of them while the need remained, that the English suspected conspiracy between the ministers and the rebels, and that, officially, the ministers had no part in the whole affair.

It is said that the Presbytery of Hamilton debated

> whether Kenmore [a leader of the rebels] or the English were the greatest enemies. It was resolved that we are; for Kenmore had done but little hurt, but we muckle evil.[91]

Another view might have been taken by the members of Synod who met at St Andrews in April 1654, for Kenmore's men carried off nearly a score of their horses.[92]

The failure of Middleton's rebellion prepared the way for a state of comparative peace in Scotland, a peace secured by a system of forts which made a successful rising almost impossible. These forts had provision for public worship, as at Leith, where there was 'a good capacious chapel'.[93]

Chaplains were stationed at each of these garrisons, and when it was proposed to abolish some appointments, Monk made strenuous efforts to have the chaplaincies continued. He argued that, in the case of Edinburgh, where there was only one company available, it would not be safe for them to attend church in the town, leaving the Castle without adequate guard. At Inverlochy, on the other hand, there were eight companies,

> and there are no Scotch ministers for that place, being the place is uncomfortable, and if there should not bee a minister allowed for it, itt would make it much more uncomfortable than it is, being a garrison wee must continue, else wee shall not bee able to keepe this countrie in peace.[94]

With this plea of General Monk for the retention of his army chaplains, we reach and bridge that period of change in which the monarchy was restored and the regular army of Britain came into being.

It is not easy to summarise the services of the ministers of Scotland with their national army during the Civil Wars.

No useful formula could be devised to express at once the religious zeal of 1639 and the suicidal schisms of 1651.. Nor can any phrase be turned to describe both the devotion of the battle-wise Robert Douglas and the caution of the politic James Na-smyth.

In very general terms it might be said that some of the Scottish ministers made excellent army chaplains but that others did not have enough love for their fellow men to make the sharing of hardship a joy and not a duty.

The complete system of Presbyterian discipline for the army, which was so carefully established by the Articles for War, was not a conspicuous success. Part of the blame for its failure has been ascribed to the chronic shortage of ministers with the army. But the prime cause for the breakdown of the whole system was that it carried into the army that disastrous division of authority between Church and State which harassed the government of Scotland.

A regimental Kirk Session which sought out and corrected the offender against the moral law, and an Army Presbytery concerned with appeals of such cases and with the wise use of the chaplains available, could have done much good and little harm.

But a Kirk Session which sought out the political heretic, and a Presbytery which purged him from the ranks could do much harm and little good.

The lesson for the Church might be fairly summed up in the words of Sir James Turner concerning military chaplains:

His duty is to have *curas animarum*, the cure of souls, and it is well if he meddle with no other buſineſs, but makes that only his care.[95]

REFERENCES

1. Baillie, *Journals*, vol. ii, pp. 300f.
2. ibid., vol. ii, p. 296.
3. Firth, *Cromwell's Army*, p. 317.
4. MSS. *Acts of the General Assembly*, Sess. 9, 1645.
5. ibid. and *Fasti*, vol. i, p. 240.
6. ibid. and *Fasti*, vol. ii, pp. 109, 260, 258.
7. *Records of the Commission*, vol. i, p. 7.
8. Terry, *Army of the Covenant*, vol. i, pp. 234-6.
    Fasti, vol. i, p. 200.
9. *Records of the Commission*, vol. i, pp. 21f.
10. ibid., vol. i, p. 36.
11. ibid., vol. i, p. 155, 19th Dec. 1646.
12. ibid., vol. i, 25th Dec. 1646.
13. ibid., vol. i, p. 177, 6th Jan. 1647.
14. *A Declaration of the Proceedings of the New Moddel'd Army in the Kingdome of Scotland* (1647).
15. *Records of the Commission*, vol. i, p. 204, 18th Feb. 1647.
16. ibid., vol. i, pp. 204f, 18th Feb. 1647.
17. ibid., 19th Feb. 1647.
18. ibid., 23rd Feb. 1647.
19. ibid., vol. i, 23rd Feb. 1647.
20. ibid., vol. i, pp. 198f, 15th Feb. 1647.
21. ibid., vol. i, 18th Mar. 1647.
22. ibid., 19th Mar. and 29th April, 1647.
23. ibid., 1st July 1647.
24. ibid., vol. i, p. 289, 14th July 1647.
25. *Memoirs of Henry Guthry*, etc. (1702), p. 199.
26. Sir James Turner, *Memoirs of his own life and times* (Bannatyne Club, 1829), p. 240.
27. Andrew Lang, *History of Scotland*, vol. iii, pp. 181, 247.
    W. L. Mathieson, *Politics and Religion*, vol. ii, p. 71.

28. *Highland Papers*, Scottish History Society, vol. ii, p. 253.

29. *Records of the Commission*, vol. i, pp. 204f.

30. *Highland Papers*, vol. ii, p. 253.

31. *The Nature . . . of the Covenant of Grace opened and Applied in LII Sermons*, by Mr John Nevay (Glasgow, 1748), p. 473.

32. *A Declaration by the Committee of Estates of the Kingdome of Scotland held at Edinburgh the 15 October 1647* (1647).

33. *Records of the Commission*, vol. ii, 19th April 1648.

34. ibid., vol. ii, 5th April 1648.

35. ibid., vol. i, p. 367.

36. ibid., vol. i, 5th May 1648.

37. ibid., vol. i, 1st June 1648.

38. Turner, *Memoirs*, p. 54.

39. Guthry, *Memoirs*, p. 229.

40. *Acts of the Parliament of Scotland*, vol. vi, part ii, p. 138.

41. G. D. Henderson, *Religious Life in Seventeenth Century Scotland* (1937), p. 172.

42. *Records of the Commission*, vol. ii, pp. 73f, 26th Sept. 1648.

43. ibid., vol. ii, 9th Sept. 1648.

44. ibid., vol. ii, 19th Sept. 1648.

45. ibid., vol. ii, p. 106.

46. ibid., vol. iii, p. 25.
    Fasti, vol. i, p. 584.

47. *Acts of the Parliament of Scotland*, vol. vi, part ii, p. 157.

48. *Records of the Commission*, vol. ii, 2nd Mar. 1649.

49. ibid., vol. ii, 13th Mar. 1649.

50. ibid., vol. ii, 2nd Mar. 1649.

51. ibid., vol. ii, 11th and 12th May 1649.

52. ibid., 23rd Nov., 1649.

53. ibid., vol. ii, p. 334, 27th Dec. 1649.

54. For a summary of the rise and fall of the parties of Church and State in Scotland during these years cf. G. D. Henderson, *Religious Life in Seventeenth Century Scotland* (1937), pp. 107f.

55. *A True relation of the proceedings of the English Army in Scotland*, etc. Letter from Mr Owen (1650).

56. *Diary of Sir Arch. Johnston of Wariston*, Scottish History Society (1919), vol. ii, p. 10.

57. *The King's Pamphlets*, British Museum, E.778.21.

58. *Records of the Commission*, vol. iii, p. 9.

59. *Diary*, pp. 19f.

60. *Records of the Commission*, vol. iii, passim.

61. *Correspondence of Sir Robert Kerr, first Earl of Ancram and his son William, third Earl of Lothian* (1875), vol. ii, p. 298.

62. *Original Memoirs . . . being the Life of Sir Henry Slingsby* (1806), Cromwell to the Speaker, 4th Sept.

63. *A True relation of the routing of the Scots* (1650).
64. R. H. Story, *William Carstares* (1874), pp. 4f.
65. R. Taylor, *Pictorial History of Scotland*, vol. ii, pp. 978f.
66. *Records of the Commission*, vol. iii, 14th Dec. 1650.
67. *Mercurius Politicus*, 12th Jan. 1651.
     W. S. Douglas, *Cromwell's Scotch Campaigns* (1898), p. 203.
68. *Records of the Commission*, vol. iii, 7th Jan. 1651.
69. ibid., vol. iii, 14th Feb. 1651.
70. ibid., vol. iii, 15th Mar. 1651.
71. *Records of the Presbyteries of Inverness and Dingwall, 1648-88*, Scottish
     History Society (1896), p. 209.
72. *Records of the Commission*, vol. iii, 13th June 1651.
73. ibid., vol. iii, 4th April 1651.
     Fasti, vol. i, pp. 94, 95, 544.
74. *Records of the Commission*, vol. iii, 23rd April, 1651.
75. ibid., vol. iii, 12th June 1651.
76. ibid., vol. iii, 23rd April 1651.
77. ibid., vol. iii, 30th June 1651.
78. Baillie, *Journals*, vol. iii, p. 122.
79. *Mercurius Scoticus*, 2-9 Sept. 1651.
     Fasti, vol. iii, passim.
80. *Calendar of State Papers, Domestic, 1651/2*, p. 191.
81. Baillie, *Journals*, vol. iii, p. 178.
82. ibid., vol. iii, p. 213 n.
83. *The Chronicle of Fife being the Diary of John Lamont* (Maitland Club, 1830),
     p. 48.
     James Walker, *The Theology and Theologians of Scotland* (1872), p. 17.
84. *Biographia Scoticana—Scots Worthies* (1816), p. 167 n.
85. For Mr Peters cf. *A Collection of State Papers, of John Thurloe Esq.* (1742),
     vol. vii, p. 249.
86. Baillie, *Journals*, vol. iii, p. 252.
87. *Clarke MSS.*, lxxxvi.70.
88. C. H. Firth, *Scotland and the Protectorate* (Scottish History Society), pp. 121f.
89. *Clarendon MSS*, xlvii.353.
90. ibid., xlvii.355.
91. *Mercurius Politicus*, 12th Nov. 1653.
92. *Lamont's Diary*, pp. 83f.
93. Edwin Lankester, *Memorials of John Ray* (1846), p. 156.
94. *Clarke MSS.*, Worcester College, Oxford, li, f. 21.
95. Sir James Turner, *Pallas Armata* (1683), p. 223.

VI

IN IRELAND

THE historian of the Scottish mercenary soldiers in Ireland has said that

although there had been Hebrideans in Ireland before 1314, the coming and consolidation of the 'galloglaigh' in Ireland is bound up closely with the Bruce invasion.[1]

Accepting this as a suitable starting-point for our study of the clergy who served the Scottish soldiers in that country we find immediate indication of their attendance. In 1317 a Papal Bull was issued against those Minorite friars who had preached rebellion in Ireland and who had urged the people to assist the Scottish invaders.[2]

The centuries which followed show little trace of any serious invasion of Scots, and the intermittent flow of Macdonalds into Antrim and of other Islesmen into Ulster and Connaught is of no importance here. In the reign of the first Queen Elizabeth, however, a priest revealed a Spanish plot to convey an army of Scots into Ireland, which might suggest that clerical aid was involved.[3] It was the arrival of Scottish regiments to assist in curbing a rebellion in Ireland in 1642 that marked the real beginning of a long and close association of Scottish soldiers with that unhappy island. The war to which they were brought had religious rivalry for background, and the clergy were prominent on both sides.

The Protestants, besieged in Drogheda, doubled their weekly Fasts, in order that by turns each Divifion of the Regiment might partake of one, and by our frequent Admonitions endeavoured to prevent thofe Vices ufually incident to Soldiers, as alfo in regard that by their continual Watches they could not attend the publick Prayers offered every Day in the Church.[4]

This religious note was re-echoed by the Scottish regiments, which were still filled with the Covenanting spirit of the Bishops' Wars. No sooner had their little force established a base at Carrickfergus, than the ministers who were with them set up Regimental Kirk Sessions.

This was done with the consent of the respective Colonels, in the regiments of Argyll, Eglinton, Glencairn and Home, and then they sought to make the next step and to create an army Presbytery.

The first meeting of this Presbytery was held at Carrickfergus on Friday 10th June 1642, and from that date the Presbyterian Church of Ireland can trace the unbroken succession of its Courts and ordinances. This historic meeting was attended by Messrs John Baird, Thomas Peebles, Hugh Cunningham and John Aird, who were the chaplains respectively of the regiments named above.

A fifth minister was Mr John Scott, chaplain to Monro's regiment. The four regimental Kirk Sessions each sent an Elder. Two more ministers were with the army in Ireland, James Simpson and John Livingstone, but were prevented by their duties from attending this meeting.

After a sermon by Mr Baird, a Moderator was appointed, and Mr Peebles was chosen as Clerk, an office which he held for thirty years. The meeting resolved that steps should be taken to set up Elderships in those regiments that lacked them, and that the Colonels should be approached to that end. Each minister was urged to begin a course of catechetical instruction in his regiment, and they agreed to meet weekly for business and to hear a discourse from one of their number from the book of Isaiah.

A Fast was appointed for the following week, for the suffering churches in Germany and Bohemia, for the differences between the King and Parliament, and for the people of Ireland. The Presbytery also wrote to the Lords Claneboy and Montgomery, inviting them to send the chaplains of their regiments to the next meeting. These Colonels willingly agreed, and John Drysdale and James Baty, the chaplains in question, were, after trial, admitted members of the Presbytery.[5]

Many applications were received from all over the country for admission to the new Presbytery, and, before long, Elderships had been set up in fifteen places, some of which had no minister of their own. The Presbytery petitioned the General Assembly for the return of the ministers who had fled from the rebellion in Ireland to Scotland. The Assembly tried to assist by sending as temporary supply some of the best ministers of Scotland, including Robert Blair, Robert Baillie and John Livingstone. These delegates were instructed to

visit, comfort, instruct and encourage the scattered flocks of Christ, to employ themsleves to their uttermost, with all faithfulness and singleness of heart, planting and watering, according to the direction of Jesus Christ, and according to the doctrine and discipline of this Church in all things; and if need be (with the concurrence of such of the ministers of the army as are there), to try and ordain such as shall be found qualified for the ministry.[6]

One of these commissioners, Mr John Livingstone, had been sent to Ireland some months previous to this appointment. In his own account of the matter, he says:

In April, 1642, I was sent, by order of the council of Scotland, to Ireland, to wait on the Scottish army, that went over with Major-General Monro; and staid for six weeks, part in Carrickfergus, where the head-quarters were; and for another six weeks most part at Antrim, with Sir John Clotworthy and his regiment, who had obtained an order from the council for me so to do. I preached for the most part in these two places; but sometimes in other parishes of the coast side about; and before I left Antrim, we had the communion celebrated there.[7]

During the summer months of 1642, the Scottish force in Ireland was increased, and the Presbytery there urged the new regiments to provide themselves with chaplains without delay, but reserving to themselves the right to confirm such appointments.[8] That some such supervision was necessary was shown in the case of Mr James Houston. He had been deposed from the charge of Glasford in the Presbytery of Hamilton, having fallen into flagrant sin.

The Presbytery of Paisley, however, granted him liberty to preach as the minister to a regiment in Ireland. When the people of Glasford heard of this, they sought for his return to the charge, but this was peremptorily refused by the Presbytery of Hamilton. The case eventually reached the Assembly and Houston was removed from the ministry.[9]

Among the commissioners from the Presbyteries who attended this Assembly was Mr John Scott, chaplain to Monro's regiment in Ireland, and representative of the Presbytery.[10]

An unnamed minister serving with the army in Ireland at this time embraced more within the scope of his duty than is customary. After a battle in June 1643, in which the Irish army was beaten,

> Con Oge got quarters and came away with a guard with the rest of the Prisoners, a minister came behind his back, unknown to the Guard, and shot him and so left him dead in the place. At which Sir Robert Stewart, who commanded that day the British, was in an extreme passion, and charged the minister never more to come abroad.[11]

Such an offence by a cleric admits of no excuse, whether of religious bigotry or personal feud, but it seems to have been utterly at variance with the accepted standard of the ministers selected for the Scottish regiments.

For example, Viscount Montgomery wrote to the General Assembly of 1643, requesting that body

> to make choice of some two grave and learned ministers of good and holy lives and conversations, and them recommend, and send over to this country, the one for the parish church

of Newton, and the other for my regiment, and by the assistance of God, they shall not want competent stipends.[12]

The victories of Montrose made it necessary to recall a part of the Scottish contingent for the defence of their own land. They were willing to return but they took advantage of the emergency to press for some redress of their many grievances, threatening that they would declare themselves for the King. The Army Presbytery hastened to denounce such conduct as 'ambiguous, scandalous, contrary to the Covenant and a divisive motion'. They debated the matter with some of the ring-leaders, and informed the Assembly of the whole affair. The Assembly endeavoured to heal the breach by sending yet more commissioners, in April 1644, who were to press upon the army in Ireland the Solemn League and Covenant.[13]

The labours of these Commissioners, and of the others who came from England on a similar errand, do not concern us, except as a revelation of the weakness of the Army Presbytery at that time.

There is a letter to the General Assembly, dated from Bangor, 27th May 1644, which states the position in full.

> Of the ministers of the regiments, two are at the utmost borders of the county of Antrim, even at Coleraine and the Route, and three are not in the Kingdom now; so that there are but three ministers of the regiments in all to join with the commissioners from Scotland, and with the two foresaid ministers of the country, in discipline, which makes our Presbytery very weak, and the peoples necessity not so supplied as their need requires every way, especially when the army is in the fields.[14]

This letter was signed by James Hamilton, one of the commissioners, as Moderator, and by James Baty, as Clerk, 'in the name of the Presbytery of the Scottish forces in Ireland'.

When James Hamilton and John Weir were returning from this service in Ireland they were captured at sea by the notorious Colkitto, and were held prisoners for a time, on board ship and in Meagrie Castle, Ardnamurchan. They improved the time, according to the Apostolic example, with spiritual exercises, and

> every day twice did both of them expound a psalm or part of a psalm, the one praying before and the other after the said exposition, in the hearing of their fellow prisoners, so long as they were together, at which time they had reached the 81st Psalm.

John Weir died of the hardships of their imprisonment, in his thirty-fourth year.[15]

Although the Army Presbytery was so weak, it continued to discharge its duty to soldiers and civilians alike, to reprove immorality and to maintain the ordinances of religion throughout the whole area. They also continued to send commissioners to the General Assembly. That Court wrote a letter of encouragement, to 'the reverend Brethren of the Presbytery unto the Army in Ireland', in 1645:

> Seeing those of your members who were sent from you to us, having carefully attended in everything that was committed to them for their despatch from this Assembly, are now to return: we think fit to write with them unto you, hearing from them of your diligence and care in promoving of the great work of the Lord, notwithstanding of manifold oppositions, that you might be encouraged without fainting to go on unto the utmost of your power to set forward that work as watchmen entrusted by God, so that you may be, in these difficult times, not only a comfort of that army whereof you have the charge; but that you may also be for the strengthening and encouragement of that poor land wherin for the time ye are.[16]

Thus encouraged the Army Presbytery continued zealously its efforts against Papists and its endeavours to recruit a sufficiency of ministers for the army and for the many vacant charges in Ireland. But they were not to be rushed into accepting any who offered, and they directed that any who sought to take up charges in the country must first produce good testimonials from those who knew them at home, and must then pass trials as to their walk and conversation in Ireland.[17] The flow of expectants was satisfactory and place after place was filled, and in 1647 there were in addition to the army ministers nearly thirty Presbyterian ministers in the Province, and for this success much credit must be given to the ministers with the army.

The Assembly continued to send its commissioners to supplement the work of the ministers in Ireland. Mr John Livingstone, for example, was there in 1646, when the Army Accounts record that there was:

> Paid to Mr Johne Livingstoune minister for his allowance at 10s. starling pr. diem being fortie eight dayes is . . . 288. 0. 0. (Scots).

Mr Livingstone also received the repayment of a sum

> qlk he lent to the sd. Captane Johnstoune and gatt not bak againe sixteine pounds sixteine schillings.[18]

The said Captain Johnstone was the commander of one of the ships conveying troops to Ireland.

One is tempted to digress into the subject of the hardships endured by the Scottish troops in Ireland, they having received five months' pay for five years' service, but such was the common complaint of all the Scots who looked to the Parliament of England for payment, and is not relevant. Of greater interest is the description in Adair's *Narrative* of the methods used by the Army Presbytery to discipline its own members. In common with other Presbyteries, they arranged that

> once or twice a year, the members of the Presbytery undergo an admonition or censure of their brethren, if need require it, as to any part of their carriage, whether in the Presbytery or otherwise, or in the discharge of their ministry, known to any of their brethren. And for that end, one or two at once were removed till the rest considered what grounds there were to admonish, censure or encourage them; and thus by degrees to be removed, and their carriage considered by the rest, till the whole members, especially the ministers

receive the mind of the rest. This was thought a fit means
for keeping the brethren more watchful in their conversing,
both with their brethren and their congregations and otherwise; as well as to keep up the authority of the Presbytery
over particular brethren.[19]

While they were thus alert to detect and to condemn any
shortcomings of the clergy, the Presbytery did not overlook the
sinners without, and particularly those of the army. In 1647 they
were particularly concerned that some of high rank seemed to be
over friendly with the Sectarian element among the English, and
they did not hesitate to voice their fear that this might lead to an
inflow of the dreaded Independency. To meet this criticism,
General Monro wrote:

> To the ministers of the severall paroches within the Scottish
> armies quarters.
> Reverend sir, I, with the officers entrusted from the several
> regiments, having taken to our consideration the mistakes
> that had beene, and may be conceived of our proceidings,
> by the ministers and people of this country, thought it
> expedient to desyre you to be confident that all our resolu-
> tions shall be such as shall in no way tend to the prejudice of
> Religion, Covenant, or what else as good Christians we are
> tyed to; and therefore wishes you would be pleased publiclie
> to assuir all these of your people who have intertained
> jealousies or fears of this nature, that the armies good inten-
> tions may no further be mistaken after this sort, and so
> recommending you to God, I rest your affectionat friend,
>   Robert Monro.[20]
> Carrickfergus, 11 August, 1647.

In spite of this assurance, the Commission of the Assembly wrote
urgently to the brethren in Ireland to warn them of the 'Anti-
nomian or Annabaptistical leaven', and:

> We also exhort you, dear brethren, to keep good corres-
> pondence with the army there, sieing they are scarce of
> ministers to attend them. Wherever they have any rende-

vouse, or wher officers meitt for publick consultations, it wer
fitt some of your number be present to blesse their meitings,
consultations and proceidings.[21]

The wheel has now revolved, and where once the ministers of
the army had supplied the many vacant parishes, the parish clergy
are called upon to make good the shortage of ministers with the
regiments.

Another source of anxiety to the Presbytery in Ireland was the
Engagement, which, in spite of the protests of the ministers, drew
away some of the Scottish regiments on that ill-fated expedition.
The failure of this effort and the execution of the King produced
in Ireland the same uneasy alliance between Covenanter and
Royalist, that it did in Scotland. The predominance of the latter
made the position of the ministers to the army more and more
difficult, for they

were yet more discountenanced by the other party, upon
which they left off frequenting the league; and employed
themselves in such parts of the country as were destitute of
ministers.[22]

The now Royalist army was not destitute of Scottish chaplains,
for Mr James Gordon was chaplain to Montgomery's regiment.
He appears on a list of officers, known as the '49 *lots*, who were
still suing for their arrears of pay in 1682.[23]

The years of Cromwellian rule in Ireland, and, indeed, those
of the restored monarchy, have little to contribute to our study,
but one indirect result of the forming of the Presbytery in Ireland
might be mentioned here.

This was the formation of the first Presbytery in North
America, for which the credit is given to an emigrant minister of
the Presbyterian Church in Ireland. He was Francis Mackemie,
who was licensed by the Presbytery of Laggan in 1681 and went
to America as pastor to a group of colonists two years later. Many
years later he was largely instrumental in drawing together a
number of ministers with their people to form a Presbytery.[24]

It might therefore be claimed with some truth that the little
band of army chaplains who met at Carrickfergus in 1642 played

an important part in establishing Presbyterianism, not only in Ireland, but also in the New World.

The long story of war in Ireland is resumed with the attempt of James II to return to power by way of that country, an attempt which might have been successful but for the stubborn resistance of two small towns. The Presbyterian Church, at the outbreak of this war, consisted of about one hundred charges and of eighty ministers.

Many of the ministers fled to Scotland but others remained to face the storm and to become, by force of circumstance, chaplains to the Protestant garrisons and regiments.

The names of these clerical stalwarts reveal in many cases their Scottish descent, as in the case of James Gordon, who advised the closing of the gates of Londonderry against the King's troops. Another Scottish name which became famous during the siege of that town was that of John Mackenzie, who wrote an account of the affair from his position as 'Chaplain to a Regiment there'.

Mr Mackenzie gives the following list of the Non-conformist clergy who were in the town during the siege, and who acted as chaplains to the townspeople and the garrison[25]:

Mr Thomas Boyd of Aghadowy,	
Mr Will. Crooks of Ballykelly,	
Mr John Rowat of Lifford,	
Mr John Mackenzie of Derilloran,	
Mr John Hamilton of Donachedie,	Dead.
Mr Robert Wilson of Strabane,	Dead.
Mr David Brown of Urnay,	Dead.
Mr Will. Gilchrist of Kilrea,	Dead.

Londonderry Cathedral was used for worship by both the Episcopalians and the Presbyterians, the latter having the afternoon on Sundays, and, according to one authority, the larger attendance.[26]

A detailed account of the efforts of the town's ministers is to be found in the *Londeriados*, as follows:

The Church and Kirk did jointly preach and pray
In St Columba's Church most lovingly;

Where Dr Walker, to their great content,
Preached stoutly against a Popish Government.
Master Mackenzie preached on the same theme,
And taught the army to fear God's great name.
The Reverend Rowat did confirm us still,
Preaching submission to God's holy will.
He likewise prophesied our relief,
When it surpassed all human belief.
The same was taught by the learned Mr Crooks,
And Master Hamilton showed it from his books.
Then Mills, a ruling elder, spoke the same
Of our relief, six weeks before it came
From sunrising to sunsetting they taught,
Whilst we against the enemy bravely fought.[27]

Seth Whittle, an Episcopal minister who did not survive the siege, also preached encouragement, closing one address with the promise:

Proceed with a ſteady aſſurance of Succeſs and Victory, for the Lord is with you and will deliver you.[28]

It was Mr John Knox of Glaslough who preached the sermon of Thanksgiving before General Kirk, when the relief of the town was made at long last.[29]

The tactics which brought the relieving ships safely up to the town seem to have been suggested by the same James Gordon who had first counselled resistance.

A footnote to the heroic exertions of the ministers and people of Londonderry is provided by the title of a pamphlet published thirty-two years later.

A View of the Danger and Folly of being Public-Spirited and Loving One's Country in the Deplorable Case of the Londonderry and Inniskilling Regiments, etc.

This pamphlet was issued by 'Mr Hamill, Gent., their agent', and it shows that the pay still due to these officers and men totalled £74,757 17s. 8d.

The other centre of resistance to the army of James II was the town of Inniskillen, and an account of its ordeal, by William McCarmick, gives a great deal of credit to Mr Robert Kelso, the Presbyterian minister. It is said that Mr Kelso

> laboured both publicly and privately in animating his hearers to take up arms and stand upon their own defence, showing example himself by wearing arms and marching at the head of them when together.

When active preparation for resistance was begun, a council was set up of

> a certain number of officers with Mr Kelso, the non-Conformist minister, to sit in council every day, to consider what measures were most proper to pursue for our preservation.[30]

The raising of these sieges did not end the war, and ministers were required with the regiments in the field.

Mr George Story, himself a chaplain to the army, tells of the efforts made by his brethren in the interests of morality and decency. He wrote:

> though our army had been much afflicted with Sickneſs and Mortality, yet this was little taken notice of by a great many who gave themſelves up to all the Wickedneſs imaginable, eſpecially that ridiculous Sin of Swearing: of which complaint being made to the Duke by ſeveral of the clergy then at Liſburn, and frequent Sermons preached againſt it; this occaſioned the Duke to ſet out a Proclamation, bearing date January 18, Strictly forbidding Curſing, Swearing and Profaneſs in Commanders and Souldiers; which, he ſaid, were Sins of much Guilt and little Temptation; but that ſeveral were ſo wicked as to invoke God more frequently to damn them than to ſave them; and that notwithſtanding the dreadful judgements of God at that time upon us for thoſe and ſuch like Sins.[31]

Mr Story has more to tell of the work of the chaplains than is usual in chaplain-historians, and one of his tales is worth telling for its touch of humour.

I cannot omit a pleaſant adventure that fell out at the taking of the Fort, between a Chaplain in the Army and a Trooper. The Chaplain happened to go down after the Fort was taken, and ſeeing a Trooper mortally wounded in all appearance, he fancied himſelf obliged to give him his beſt advice: The other was very thankful for it; and whilſt they were about the matter, comes the Sally. Our Horſe came thundering down, at which the Clergyman making haſte to get out of their way, he ſtumbled and fell down. The wounded trooper ſeeing him fall, judg'd he had been kill'd and ſtept to him immediately to ſtrip him, and in a trice had got his Coat off on one side: The other call'd to him to hold, and aſk'd what he meant. 'Sir,' ſays the other, 'I beg your pardon; for I believed you were killed and therefore I thought myſelf obliged to take care of your Clothes, as well as you did of my Soul.'[32]

In the second volume of his history of the War in Ireland, Mr Story shows that the arrangements for the care of the sick and the wounded were greatly improved under the severe lessons of experience. He wrote:

we had much better conveniences for our Sick and wounded than formerly, having a great many tents ſet up in form of a Quadrangle with Quilts and other conveniences for every Soldier.[33]

This can be endorsed from official sources, for Dalton's *Army Lists* show that a complete Staff, including a Chaplain, was commissioned for 'Our Marching Hospital in Our Kingdom of Ireland'.[34]

From official sources also comes the curious case of the man who held a double commission as Captain and Chaplain, in 1690. The case is mentioned by Colonel Clifford Walton, who quotes as follows from the Treasury State Papers:

Petition, 1690, of C. Jenney, Clerk, complaining that although he was captain and chaplain in Colonel Monroe's Regiment at Londonderry and the same when reformed, he is inserted in the list lately made up as captain only, and desiring to be paid as chaplain too; Minuted, 'Cannot be done'.[35]

Thus was Mr Jenney deprived of his clerical status by a stroke of the pen, and, perhaps, made a captain for ever.

To close this note of the chaplaincy services of the wars in Ireland of 1689 and 1690, mention should be made of the clergy who served James II.

The deaths of two friars in the army besieging Londonderry, and the capture of a priest with the garrison of Charlemont, indicate the presence of chaplains with that army.[36]

Specific information may also be found in the published lists of the officers of King James's army. A search of these reveals that the eight regiments of horse had five chaplains, that the seven regiments of dragoons had three, and that the fifty-two regiments of foot had some thirty clergymen among them.[37]

The *Journal* of John Steven, who marched with this army, shows that religious observance had its place even on the march. For example, he declares that

> at length having passed what was left of the solitude we came to a small place the English call Woodford . . . where it being St James's Day we halted and heard Mass.[38]

Steven has much to say concerning the disregard for the realities of religion which prevailed throughout the force, even among those who paid lip service to its claims.[39]

It does not appear that there was much to choose between the armies contesting for the Kingdom of Ireland in the sphere of moral worth, the chaplains of both having an uphill and thankless task.

The story of Scottish army chaplains in Ireland might be resumed from the defeat of the Stewart attempt, for many Scottish regiments were to be stationed in that country in the years that followed, but these will be dealt with in the wider sphere of the service at home and abroad of these regiments and their chaplains.

To conclude this chapter with a word on the comparative success of the Army Presbytery in Ireland, we would suggest that this was due to a local need being met by the setting up of the Presbytery at Carrickfergus. Round this nucleus organisation was possible. Elderships could be established and the supply of suitable ministers for the many vacant charges properly supervised. The Presbytery was less successful in its proper military sphere for the reason that crippled the effectiveness of the other Army Presbyteries, a chronic shortage of ministers with the regiments.

REFERENCES

1. G. A. Hayes-McCoy, *Scots Mercenary Forces in Ireland* (1937), p. 13.
2. *Foedera*, vol. iii, p. 630.
3. *Calendar of State Papers, Ireland, 1588-1592*, p. 453.
   Register of the Privy Council, vol. iv, p. 739.
4. Nicholas Bernard, Dean of Ardagh, *The Whole Proceedings of the Siege of Drogheda in Ireland*, etc. (1736), pp. 10f.
5. J. S. Reid, *History of the Presbyterian Church in Ireland* (1867), vol. i, pp. 372f.
   Cf. Patrick Adair, *A True Narrative of the Rise and Progress of the Presbyterian Government in the North of Ireland*, ed. W. D Killen (1866), pp. 92f.
6. Acts of the Assembly, 30th July 1642.
7. *A Brief Historical relation of the Life of Mr John Livingstone, minister of the Gospel* (1754), p. 371.
8. Adair, *Narrative*, p. 100.
9. Baillie, *Journals*, vol. i, pp. 387f.
10. Acts of the Assembly, 1643.
11. *The Warr in Ireland by a British Officer* (Dublin, 1873), p. 30.
12. *MSS. Records of the Church of Scotland*, quoted in Reid, *The Church in Ireland*, vol. i, p. 394 n.
13. Adair, *Narrative*, pp. 102ff.
14. *MSS. Records of the Church of Scotland*, quoted in Reid, *The Church in Ireland*, vol. i, p. 466.
15. *Fasti*, vol. ii, p. 277.
16. Acts of the Assembly, 1645, quoted in Reid, *The Church in Ireland*, vol. ii, pp. 8f.
17. Adair, *Narrative*, p. 211.
18. *Papers relating to the Army*, pp. 402 and 397.
19. Adair, *Narrative*, p. 138.
20. Quoted, Reid, *The Church in Ireland*, pp. 57f and n.
21. *Records of the Commission*, vol. i, 15th Oct. 1647.
22. Adair, *Narrative*, p. 164.

23. *Irish Exchequer Bills*, 1682/3, Nov. 25, P.83.A.
    Gordons under Arms (Spalding Club), No. 691.
    Reid, *The Church in Ireland*, vol. ii, p. 44 and n.
24. Leonard J. Trinterud, *The Forming of an American Tradition* (1949),
    pp. 27-33.
25. John Mackenzie, *A Narrative of the Siege of Londonderry*, etc. (1690).
26. J. Boyse, *A Vindication of the Reverend Mr Alexander Osborn*, etc. (1690),
    p. 25.
27. 'Londeriados, commonly called the Armagh Manuscript', Lib. iii, Sec. v,
    in *The Siege and History of Londonderry*, ed. John Hempton (1864),
    p. 58.
28. Seth Whittle, *A Sermon preached before the Garrison*, etc. (1689).
29. Thomas Ash, *Diary*, in Hempton, *Siege of Londonderry*, p. 304.
30. William McCarmick, *A farther Impartial Account of the Actions of the
    Inniskilling Men* (1691), p. 17.
31. *A True and Impartial History of the Most Material Occurrences in the Kingdom
    of Ireland during the two Last Years, written by an Eyewitness* (1691), p. 52.
32. ibid., p. 126.
33. *A Continuation of the Impartial History of the Wars in Ireland, by George
    Story, Chaplain to the Regiment*, etc. (1693), p. 115.
34. Charles Dalton, *English Army Lists and Commission Registers, 1661-1714*
    (1896), vol. iii, p. 161.
35. Col. Clifford Walton, *History of the British Standing Army, 1660-1700*
    (1894), p. 764.
36. *A True and Impartial History*, p. 63.
37. John D'Alton, *King James's Irish Army List, 1689* (1861), passim.
38. *The Journal of John Stevens containing a brief Account of the War in Ireland*,
    ed. R. N. Murray (1912), p. 154.
39. ibid., p. 94.

VII

THE RESTORATION AND THE REVOLUTION

DURING the thirty years of Scottish history which lie between the Restoration and the Revolution, the clergy appear as military chaplains in three distinct groups. First are the chaplains appointed to the regiments of the standing army of Charles II and James II. Second, those ministers who acted as chaplains to the irregular armies of the Covenanters when in arms against the Government. Third, those Scottish churchmen who took part for or against the Revolution.

Taking these groups in this order, we find that the standing army grew very slowly in Scotland. Various causes delayed the formation of the five companies who became the Scots Foot Guards until August 1662, and subsequent development was so slow and so erratic that in 1688 the whole Scottish force numbered less than 4,000 men, who were all quartered near London.[1]

The position and the duties of the chaplains to the standing army of the Stewart Kings were clearly defined.

They were granted a military commission similar to that of Commissariat Officers and unlike the warrants by which Doctors, Engineers, Artillery, Quartermaster and Ordnance Officers were appointed.[2] In 1662, for example, a chaplain was commissioned as follows:

CHARLES, etc., to Dr Herbert Astley, Greeting, We do by these presents constitute and appoint you to be Chaplain of that Regiment of Horse raised or to be raised for Our service,

wherof Our right trusty and right well-beloved cousin
James, earl of Northampton is Colonel.

You are therefore diligently to teach and instruct the
officers and soldiers of the said regiment, who are to observe
you as their Chaplain; and you are likewise to observe and
follow such orders and directions as you shall from time to
time receive from your said Colonel or other your superior
officers of that regiment. Given, etc., the first day of October,
in the 14th year of Our Reign, etc.[3]

The Chaplain, so commissioned, found that there were rules
laid down in the *Articles for War* for the guidance of both pastor
and flock. The *Articles* for 1663 insist upon daily prayers, while
those for 1666 give the following instructions:

3. That the service of Almighty God be not neglected, it
is ordained that prayers be orderly read every day to each
troop of Our Guards, Troops or Companies who have
chaplains allowed to them. And once each week, on each
Sunday or holy-day, a sermon shall be preached, or some
place of scripture or catechisme expounded to them. And
every chaplain that omits his duty herein, and provides not
some minister in orders to officiate for him, shall for the first
offence forfeit half a week's pay, and for the second offence a
week's pay, and for the third offence be cashiered; and all
officers and soldiers that shall often and wilfully absent
themselves from publique prayers and sermons, and all such
as shall abuse or prophane any the places of God's worship,
in any church or chapel, or shall offer violence to any chaplains in the Army, or any other minister, shall be punished in
the same manner, or otherwise at discretion, according to
the nature and aggravation of the offence.[4]

The *Articles* for 1673, 1686 and 1692, however, refer to Divine
Worship in more general terms, and the order for Daily Prayers
was discontinued, though it could be revived at discretion, as was
done in 1691, as part of the campaign against the depravity of the
troops in Ireland.[5]

A set of such *Articles for War* for the Army in Scotland was ratified by the King on 4th January 1667. These Rules were, apparently, drawn up by General Dalyell, and offer a strange contrast to the usually accepted view of this persecutor of the Covenanters. These *Articles* begin with a section devoted to 'Christian and Moral Duties'.

1. Forasmuch as all Lawes, Acts and Ordinances ought to be founded upon and have their Originals from the Law of Almighty God; to the end therefore, that with ye more Confidence Wee may depend upon this Our God for a blessing upon Our selves and Our Army in all its undertakings and atchievments.

Whosoever shall be so desperatlie mad as to blasphem or speake against the Holy, Glorious and Blessed Trinitie, one GOD in three Persons, Father, Sonne and Holy-Ghost, shall die without mercy.

2. All such and unlawful Oaths and imprecations and Curses shall be punished with amercing and fyning every such swearer and Curser, For the first Transgression, in one day's pay, For the second in two, etc. And if any shall be found incorrigible, let him be left to the Courts severest Censures usuall in such cases.

3. Whosoeuer upon the Lord's Day shall unnecessarily absent themselves from Divine Worship, shall lose a month's pay.

The *Articles* continue under five more 'heads' to condemn all 'wilfull Murders, Rapes, raising of fyre, Thefts, Outrages, unnatural abuses and other notorious Crimes and abominable', all of which shall be punishable by death.[6]

The savage death penalty for Blasphemy reflects the Civil Law under which, in 1697, Thomas Aitkenhead was put to death, in spite of the protests of the ministers.[7]

These Scottish *Articles* contain an instruction for officers which indicates that the troops were normally expected to attend the nearest church. The Article in question directs:

Let all and euerie Officer of Whatsoeuer qualitie or Degree, take care that all under his command behave themselves civillie and Christianly, Namelie that they frequent God's publict Worship, when they are, where they may have it, as they will be answerable to the Generall.[8]

The small force available in Scotland was necessarily scattered throughout the whole country, in detachments, and these would each attend the parish church. It does not appear that a chaplain was appointed to a regiment except it were being sent out of Scotland. There is a statement of the military establishment for Scotland for 1684 in the General Register House, Edinburgh, and this shows that there was then only one military chaplain in the country. He was appointed to the Castle of Edinburgh at a salary of two shillings per day. According to *Fasti* this post was held during the period of the Restoration by John Brown from 1661, Alexander Smith from 1668, Gilbert Simpson from 1673, John Barclay from 1680 and Charles Forrester from 1682. The last of these served during the siege of the last fortress in Scotland to hold out for King James, and thereafter fled abroad.[9] The garrison normally consisted of one company of the regiment which is now the Scots Guards, but, in the absence of their early records, nothing is known of the activities of their chaplains. The commanding officer of the regiment was Sir James Turner, who, as we have seen, held strong views on the subject of those chaplains who meddled with other affairs than the 'cure of souls', so, it may be supposed that the Castle chaplains were not encouraged to trespass.

Apart from this garrison, the Army of Scotland consisted of sundry troops of horse and of dragoons who had no chaplains attached to them. There were also certain regiments of foot, most of which had a very short existence. One such regiment was raised in 1672 by Sir William Lockhart for service with the Fleet, It continued for two years and does not seem to have had a chaplain. Sir George Monro raised another regiment in 1674, to serve in Scotland, which continued for two years and had no chaplain. In 1678, however, Lord James Douglas raised a regiment in Scotland for service in England, and a chaplain appears in its list of commissioned officers. His name is given as 'Jon.

Campbell', and he may have continued with the regiment until it was disbanded in 1679. The Earl of Mar raised a regiment in 1678 which has had a longer lease of life, for it continued as the Royal Scots Fusiliers, but it does not seem to have had a chaplain in the early years of its long history.[10]

Mention must also be made of the regiment of Scots in the service of France, for they were recalled to England for two years in 1666. While they were at home they, who are now the Royal Scots, had a chaplain, David Whitford, the son of the Bishop of Brechin. Mr Whitford's commission was dated 16th July 1666.[11] He had no easy task, for Pepys says of this regiment, when they were guarding Chatham against the Dutch, that they were

far more terrible to these people of the country towns than the Dutch themselves.[12]

This regiment returned to France, but in 1678 it was finally recalled and began its long career as the 'First of Foot'. They had a Chaplain on their 'establishment' when at home, 1678-80, but the place may have been vacant, for no name is given. They were then sent to the difficult garrison of Tangier, where, according to their own records, the regiment attended daily prayers in the market place.[13] These prayers would be conducted by the chaplains to the garrison, who were appointed by the Bishop of London, and who are unique in the Army Lists from the fact that they are not listed as Chaplains but as Ministers, and had a stipend of 10s. per diem. This office was held in turn by Lancelot Addison, Marius d'Assigny, Dr Turner and Dr Hughes. A statement of the strength of the Garrison, in 1676, shows, under the heading 'Churchmen':

Priests and Fryers	18
Ministers	2
In all	20

Miss Routh, in her description of this garrison, gives a considerable amount of information concerning these ministers, not relevant here, but incidentally informs us of a sermon preached there against the too strict observance of the Sabbath. One hearer thought this unseasonable:

> this place being without doubt inclined rather to too much liberty than an over severe strictness.[14]

The Royal Scots were relieved of duty in Tangier in 1684, and returned home. Mr Roderick Mackenzie was commissioned as their chaplain in that year, and was succeeded, in 1686, by one whose name is given variously as John Gilder, Gildon or Graham.[15]

Setting aside, for a time, the history of the Royal Scots, we must mention another Scottish regiment raised in the reign of James II. This was known as Colonel John Wachop's (Scotch) Regiment of Foot. The officers of this corps were mostly Roman Catholics who had thrown up their commissions in the British regiments in Dutch service.

The regimental lists show that they had a chaplain, commissioned on 30th March 1688, named Maxwell.[16]

In addition to this handful of chaplains serving the Scottish regiments of the restored monarchy, the Army Lists suggest that other clergy of Scots descent were serving with the Army. For instance, an Alexander Mackintosh was commissioned to the King's Own Regiment of Dragoons in 1678, to the Holland Regiment in 1685, and to the First Troop of Horse Guards in 1686.[17]

Another possible Scot was Alexander Innes, who was commissioned in 1673 to the 'New Royal English Regiment', sent to France in that year. He appears again in the interesting appointment, 'chaplain to Our garrison of New York', in 1686. It is possible that he continued in the Army after the Revolution, for there was a Chaplain of his name in Colonel John Buchan's Regiment in 1695. This regiment had been formed out of the remains of the standing forces of Scotland after the Revolution. If this is the same chaplain, he continues, in 1703, as 'Chaplain General of Our Forces to be sent to Portugal'.[18]

The number of chaplains in attendance upon the Scottish regiments, however, was negligible. When James II called all the available Scottish troops to London to meet the dangers of 1688

—one regiment each of horse and dragoons, one regiment of Foot Guards, and two regiments of infantry—they had no commissioned chaplain with them, except Mr Maxwell of Wachop's Regiment.[19]

Before we enter upon the subject of the chaplains of the Revolution armies, we must consider that group of ministers who were, in effect, military chaplains to the Covenanters, when in arms against the Crown. We are not concerned to tell again of the royal attempts to establish an effective Episcopal Church in Scotland, by law, by force and by conciliation, nor are we to tell again of the part played by the ministers who resisted these attempts, save where and when they were chaplains to men at war.

Many of the Presbyterian ministers of Scotland could not conform to the new ecclesiastical arrangements and, being deprived of their charges, continued a semi-private ministry to their families and friends. These gatherings tended to grow and could not be contained within the walls of any dwelling house. The inevitable development was the preaching in fields, begun, it is said, by Mr John Welsh and Mr Gabriel Semple, who had been ministers in the Presbytery of Dumfries.[20]

The Government tried to suppress such gatherings by a show of force, but they had few troops available, and the attempt at repression touched off the first overt act of rebellion. The occasion of this rising is of no importance here, but the capture by the rebels of Sir James Turner, the local commander of the military, provides us with some information on the capacity of the Covenanting minister as a Chaplain to the Forces.

The captive commander is very careful to give all the credit he can to the ministers whom he met while in the hands of the rebels. He tells how Mr Hugh Henderson, who had himself been a chaplain to the Galloway regiment, had him to dinner and entertained him with real kindness.[21] He also speaks of discussions he had with John Welsh and Gabriel Semple, in which he was allowed to speak freely.

In spite of this willingness to praise he still finds much to criticise in the conduct of the rebel preachers. Much of his criticism is what might be expected from an enemy of their cause and creed. For instance, he did not like their long prayers, and describes one grace before ale as 'one of the moſt bombaſtic graces that ever I heard in my life'.[22]

Such criticism from such a source is of little weight, but, on two separate occasions, Turner has unexpected comment to make in a matter of which he had some professional knowledge, and that is the work of the preachers as chaplains to their army. In the first of these he declares:

> I have not ſeene leſſe of divine worſhip anywhere, than I ſaw in that army of theirs; foi though at their rendevouſes and halts they had opportunitie enough everie day for it, yet I never did heare any of their miniſters (and as they them-ſelves told me, there was not ſo few as tuo and threttie of them, wherof onlie five or ſixe converſed with me), either pray, preach or ſing pſalmes; neither could I learne that was ever practiſd publicklie, except once by Mr Robbiſone at Corſfairne, ane other time by Mr Welch at Dalmellinton, and now the third time by Mr Semple at Lanrick, where the laufull paſtor, was forced to reſigne his pulpit to him. What they did in ſeverall quarters I know not; perhaps they had some familie exerciſe there.[23]

And later, when the Covenanters were near Edinburgh, he says:

> At this place, I neither heard prayers, psalmes or preaching; yet one of their miniſters, (and they ſaid, it was either one Guthrie or one Oglebie), made a ſpeech to them, which, if his cauſe had beene good, had not been evill. 'Bot I intreate you', ſaid he, 'to uſe all imaginable diſcretion to thoſe who are not of your perſuaſion; to endeavour to gaine them with love, and by your good carriage, ſtop the mouths of your adverſaries.'[24]

If we accept these criticisms from such a source, they are of interest and importance, for they are the judgement of the pro-fessional soldier, who can find time, even on a campaign, for all the duties laid down in his orders, including Daily Prayers. Such a 'man under authority' would be a little contemptuous of amateur soldiers, who loudly professed to serve God, but who postponed his worship to a more convenient season.

Turner's criticism receives a measure of support from Colonel Wallace, the military leader of the insurgents.

His account of the rising states that at their many consultations they prayed for divine guidance, but he only mentions formal preaching on two occasions. The first of these was conducted by Mr Semple, near Ochiltree, on 22nd November 1666, and the second was at Lanark on the 26th of that month. At the latter place the Covenant was renewed, and Messrs Guthrie, Semple and Crookshank all took part.[25]

The little rebel army was faced with the Government forces on the slopes of the Pentland Hills, and made a stout but vain resistance, under the leadership of their ministers, whom General Drummond refers to as 'cashiered preachers'.[26]

The Earl of Rothes wrote to the Earl of Lauderdale, after the battle:

> The Nonconforme Ministers were cheife comanders amongst them; and the gallanteste amongst them, whose name was Crukshanck receaved the just reward for rebellioun, upon the feild, which is death and damna'ne.

In the same letter Rothes regrets that he has not been able to locate Andrew McCormick, another of the preacher leaders, but, from other sources we learn that he too had fallen in the fight.[27]

A few weeks later Rothes again wrote to Lauderdale, and quotes a deposition by a servant of 'that arch willan Welsh', which belittles the part played by Welsh and Semple in the battle. He says that

> ther ffathes haveinge ffailed them, they stood at a distance, and called allowd, with ther hondes stretched out (the whole tyme of the ingagement) the Great God of Jacob, the Great God of Jacob, not utering on other silabill, whilst the rest of ther brethren were in action, some under the notione of Captaines, and some Levantes.[28]

The evidence of a servant, transmitted by an enemy, that two of the ministers held out their hands like Moses over the battlefield, is confirmed by the prisoner, Sir James Turner, who says that Semple and Welsh occupied a post on a hill overlooking the combat

> and by doing ſo, I thought both of them had provided indifferentlie well for their oune ſaftie.[29]

Several other ministers escaped from the field, including John Scot, one time minister of Oxnam,[30] and William Veitch, who survived many adventures to become minister of Peebles in 1690.[31]

Two of their brethren were not so fortunate, for Alexander Robertson, son of the minister of Urr, who had advised the abandonment of the enterprise,[32] was arrested and put to death on the scaffold, and Hugh McKail, who had been forced to leave the ranks through ill-health, shared the same fate.[33]

The presence of one cleric with the royal army of 1666 is shown by the tale that, in the heat of the action

> Duke Hamilton hardly escaped, by Ramsay, dean of Hamilton, laying his sword upon the Duke's back, to ward off the countryman's stroke, that he saw he was bringing on him.[34]

The Covenanters who were imprisoned after the defeat received gifts of food from Wishart, now Bishop of Edinburgh, the former chaplain to Montrose.[35]

The complete failure of this premature rising might have meant the end of serious resistance to the new order in the Church, but, in spite of conciliation and Indulgence, and the billeting of soldiers and Highland levies upon the suspect, a hard core of resistance to all that pertained to Episcopacy continued to trouble the Administrators of the country. The field preachings continued, and grew bigger and bolder. The description of one such series of meetings, by John Blackadder, reveals the strength they could muster. These meetings were being held at East Nisbet when an alarm was given of a possible attempt at disturbance by the Earl of Hume:

upon this we hastily drew together about seven or eightscore of horse, on the Saturday, equipped with such furniture as they had. Pickets of twelve or sixteen men were appointed to reconnoitre and ride towards the suspected parts. Single horsemen were despatched to greater distances to view the country and give warning in case of attack. The remainder of the horse were drawn round to be a defence, at such distance as they might hear sermon, and be ready to act if need be. Every means was taken to compose the multitude from needless alarm, and prevent, in a harmless defensive way, any affront that might be offered to so solemn and sacred a work.[36]

Then follows a long description of the Communion feast celebrated within this guardian ring, and:

Each day at the congregations dismissing the ministers with their guards and as many of the people as could, retired to their quarters in three several country towns ... the horsemen drew up in a body till the people left the place, and then marched in goodly array behind at a little distance untill all were safely lodged in their quarters.[37]

These 'Armed Conventicles' as they were called were defensive in concept, but the danger of a skirmish which would develop into rebellion was ever present. Various minor clashes did take place between the Covenanters and small bodies of soldiers before one such developed into a sharp defeat for the government troops at Drumclog, in 1679. The nature of this unpremeditated rising made the ministers at once the chaplains and the captains of the rebel army. Thomas Douglas was preaching when the alarm was given of the approaching danger and Donald Cargill,[38] formerly minister of the Barony of Glasgow, was active in the fight which followed.[39] On the rout of the dragoons, Mr John King, whom they had held a prisoner, was free to join the rebels,[40] and the little group was made four by the accession of John Kid, who was to die on the scaffold with his colleague, King. The names of the ministers who joined the rebels were:

Mr John Welch, Mr David Hume, Mr Gabriel Semple, Mr John Rae, Mr Samuel Arnot, Mr Andrew Morton, Mr Hugh Kennedy, Mr John Blackader, Mr Archibald Riddell, Mr Lamb, Mr Thomas Black, Mr Forrester, Mr Robert Muir and Mr George Barclay.[41]

This clerical influx proved to be fruitful of weakness rather than of strength. The original group of four had been united in detestation of any ministers who had returned to their charges under the Indulgence, but the new, and larger group, while not accepting the Indulgence for themselves, were not so severe in condemnation of those who had done so. The extreme party had a considerable following among the laity, and the rebel camp was torn by the quarrels which resulted.

The Lord's Day saw these disputes reach a height, when each party claimed the right to preach, and rival chaplains came almost to grips with one another. One partisan describes the scene:

> This day the Lord was grievouſly diſhonouıed, and his people ſadly diſcouraged with the unchriſtian carriage and corrupt doctrine of Mr Hume; foı (1) When Mr John Kid was going to preach, Mr Hume in a great rage, had the impudence to come where he was, and commanded him to begone out of his ſight, and called him a troubler of the church, for no reaſon I know of, but becauſe he preached faithfully againſt their idol, the indulgence.
>
> (2) After Mr Hume had driven away Mr Kid, he went, in a great fury, to the place where Mr Douglas was going to preach to a meeting of the honeſt party, who had called him to preach to them; and after Mr Douglas had opened his book to ſing a pſalm, Mr Hume thruſt him away by vio-lence, and then, by uſurpation, ſtepped in himſelf in his place.[42]

The other side in this contention was expressed by Mr John Rae, who refused to preach against the Indulgence when com-manded to do so by the rebel leaders. Mr Rae declared that he had refused to preach to the bidding of the magistrate and would refuse to preach to the bidding of the people.[43]

There is an undated pamphlet in the National Library of Scotland, entitled *A Sermon preached at Glafgow in Scotland, to the Rebels in Arms*. This was preached on the text, 'Sion is Wounded', by John Kea, not to be identified, unless it should read John Rae. The preacher laments that the poor Church of Scotland is also 'wonded'.

The Kirk was indeed wounded, and that by the hands of her friends, who sacrificed any hope of victory in the field for the pleasures of endless legalistic debate. While the Covenanters debated the expulsion of an Achan from the camp, the government was hastily mustering troops, wherever they could be got quickly and cheaply. A strong force of horse and foot was ordered to accompany the new commander, Monmouth, from England, but the bulk of these were never raised, and only five troops of horse marched north.

Sir Walter Scott would have us believe that the royal army had with it a complete artillery train, but Lieutenant John Slezer, who commanded the guns in the final battle, states that he had four pieces of artillery, but only one gunner.[44]

Before this battle joined at Bothwell Bridge, an effort was made by Mr David Hume to obtain a settlement on terms, but this was refused, and firing commenced. The rebels made a stout defence of the bridge, but when this was lost the bulk of their army broke and fled. The ministers present shared the fate of the laity, some escaping and some falling into the hands of the enemy. A list of the preachers present is given in a contemporary account as follows:

Mr Welfh,	Mr Ray,
Mr King,	Mr Douglas,
Mr Cargill,	Mr Forrefter,
Mr Baxley, [Barclay?]	Mr Mury. [Muir?][45]

Many of those named in this list escaped from the defeat, although Mr Cargill only did so after being left for dead on the field.[46] Messrs King and Kid were less fortunate, being made prisoners and brought to trial. They petitioned the Court, that though found among the insurgents, they had taken no share in their proceedings; that they were, in fact, detained among them by force; that they had refused to preach to them, and so far from encouraging them to rebellion, had used every argument to persuade them to return to their former loyalty and obedience; and that they had seized the first opportunity of escaping after the battle of Bothwell Bridge.[47]

Their judges found some difficulty in accepting this defence, and ordered their execution on the afternoon of the trial.

The hopes of the Covenanters were thus dashed once more, and the leaders once more in hiding or in exile. The flame of resistance was kindled again, however, after the shortest interval and burned fiercely when fanned by Donald Cargill and Richard Cameron. It became fashionable in later years to disparage the words and deeds of the little band of zealots who gathered round these men.

Their solemn deposition of the King, for instance, has been held up to ridicule, but Daniel Defoe saw more clearly. Of this incident he said they deposed the King

upon the same grounds as was afterwards the renouncing of the King by the Revolution, and was abundantly justified by the practice of the whole nation in the Revolution.[48]

Judge the Cameronians by the words of the Queensferry Paper, calling men to a battle for freedom that shall continue down the generations if need be.

We bind and oblige our ſelves to defend our ſelves and one another in our worſhipping of God, and in our natural, civil and divine Rights and Liberties, till we ſhall overcome, or ſend them down under Debate to our Poſterity, that they may begin where we end. . . .[49]

Cameron and Cargill were not long spared to lead their people, for at Ayrsmoss, in July 1680, the dragoons came upon them. Cameron was slain in the fight, Cargill escaped but was captured later and executed. A witness at the trial of Cargill declared that he was a rebel at Airdsmoss with Mr Cameron and had a sword and two pistols.[50]

This success must have seemed decisive to the rulers of Scotland but the peace they might have expected was broken again and again. The invasions of England by Monmouth and of Scotland by Argyll were linked by the appointment of two Englishmen to the Scottish attempt, and of two Scots,

Fletcher and Ferguson, an Independent minister, to the English expedition.[51]

Other ministers were directly involved in the Scottish affair. For instance, the confidential secretary of Argyll was William Spence, the outed minister of Glendevon.[52]

An active agent and messenger of the rebels was William Veitch, who had, indeed, some part in nearly every plot against the Crown. George Barclay and Robert Langlands came over from Holland with the expedition, and continued with the 'Hillmen' after the failure of that attempt.[53]

The presence of ministers in the camp of Argyll is confirmed in the preamble to the official Declaration which was printed in 'Campbell-town in Kintyre', and read in the church of that place on 21st May 1685 thus:

The Declaration and Apology of the Protestant people, that is, of the Noblemen, Barrons, Gentlemen, Burgesses & Commons of allsorts now in armes within the Kingdome of Scotland, with the concurrence of their true and faithfull Pastors & of severall Gentlemen of the English Nation joined with them in the same cause, etc.[54]

This attempt had as little success as the more spontaneous affairs that had gone before, but it pointed the way to the successful invasion under William of Orange, and with it we come to the last of the three groups of Scottish military chaplains of this period.

A considerable part of the force on which William relied for victory was made up of the English and Scottish regiments in the pay of Holland, and these had with them some chaplains. To one of these, who later claimed to be the only English chaplain with the Fleet, we owe a story of the whole adventure with a wealth of interesting detail.[55]

He gives the price regulations which were made in Holland to curb the profiteering as the army was assembled, and continues with a most graphic account of his experiences during the storm which prevented the first attempt.

> Sundry ſoldiers cried out, I am ſure I can feel the Hole where the ſea comes in at; when (as in truth) it was the Water and the Beir together, ſlaſhing within the Ship; for you muſt know we were moſt of us all in darkneſs (no candle being permitted to come under Deck) becauſe of the Magazine.[56]

The Fleet put back to port and refitted and our chaplain tells of the orderly arrangements which were made for the conduct of public worship for the troops.

> It was ordered here that the Dutch ſhould begin their prayers in the Church every morning at Nine of the Clock, the Engliſhe at Ten, and the French at Eleven: The Dutch begin their prayers in the afternoon at Two, the English at Three, and the French at Four of the Clock; which order was punctually obſerved ſo long as we were here.[57]

The second venture was more fortunate, and the Fleet approached the coast of England, and our informant says that

> a certain Miniſter in the Fleet, on board the Ship called the Golden Sun, went up to the top of the uppermoſt Cabin, where the Colours hang out, a place where he could eaſily behold all the People on the Shore and where they might moſt perfectly ſee him, and pulling a Bible out of his Pocket, he opened it, and held it ſo in his right hand making many flouriſhes with it unto the People, whoſe eyes were fixed on him, and duly obſerved him; thereby ſignifying to the People the flouriſhing of the Holy Goſpel (by God's Bleſſing upon the Prince of Orange's Endeavours), and calling out as loud as he was able, ſaid unto them on the top of the Rock;

For the Proteſtant Religion, and maintaining of the Goſpel in the Truth and Purity thereof, are we all by the Goodneſs and Providence of God come hither, after ſo many Storms and Tempeſts.[58]

What the people made of his flourishings and pompous message would be interesting but has not been preserved.

The Diary continues until the Prince is safely in London, and, from a second volume, we learn that Mr John Whittie or Wittel, remained in the Army and was wounded during the campaign in Ireland.[59]

From this Diary, and from other sources, it becomes evident that one part of the duties of the clergy with the invasion force was propaganda for the Cause, and the public announcement of William's intentions, and, later, of his Accession. William Boyd, a Scots minister who came from Holland with the army, is said to have made his way to Glasgow and there proclaimed William as King. Boyd preached in the Castle of Edinburgh in June 1691, so he did not lose all touch with affairs military.[60]

There were two other Scottish ministers in the invasion army who have more claim for notice, William Carstares and Gilbert Burnet; the former had for many years a very real influence upon William's handling of Scottish affairs, and the latter, who became Bishop of Salisbury, recorded the history of his own time.

As a military chaplain, Mr Carstares landed at Torbay with the Prince, and, at his suggestion, a service of Thanksgiving was held on the beach. Mr Burnet was also present and had some conversation with the Prince, but he makes no mention of his colleague or of the service.[61]

In the northern kingdom the only real resistance to the new regime was that of the Duke of Gordon, who held the Castle of Edinburgh, and of John Graham of Claverhouse, Viscount Dundee.

The minister of Edinburgh Castle at the time was Charles Forrester, and he seems to have done his duty throughout the siege. The Castle Church was itself so badly damaged by shot that the services had to be conducted in the vaults.

It was Mr Forrester who put to each member of the garrison in turn an oath of loyalty.[62] According to *Scotichronicon* there was also a priest, Alexander Winster, in the garrison, who was released after the capitulation and died at Banff in 1708.[63]

A more active effort on behalf of King James was made by Viscount Dundee. He, with a few troopers of his old regiment, raised the standard of revolt in the Highlands and were formidable in the absence of any regular army. This little band of Royalists did not lack for chaplains. An officer of their number declared that Dundee 'took the Sacrament in the Church of England, two days before he was killed'.[64] A modern historian finds reason to doubt this as it does not fit in with his ideas of the Viscount's movements.

The same historian finds more credible the tradition that:

> in 1715 the Earl of Mar listened to a sermon which its author had preached before Dundee a few days before Killiecrankie.[6]

This must refer to the sermon preached by William Irvine, some-time minister of Kirkmichael, which he repeated to that part of the Rebel army of 1715 which invaded England. That sermon was preached at Kelso and the Earl of Mar was not present.[66]

The records of the Church of Scotland show that several ministers joined the army of Claverhouse. Sweyn McSweyn, minister of Kilcalmonell, Alexander Balnevis, minister of Lundieff, James Taylor, minister of Kinettles, were all deprived of their livings for joining his forces. Nor must we omit Robert Stewart, minister of Balquidder, who traditionally wielded a mighty broadsword at Killiecrankie.[67]

A party of Dundee's men threatened for a time the town of Inverness, and the Kirk Session records show ministers and townsfolk standing ready for fight, with public worship conducted in the open air.[68]

Perhaps the mobilised manhood of Inverness with its ministers cannot be called a regiment with its chaplains, but it is typical of the feeling which made it possible for Scotland to raise, in a very short space of time, eleven troops of horse, one regiment of dragoons and eleven regiments of foot, to meet the emergency and to preserve the new government.[69]   One of the regiments of foot was raised by the United Societies or Cameronians, from among their own adherents, and it had for its chaplain Alexander Shields.

He has been called 'a rampant hill-preacher',[70] but such casual condemnation is much less than just. Mr Shields was a hill-preacher from necessity, for he was one of the many who could not conform to the Church as then established. That he was a man of some real depth of scholarship is shown by his published works, and that he was no lover of violence is made plain by his urgency that the clergy of the Episcopal Church should not be 'rabbled', but removed by some more legal and decent method, if necessary.[71] As chaplain to the regiment raised by these fiercely religious 'hill-men', Mr Shields undertook a difficult charge. The regiment was in danger of dissolution almost at once, for many in its ranks doubted whether it was right for them to associate with the less religious regiments around them. Colonel Cleland, who was in command, had almost lost all patience with them, when a compromise was reached, largely through the efforts of the chaplain.[72] The first action in which they took part was the defence of Dunkeld against the Highlanders who had been victorious at Killiecrankie. Mr Shields was not present at this successful stand, but his account of events which preceded the fight is illuminating.

August 20. Duke Hamiltoun, before he went to London, ordered our regiment to be posted near the enimy, and discharged them correspondence with the rest of the forces. At Dunkell they wer betrayed, and the horse retired at Ramsey's orders, August 21, and they had a barrel of figgs instead of pouder; the souldiers were combining to leave the post, and goe off, and had mounted their baggage, but I prevailed with them to stay.[73]

The dispersal of the Highland army and the end of all overt support for King James in Scotland did not end the troubles of the Cameronians' chaplain. He had to endure bitter criticism from his own sect, receiving three letters from the West, all of them accusing me of defection, in uniting with the ministers, and associating with the army.[74]

Nor was there peace within the regiment. Controversy was as meat and drink to these soldiers, and they produced a list of grievances against their commander, of which the first declared

that he put in prophane officers and some of them that had not been sogers.[75]

A few weeks later, in December 1689, someone put their woes into verse, addressed to King William. This ends:

> Great Sir, we close hoping you will remember
> We're in the North, and now it is December,
> Our cloaths are thinn, our Purses are right bare
> To bide these two, Great Sir, it is right sere:
> And also Sir, we lye among our foes;
> Given and subscribed, at Montrose.[76]

The regiment and its chaplain weathered these storms and departed together to the battlefields of Flanders, where we shall meet them again.

From this summary of the occasions on which the ministers of Scotland took their place with men at war, it is evident and important here that, from the earliest beginnings of the Regular Army of Britain, the Chaplain has his place on the military establishment. We shall see how that place was exalted and debased in the century which followed upon the Revolution.

REFERENCES

1. Charles Dalton, *The Scots Army, 1661-1688* (1909), Introduction, passim.
2. Clifford Walton, *British Army*, p. 760.
3. C. M. Clode, *Military Forces of the Crown* (1869), vol. ii, p. 367.
4. ibid., vol. ii, pp. 367f.
5. Clifford Walton, *British Army*, p. 759.

6. Dalton, *Scots Army*, pp. 84f.
7. Thomas McCrie, *The Story of the Scottish Church* (1875), pp. 432f; William
   Lorimer, *Two Discourses*, etc. (1713), Preface.
   Another view is taken by T. B. Macaulay, *The History of England* (1855),
   vol. iv, pp. 781f.
8. Dalton, *Scots Army*, p. 86.
9. *Fasti*, vol. i, p. 92.
10. Dalton, *Scots Army*, Part ii, pp. 95, 100, 102, 113f.
11. Dalton, *Army Lists*, vol. i, p. 71.
12. Pepys, *Diary*, 30th June 1667.
13. J. C. Leask, *The Regimental Records of the Royal Scots* (1915), pp. 19, 21,
    24, 43.
14. E. C. M. Routh, *Tangier, England's Last Atlantic Outpost* (1912), pp. 305,
    306, 370.
15. Dalton, *Army Lists*, vol. ii, pp. 23, 84, 131.
    Leask, *Records of the Royal Scots*, p. 54.
16. Dalton, *Army Lists*, vol. ii, p. 153.
17. ibid., vol. i, pp. 204, 255; vol. ii, pp. 61, 73, 115.
18. ibid., vol. i, p. 162; vol. iv, p. 100; vol. v, p. 157.
19. ibid., vol. ii, pp. 210ff.
20. James Kirkton, *The Secret and True History of the Church of Scotland*, ed.
    C. K. Sharpe (1817), p. 164.
    Fasti, vol. i, pp. 590, 592.
21. Sir James Turner, *Memoirs*, pp. 152f.
22. ibid., p. 158.
23. ibid., pp. 168f.
24. ibid., pp. 176f.
25. *Memoirs of Mr William Veitch and George Brysson*, ed. Thomas McCrie
    (1825), pp. 395, 397, 401, 405, 408.
26. Dalton, *Scots Army*, p. 25. Gen. Drummond's Despatch. *London Gazette*,
    30th Nov. 1666.
27. *Lauderdale Papers*, ed. O. Airy (Camden Society, 1884), vol. i, p. 254.
28. ibid., vol. i, pp. 267f.
29. Sir James Turner, *Memoirs*, p. 185.
30. *Fasti*, vol. i, p. 510.
31. ibid., vol. i, p. 466; cf. *Memoir of Veitch*, ed. McCrie.
32. ibid., vol. i, p. 607; Kirkton, *History*, p. 234, passim.
33. *Naphtali*, ed. W. Wilson (1845), pp. 257ff.
34. *Fasti*, vol. ii, p. 258; *Memoir of Veitch*, p. 42.
35. Kirkton, *History*, p. 247.
36. *Memoirs of the Rev. John Blackader*, ed. A. Chrichton (1823), pp. 198f.
37. ibid., p. 202.
38. *Fasti*, vol. i, p. 664.
39. ibid., vol. ii, p. 39.

40. William Aiton, *A History of the Rencounter at . . . Bothwell Bridge* (1821), pp. 57ff.

41. William Wilson, *A True and Impartial Relation of the . . . defeat at Bothwell Bridge* (1797), p. 15.
   Fasti, vol. i, p. 592; vol i, p. 430; vol. i, p. 590; vol. i, p. 230; vol. i, pp. 723f; vol. i, p. 32; vol. i, p. 603; vol. ii, p. 730; vol. ii, p. 275; vol. ii, p. 550; vol. i, p. 660; vol. ii, p. 290; vol. ii, p. 703.

42. Wilson, *Bothwell Bridge*, p. 26.

43. *Fasti*, vol. i, p. 230.

44. Dalton, *Scots Army*, Introduction, p. xix.

45. *A True Account of the Great Victory obtained over the Rebels in Scotland by His Majesties Forces under the command of the Duke of Monmouth, the 22nd of this instant June, 1679*, p. 4.

46. W. H. Carslaw, *Life and Times of Donald Cargill* (Paisley, no date), p. 89 and passim.

47. *Lauderdale Papers*, vol. iii, pp. 176f.

48. Daniel Defoe, *Memoirs of the Church of Scotland* (1717), p. 224.

49. Robert Wodrow, *The History of the Sufferings of the Church of Scotland* (1722), vol. ii, Appendix xlvi, p. 47.

50. *A True and Impartial account of the Examinations and Confessions of several Execrable Conspirators against the King* (1681).

51. Sibbald D. Scott, *The British Army, its Origins*, etc. (1868-80), vol. iii, p. 462.

52. *Fasti*, vol. ii, p. 766.

53. ibid., vol. ii, pp. 703 and 40.

54. Quoted, W. J. Couper, *Scottish Rebel Printers* (privately printed, Edinburgh, 1912).

55. *An Exact Diary of the late Expedition of his Illustrious Highneſs the Prince of Orange*, etc. By a Miniſter, Chaplain in the Army (1689). (The Epistle Dedicatory is signed John Whittie.)

56. ibid., pp. 19f.

57. ibid., p. 23.

58. ibid., pp. 34f.

59. *Conſtantius Redivivus, or a Full Account—of the Succeſſes . . . of the Heroical Prince William*, etc. by John Wittel, Sometyme the only Engliſh Chaplain to the Army (1693), Epistle Dedicatory.

60. *Fasti*, vol. i, p. 712.
   One of King William's Men, ed. H. M. B. Reid (1898), p. 171.

61. R. H. Story, *William Carstares* (1874), pp. 156f.
   Gilbert Burnet, *History of His Own Time* (1838), vol. i, p. 379.

62. *Fasti*, vol. i, p. 92; James Grant, *Memorials of the Castle of Edinburgh* (1850), p. 188.

63. J. F. S. Gordon, *Ecclesiastical Chronicle for Scotland, Scotichronicon* (1875) vol. iv.

64. *Memoirs of the Lord Viscount Dundee*, etc. by an Officer of the Army (London, n.d.), p. vi.

65. C. S. Terry, *John Graham of Claverhouse* (1905), p. 331 n.

66. *Fasti*, vol. ii, p. 119; Robert Patten, *The History of the late Rebellion*, etc. (1717), pp. 39f.

67. *Fasti*, vol. iii, p. 43; vol. ii, p. 807; vol. iii, p. 775; vol. ii, p. 721.

68. *Inverness Kirk Session Records*, ed. Alex. Mitchell, p. 8.

69. Dalton, *Army Lists*, vol. iii, Introduction passim.

70. ibid., vol. ii, p. 88.

71. Hector Macpherson, *The Cameronian Philosopher; Alexander Shields* (1932), passim.

72. McCrie, *The Story of the Scottish Church*, p. 400.

73. Wodrow, *Analecta*, vol. i, p. 192.

74. ibid., vol. i, p. 193.

75. Dalton, *Army Lists*, vol. iii, p. 406.

76. *To his most Excellent Majesty, William, King of Great Britain, the Humble Address of the Regimented Cameronian Presbyterians, lying at Montrose and adjacent cities in Angus, December 12th 1689.* Quoted, *Various Pieces of Fugitive Scottish Poetry*, Second Series (1853).

VIII

WILLIAM III AND ANNE

W ITH the accession of William and Mary a new chapter opened in Scottish military history. Regiments were still raised in the northern kingdom, but they were no longer necessarily attached to the Scottish military establishment, and were frequently transferred to that of England or of Ireland, and might be used abroad in the war against France. This policy had much to do with the gradual appearance of English and Episcopalian clergy as chaplains to regiments primarily raised in Scotland.

Many of the regiments which were so hastily levied in Scotland in 1689, were as quickly disbanded as the danger passed away, and the need for economy grew, and, at the close of 1690, there remained of the new regiments only one regiment of dragoons, now the 7th Hussars, and five regiments of foot, two of which continue, the King's Own Scottish Borderers and the Cameronians.[1] These new regiments, in common with the older Scottish formations which survived the Revolution, were each entitled to a chaplain, who was paid 6s. 8d. per day,[2] with an extra allowance for a servant. Thus the chaplain attached to the regiment which is now the Royal Scots Greys received £134 as his salary for the year 1689.[3] In addition to the regimental chaplains, the needs of the scattered garrisons throughout Scotland were met by the parochial ministers, as, for example, David Guthrie, minister of Glenmuik, served the garrison of the Castle of Abergeldie.[4]

The Scottish regiments which were involved in the long wars

with France in Flanders were accompanied by their chaplains. Indeed, the chaplaincy service of the British element of the Allied Army was organised to the extent of having a Chaplain General, for 'Jno. Wickhart' was commissioned as such in March 1692, with a salary of 10s. per day. Mr Wickhart became Dean of Westminster, and was succeeded as Chaplain General by Richard Willis.[5] Among the Scottish chaplains with the army in Flanders, the pride of place must be given to William Carstares.

He was one of the Chaplains to the King, and accompanied him in his carriage even to the battlefield. It is said that, for this attendance, he had the princely stipend of £500 per annum.[6] This may not be accurate, for he wrote from the camp, in 1692, expressing the hope that his rents for the previous year had come in, for

campaigns are expensive; and three horses and two servants, which are absolutely necessary for me, will be expensive.

In this letter he makes one of his few references to the performance of chaplaincy duty with the troops:

I have access often in Angus' and Leven's regiments to be employed in my proper work.[7]

The regiments he names are now the Cameronians and the Scottish Borderers, respectively. Carstares was a preacher in the camp on the Sunday which followed upon the heavy losses sustained by the Scots at Steinkirk, and spoke on the worthy text, 'And it is appointed unto men once to die.'[8]

Mr Shields appears again with his regiment on the fields of Flanders. He was now a minister of the Church of Scotland, and he notes in his Diary in 1691:

February. A.S. gote a call to Angus' regiment; and on the 4th was ordeaned in the Cannongate meeting-house; and the officers of the regiment received him.

This ecclesiastical commission to the spiritual care of the regiment was reinforced by a military one, dated 1st April of that year, but on 10th February he had preached his last sermon in the Cannongate before going abroad.[9]

In a letter home Mr Shields says that the King met the regiment on the march, and inquired kindly for their chaplain. He shows, however, that others in the army were less kind, for

> as we marched through the army, the Scots mocked us, especially D'Offarels regiment (now Royal Scots Fusiliers) . . . jeering us with 'Presbytery', . . . and said we would get no hills here to preach and pray upon.[10]

The Cameronian chaplain continued his militant Protestantism while with the army, for he was complained upon at Bruges

> to the Bishop, Governor and Commanding Officer of the forces in this town for the sermon I preached last Sabbath, and my testimony therein offered against Popery. They trouble me, but I trust in God and do not fear them.[11]

One of his letters was addressed to the General Assembly which should have met in 1693. In it he pleads that that Court have a thought for the soldiers. He says:

> The war in it ſelf be no deſirable thing. Yet in the preſent conſtitution of the World, the management and proſecution of it for a good Cauſe, is a good and lawful vocation ſuitable to Chriſtians and Conſiſtent with Piety.

He continues with a plea that the Assembly should use its influence to secure a better type of recruit for the Scottish regiments for the fair name of the Presbyterian Church. People abroad are judging the Church of Scotland by the

> profanity in Officers and Souldiers and Chaplains too, of ſo many Scots Regiments, thinking them to be all Preſbyterians, becauſe coming from a Country where Preſbytery is the Order.[12]

The work of a conscientious chaplain to the army in Flanders is shown in yet another of his letters, dated 18th May 1691.

> Our new men, eſpecially the recruits, can hardly be reſtrained from groſs profanity. But I have been every day exerciſed in catechiſing ſome of the companies, wherein I

find ſome of the profane more knowing than ſome of the
profeſſors. Orders and laws are given out againſt ſwearing
and all debaucheries, aſſigning delinquents to loſe a days
pay and the informer to get it. Some have been ſcourged
for Sabbath breaking, drunkenneſs and ſwearing, whereby
there might be hope of repreſſing open profanity if the
officers would bear a hand. But it is a matter of diſcourage-
ment and of great difference and debate among the officers
that the Lieut. Colonel brings in ſo many new officers and
ſome of them ill men, whereupon ſome have offered to
demitt.

He goes on to say that he intends to

expend a great deal of my pay upon Bibles and Catechiſms
for the Regiment, which we think to get from Holland.[13]

A few weeks later he reports that

the Dutch and Germans are keeping a faſt; the Scots and
Engliſh their careleſs damning and ſwearing. When we
ſhall keep ours I know not; few mind it except ſome of the
old men who yet keep their ſocieties.[14]

The regimented Cameronians had fallen on evil days. They
could not count on any support from the Societies at home, in fact
a hostile mob stopped an attempt at recruiting in Ayr in February
1692. The corps was now hindered by its associations from a
normal supply of recruits and denied help by those who had first
brought it into being, but it had done well in Scotland, it was to
do better in Flanders and was to win in military circles new
laurels for an honoured name. Much more could be told of the
life of Mr Shields, of his strange dreams and merciful escapes
from peril while in Flanders, of his becoming minister of St
Andrews in Scotland, of his scholarly publications; but these, and
his appointment as a chaplain to the Expedition to Darien, are
not relevant and are to be found elsewhere.[15]

There were other chaplains with the Scottish regiments fighting
the French, and some of these are well worthy of mention.

The chaplain to the Royal Scots during the campaigns from

1692 to 1709 was Mr Samuel Noyes. He kept a Diary which has never been published. This little book is in the Library of Welbeck Abbey, according to the Bibliography of Winston Churchill's *Marlborough*. There is, however, a typewritten copy in the Military Library of Edinburgh Castle. Noyes does not give much information concerning his work as a Chaplain, but he does make it plain that he was in attendance upon his regiment, on the march and in action. He tells of his tent being so stiffly frozen that it could scarcely be struck and stowed away.[16] On another occasion he says that there was

> a battery of 7 or 8 pieces of cannon firing upon us as we marcht off but to little or no effect. One of their Balls light between my Horses Leggs & another at ye same time went just behind my back.[17]

In 1731, Noyes became a Prebendary of Winchester, being so preferred by Richard Willis, the Bishop, who had been Chaplain General in 1694.[18]

The Chaplain of the Scots Guards at this time was Edward d'Auvergne, who achieved fame as one of the best of contemporary historians; he became Rector of Great Hallingbury in Essex.[19] According to Dalton he was followed in the regiment by his son of the same name, but the *Dictionary of National Biography* and the University lists are silent as to the existence of this son. It is possible that the historian's commission was renewed in 1713, so causing this confusion.[20]

The Scottish regiments that fought for William were served by some fifteen chaplains. It may be noted that the chaplain to Strathnaver's regiment, Mr John Good, was ordained to that charge by 'the Scots Presbytery in London'. His commission was dated 1695; he became minister of Carnwath.[21] John Milling, the chaplain of Maitland's Regiment, now the King's Own Scottish Borderers, from 1694 became minister of Leyden in the Netherlands.[22] He was followed in the regiment by John Chalmers, the brother of Principal George Chalmers of Aberdeen. Mr Chalmers became minister of Campvere in the Netherlands in 1699, and of Duffus in Scotland, in 1722.[23]

These illustrations make it clear that the regimental chaplain of this period normally accompanied his men on the campaign. Carstares, Shields, Noyes and d'Auvergne leave no doubt of their participation in march and battle, and Chalmers and Milling were called from their regiments to charges abroad.

In addition to the commissioned chaplains with regiments other ministers were required for the troops stationed at home. The Castle of Edinburgh was served by Walter Smith from 1692 until 1709,[24] and the important garrison at Inverlochy called Daniel McKay to be their minister in 1692, and he continued with them until he was called to Inverary in 1699.[25]

There were, however, many detachments of troops in Scotland who could not be brought under the care of the garrison chaplains, and the General Assembly was asked, in 1697, to find some means for their spiritual oversight.

On the 12th January of that year

there was prefented to the General Affembly, a letter from the Right Honourable, The Vifcount of Teviot, Commander in Chief of His Majeftie's Forces within this Kingdom, Defiring them to fall upon fome way, how the faid ftanding forces may be provided with Preachers, and untill that be obtained, that they ferioufly Recommend to the Refpective Minifterf and Church-Seffions, where they are or fhall be ordered to quarter, to provide them with convenient Seats; for hearing with the faid Congregations, and to infpect and notice them as they do other Parifhioners during their abode there. . . .

The Assembly agreed to do all that they could to meet the desires of the Commander in Chief, and further recommended their Commissioners

to fall upon all expedient ways competent for them, how the faid Forces may be provided with Preachers and upon Application to fettle Minifters in Regiments belonging to this Kingdom.[26]

This request for a better supply of chaplains in the field must have been embarrassing to the Assembly, for the great difficulty that year and for many years to come was to provide for the many vacant charges throughout the country, particularly in the North. The Peace of Ryswick and the consequent reduction of many regiments relieved them of the additional burden of providing for these.

Before we follow the fortunes of the Scottish chaplains beyond this point, it must be admitted that, in spite of the ability of such men as d'Auvergne, and the enthusiasm of such a chaplain as Alexander Shields, there was already some criticism of the zeal and of the motives of those who pretended to be the spiritual guides of the army. There is a poem of 1693, which is much too long for quotation, but of which a part is relevant and illuminating. The whole production professes to be a petition from the chaplains to Parliament for the redress of their grievances, and in it they cry:

13

And if't be our chance
To ſerve againſt *France*,
At Sea, on the *Rhine*, or in *Flanders*:
We earneſtly ſue t' ye,
That exempt from all duty
We may Dine with our Pious Commanders.

14

Then Brandy good ſtore,
With ſeveral things more,
Which we Sons o' th' Church have a right in:
But chiefly w' intreat,
You'll never forget
To excuſe us from Preaching and Fighting.

15

Let not a Commiſſion
So change the condition
Of him that juſt carried a Halbert;
That a Dunce of no letters
Should Hector his Betters,
For truly we cannot at all bear't.

16

Nor when the War's done,
Let's be broke ev'ry one,
To languish in Rags and lye idle;
Nor be ſo ill ſerv'd.
To be left to be ſtarv'd,
And kept by a Bear, and a Fiddle.[27]

We have shown that such jibes were wide of the mark in the case of a considerable part of the Scottish chaplains, and even the derogatory 'Pious Commanders' loses weight when it is remembered that one such was General Hugh Mackay, who fell at Steinkirk. Not long before that battle he issued his *Rules of War for the Infantry . . . encountering with the Enemy upon the Day of Battel.* These consist of twenty-two rules, with:

> Lastly, when all dispositions are made, and the army waiting for the signal to move toward the enemy, both officers and soldiers ought seriously to recommend, together with their souls and bodies, the care and protection of the cause for which they so freely expose their lives, to God who overruleth the deliberations and councils, designs and enterprises of his creatures, and on whose blessing alone, the success of all undertakings doth depend.[28]

The prayer he then suggests as suitable for the occasion need not be quoted, but it does seem that the piety of this commander was as real as the work of his chaplains was faithful.

Although we may fairly claim that the chaplains of the armies of William were normally diligent in their duty, there are signs discoverable of the beginnings of carelessness and of corruption that suggest worse things to come.

One such hint of lack of care may be taken from the records of the General Assembly for 1707. In that year the Commission of the Assembly was asked for a decision in the case of Alexander Borthwick, minister of Greenlaw in the Presbytery of Duns. He also held a commission as Chaplain to Lord Polworth's Dragoons, and this plurality had been challenged in the Presbytery. The Commission advised that the Presbytery need not make any question about Mr Borthwuick seeing the Parish of Greenlaw was, and is, under no disadvantage thereby, and the regiment sustains as little prejudice, they being quartered at several places of great distance, each troop being proper parishioners in the congregations where they are quartered.[29]

The argument of the Commission is perfectly plausible and almost incontrovertible, but it opens a wide door for abuse, and it makes no provision for the day when the regiment must be drawn together for foreign service.

An early instance of corruption in the matter of a regimental chaplaincy comes from the private papers of a Colonel of Dragoons. This document was written by a cleric, who may have seen service with the Scots Guards, and it explains itself.

I, James Johnson, Chaplain of the Royal Regiment of Dragoons commanded by the Right Honourable the Lord Raby, being desirous to live at home, Do hereby promise to his Lordship upon consideration of his leave thereto, forever to quit all claims and demands whatsoever from the Regiment as Chaplain to the same, from the first day of January next ensuing inclusive, and do further promise never to make interest either for myself or any other to be Chaplain to the said Regiment. Witness my hand, this 2nd day of November, 1700.[30]

One may presume that the cleric stayed at home, the regiment went abroad without a chaplain, and the Honourable Colonel pocketed the chaplain's pay.

Long before such practices could become common, the war with France was resumed, and the regimental chaplain is found with the armies led to victory by Marlborough.

The *Blenheim Bounty Roll* is a list of those who qualified to receive a grant of money for having shared in the battle, and it is of obvious importance here as evidence of the presence of chaplains in the field that day.

The British regiments involved at Blenheim included five of horse, two of dragoons and fourteen battalions of foot. These were accompanied by thirteen chaplains who each received a bounty of £20. There were five Scottish units among these, and, according to the Roll, Samuel Noyes of the Royal Scots and David Pitcairn with the Cameronians were present at the battle. Mr Pitcairn was also at Ramillies, became minister of Dysart, and died Father of the Church in 1757.[31]

The rolls of the regiments which fought at Malplaquet are less conclusive of personal presence at the battle, but, with that reservation, it shows that once more there were five Scottish units engaged, exclusive of those in Dutch pay, and that these had four chaplains between them. They were George Anderson of the Scots Greys, Joseph Loveday of the Royal Scots, Robert Middleton of the Royal Scots Fusiliers and Samuel Halliday of the Cameronians.[32]

The Chaplain General of the army at the time of Blenheim and Malplaquet was Francis Hare, who had been a domestic chaplain to the Commander in Chief, and who seems also to have held a commission as a regimental chaplain.[33]

Francis Hare, who became Bishop of Chichester, wrote long letters home, which are of some value as history, but these are largely useless here. Mr Hare does mention the holding of services of Thanksgiving[34] after the various victories, but even this information can be found in other places. Marlborough's Dispatches show that such celebrations were held after Schellenberg, Blenheim, Oudenarde and Malplaquet and on other similar occasions. The reference to that after Malplaquet is typical of them all.

> According to the orders given on Friday, yesterday was observed very devoutly through the whole army as a day of Thanksgiving to Almighty God for our victory, and the evening concluded with a triple discharge of all our artillery and small arms.[35]

Colonel Blackader, of the Cameronians, had his own opinion of these Thanksgivings, and wrote gloomily of one such:

> Tomorrow is appointed by the General to be obſerved through the army in thankſgiving for our ſucceſs and

prayer. God grant that we be not found mocking him in this exerciſe, when theſe mouths come hot from curſing and ſwearing to the ſervice of God, pretending to thank him for mercies which they have no ſenſe of, and when the work is over, return to ſwearing and blasfemy. But, Lord, whatever the army do, make me ſingle and fervent, and tune my heart to praiſe and gratitude.[36]

These days of Thanksgiving are also mentioned by the author of the long poem *The Remembrance*, who incidently tells us more about the activities of the army chaplains than most of his contemporaries. He says that in

> Finelo toun when we first came in
> They aloued us a good preaching housse,
> On Sundayes afternoon Mr George Andersoun
> He always preached to us
> And after Ramelie we had a fast day
> And preaching throu al our armie.[37]

Some impression of the elaborate drill involved in a parade for church may be gathered from that which governed the regiments of dragoons. These drew up for prayers as if for battle, that is to say, they paraded mounted, left their horses linked together, and marched forward on foot to the chaplain. The orders necessary for such a movement are given in a drill manual, as follows[38]:

1. Return your swords.
2. Files to the right, Double march.
3. Make ready your carbines.
4. Handle your carbines.
5. Sling your carbines.
6. Throw back your carbines.
7. Make ready your links.
8. Drop your links.
9. Quit your right stirrup.
10. Dismount.
11. Files that doubled, as you were, march.

12. Link your horses.
13. Face to your proper front.
14. Move clear of your horses, march.
15. Rest your carbines.
16. Unsling your carbines.
17. Shoulder.
18. Squadrons face to the right.
19. March.
20. Halt.

When all this military ritual had been performed to the satisfaction of those in command, the worship of God might begin.

If the worth of Marlborough's chaplains is measured by the moral standard of his troops a wide variety of estimate is possible. If we accept the testimony of Thomas Lediard, one of the Staff Officers, we must believe that his General made the camp like a well-governed city, driving out all loose women and insisting upon a high standard of discipline and upon the regular conduct of public worship. In fact, according to Lediard, the camp was the best academy in the world for the training of a gentleman.[39]

The Colonel of the Cameronians would not have agreed, for he wrote:

A ſad ſabbath. We are far from knowing a ſabbath or ſeeing any marks of it here, that it is more like hell that day than on any other. Oh how long ſhall I dwell in the tents of wickedneſs.[40]

Perhaps the truth lies somewhere between these extremes, and was expressed by Corporal Trim, who would have agreed with Colonel Blackader on the subject of swearing soldiers, but who also said to the Curate:

A soldier, an' please your Reverence, prays as often (of his own accord) as a parson: and, when he is fighting for his king, and for his own life, and for his honour too, he has the most reason to pray to God of any one in the whole world.[41]

The conduct of Marlborough's men, when at home in Scotland,

gave rise to some criticism, and in 1710 the General Assembly had to take notice of these, as follows:

> The General Assembly, finding that there are several Refer-ences made to them, by inferiour Judicatories of the Church concerning Soldiers under Scandals, who refuse to submit to the Discipline of the Church for removing the said Scandals; for remedy thereof, they do Resolve that this matter should be represented to the Earl of Leven, Com-mander in Chief of Her Majesties forces in Scotland.[42]

The Earl of Leven was present at this meeting of the Assembly and promised to do what he could in this affair, but the scandals continued, and the Assembly had to complain on the same grounds in 1712 and in 1718. In 1724 they approached the Commander in Chief to request his active help in the suppression of

> cursing, Swearing, breaking of the Lord's Day and other Immoralities of the Soldiery, by a due Execution of the *Articles of War* against Immorality.[43]

The *Articles for War* which the Assembly invoked were those which had been read in the House of Commons and inscribed in its Journals on 4th February 1717.

These *Articles* ordered all officers and men to 'diligently fre-quent Divine Service and Sermon', and laid down fines for non-attendance, the said fines to be applied for the 'Relief of the Sick Soldiers of ſuch Troop or Company, to which the Offender does belong'. Similar penalties were to be imposed for unlawful oaths, and violence toward a chaplain or any other minister was to be dealt with by Court Martial.[44]

The jealous watch kept by the Presbyterians after the Revolu-tion, against any intrusion of Episcopacy, was bound to take note of any regiment which brought an Episcopal chaplain into Scotland. Such a case was mentioned in the letter from an officer in Scotland which was forwarded to William Carstares in February 1709/10. The writer complains of the violence and inveteracy of the Presbyterians against the Church of England, and pleads for a measure of toleration; he continues:

> Though our chaplain was here, yet he was not suffered to preach; which is what we were never denied in the most rigid Roman Catholic countries.[45]

This difficulty was not new for Alexander Shields had protested against the reading of the English service in Perth by the army chaplain, Thomas Morer, and had told his audience

> that there was no difference betwixt the Church of England and the Church of Rome, but that the one ſaid Maſs in Engliſh and the other in Latin.[46]

This quarrel continued down the years until the Army established a compromise, that soldiers should attend the Church established by law in that part of Britain where they were quartered.

The practice of appointing garrison chaplains in Scotland was continued, but not because of any provision in the Act of Union of 1707. In spite of the popular opinion, the garrisons of the country were not guaranteed by that Act and, indeed, in 1709 they were found in a parlous state.

On the occasion of an invasion scare in that year, it was reported that the Castle of Dumbarton had several breaches in the walls, that none of the twelve guns was mounted and that there was no ammunition available.[47] This wretched condition of things did not extend to the chaplaincy services, for the posts at Edinburgh, Stirling, Dumbarton and Fort William were supplied more or less regularly with chaplains, although the office was in some danger of becoming a sinecure where all else was neglected and ruinous. The smaller posts had the services of the local clergy; thus in 1740 the General Assembly allowed £10 to Mr William Blair, minister of Kingussie, for his preaching in a barrack at Ruthven.[48]

Such an arrangement was reversed in the case of Fort William, for here the chaplain to the garrison supplied the needs of the local population. Thus we find that Daniel McKay was called by the garrison in 1692. He was ordained to the charge by the

Presbytery of Abertarff, and continued until 1699. It is noted that he made no use of the Gaelic while incumbent there. His successor as chaplain was Neil McVicar, who became minister of St Cuthbert's, Edinburgh. and who only once used Gaelic. The appointment of William Brodie as chaplain gave rise to opposition in the Presbytery on the grounds that he had no knowledge of Gaelic. The military authorities replied that

> the Government have firmly resolved never to call a minister that will make use of Irish, it being the Queen's orders to purge the regiment of all Highland soldiers.[49]

This answer, and the small chance of any other suitable candidate being found, coupled with the fact that Brodie was otherwise qualified, induced the Synod to move the Presbytery to settle him in the charge. Brodie accompanied the regiment, which is now the King's Own Scottish Borderers, when they went to Flanders, and continued with them in 1715, when he was on a leet for the Scots Church in Rotterdam.[50]

Thus we have parish ministers acting as part-time army chaplains, and an army chaplain acting as parish minister.

The case of the chaplaincy of Edinburgh Castle differs from both of these. From the Revolution a series of ministers, Walter Smith, John Fleming and Alexander Ker, were ordained to the charge of the great Kirk of the Castle, which stood on the site now occupied by the Scottish National War Memorial. These ministers had a seat in the Presbytery and were referred to as ministers and not as chaplains.[51]

The salaries of the garrison chaplains varied considerably, for the chaplain to the regiment stationed at Fort William received five shillings per day in 1702, while his colleague in Edinburgh had to be content with half of that amount.[52] An official report for 1746 shows that the chaplain at Berwick received £121 per annum and the chaplain of Stirling Castle had £45 12s. 6d. From the same source it appears that the widow of a chaplain was entitled to a pension of £16, in common with the widow of an ensign or of a doctor; and that the price of a chaplain's commission ranged from £300 to £400.[53]

We now reach a period in the history of the British Army for which even the labours of the indefatigable Dalton could do little. He confesses:

I cannot hope to bridge the first twelve and a half years of George II's reign. In the first place the period from June 1727 to December 1739 is one of the most stagnant in British history. Secondly the military MSS for the years in question at the Public Record Office, London, are few in number and lamentably incomplete.[54]

There is therefore a gap in our roll of Scottish army chaplains, a gap which can be filled only in part from other sources. For example, the regimental records of the Royal Scots give the names of Henry Herbert and Samuel Groves, and *Fasti* provides one, James Thomson, for the Cameronians, during these lean years.[55]

Before passing over this gap, reference might be made to a gap which yawns in our particular study, and that is the absence of any attempt to define the duties of the chaplains to the army. The various *Articles for War* insist upon the decent conduct and the regular attendance of the troops at public worship, but there is no programme of duty for the chaplain apart from these appearances at prayers or sermon. We have seen that Mr Shields went catechising round the companies, and that, as early as the Civil Wars, the clergy were expected to have some care of the sick, but these duties were never prescribed until one of Wellington's generals undertook the task of teaching all departments to know their duty. The absence of such a code is made more apparent against the very thorough *Compilation des Ordonnances des Roys de France, Concernant les Gens de Guerre*, which was published in Paris in 1728.

Those sections which instruct the chaplain in his duty to the sick and the dying will illustrate the thoroughness of the whole.

Art. LVII

L'Aumonier, confeſſera tous les malades à leur arrivée, ou du moins avant les vingt-quatre heures expirées; il dira tous les jours la Messe à heure réglée, fera la Prière tous les soirs, et en son absence il la fera faire par les servens, & ne negligera rien de l'administration des Sacremens.

Art. LVIII

Quoyque sa principale occupation consiste dans le spirituel, il fera cependant admis, dans l'Assemblée de chaque mois, à proposer avec les autres Officiers ce qu'il croira convenable au bien du service de Sa Majesté; & il Signera comme eux les Stats qui y seront arrêtéz.

Art. LIX

Il tiendra un Registre fidelle des morts, qu'il fera signer à la fin de chaque mois, par deux Officiers de l'Hôpital, & par le Commissaire des Guerres, & qui devra être conforme à celuy de l'Entrepreneur; il tirera de ce Registre deux certificats signez & légaliséz par le Commissairs des Guerres pour en envoyer un au Regiment, & l'autre à la famille du défunt; & pour les Troupes étrangères, il suffira d'en adresser un au Régiment.

Art. LX

Nul ne pourra tester en faveur des Officiers de l'Hôpital où il fera, pas meme l'Aumonier ni de son Couvent, sous prétext de legs pieux: l'Aumonier pourra cependant, en envoyant l'Extrait mortuaire, avertir la famille des intentions du défunt.[56]

Although they lacked the guidance of such a Code, the chaplains of the British Army gave, on the whole, good and devoted service during the early years of the eighteenth century. There were signs, however, of that slackness and simony which could ruin that reputation if allowed to develop. But before we continue with the general history of the clergy with the regiments of Scotland, we must give a little time to consider those who were involved in the various attempts to restore the House of Stuart to the throne.

REFERENCES

1. Dalton, *Army Lists*, vol. iii, Introduction, passim.
2. Grose, *Military Antiquities*, vol. v, p. 309.
3. *Historical Records of the Royal Scots Greys* (1840), p. 19.
4. *Fasti*, vol. iii, p. 533.
5. Dalton, *Army Lists*, vol. iii, p. 283; vol. iv, p. 49.
6. Joseph McCormick, *State Papers and Letters addressed to William Carstares* (1774), p. 38.
7. Story, *William Carstares*, pp. 211, 226f.
8. *One of King William's Men*, p. 199.
9. Wodrow, *Analecta*, vol. i, p. 202.
   Dalton, *Army Lists*, vol. iii, p. 210.
   A Sermon preached by Mr Alexander Shields, etc. (1702).
10. *Laing MSS, Cameronian Papers*, vol. iii, 344, No. 280, 13th April 1691.
11. ibid., vol. iii, 344, No. 281.
12. ibid., vol. iii:
    'A letter from Mr Alexander Shields, minister of the regiment whereof the late noble Earl of Angus was Colonel, now in Flanders, directed to the General Assembly of the Church of Scotland which was to have met at Edinburgh in December, 1693.'
13. ibid., vol. iii, 344, No. 282.
14. ibid., vol. iii, 350, No. 285.
15. Cf. Article by Hector Macpherson in *Scottish Church History Society*, vol. iii, pp. 55ff.
16. *The Pocket Book of Dr Samuel Noyes*, etc., Edinburgh Castle copy, p. 4.
17. ibid., p. 16.
18. ibid., Introduction.
19. F. Maurice, *The History of the Scots Guards* (1934), vol. i, pp. 57, 65; Dalton, *Army Lists*, vol. iii, p. 309.
20. Maurice, vol. i, p. 110; Dalton, vol. vi, p. 60.
21. *Fasti*, vol. ii, p. 316.
    Dalton, *Army Lists*, vol. iv, p. 105.
22. ibid., vol. iv, p. 42.
    Scottish Church Rotterdam, pp. 123 and 315.
23. Dalton, *Army Lists*, vol. iv, p. 97; *Fasti*, vol. i, p. 153.
24. *Fasti*, vol. i, p. 92.
25. ibid., vol. iii, p. 114.
26. *XIII, Act and Recommendation anent Ministers to the Army, Edinburgh 12 January 1697, ante Meridien*, Session 9.
27. *The Chaplains Petition to the Honourable House for Redress of Grievances*. By one of the Camp Chaplains (1693).
28. John Mackay, *The Life of Lt. Gen. Hugh Mackay* (Bannatyne Club), pp. 134f.

29. *Fasti*, vol. i, p. 416.
30. Clifford Walton, *British Army*, pp. 760f.
31. Dalton, *Army Lists*, vol. v, Part II, pp. 33 and 66.
    Fasti, vol. ii, pp. 482 and 535.
32. Dalton, *Army Lists*, vol. vi, pp. 314, 323, 339, 345.
33. ibid., vol. v, p. 178; vol. vi, p. 300.
    Marlborough, *Dispatches*, vol. iii, p. 311.
34. *Hare MSS., Fourteenth Report of the Historical MSS. Commission* (1895), Part ix, pp. 200-35.
35. *Dispatches*, vol. i, pp. 344 and 416; vol. iv, pp. 120 and 560; vol. v, p. 115.
36. *Select passages from the Diary and Letters of the late John Blackader, Esq., formerly colonell of the xxvi.th or Cameronian Regiment of Foot* (1806), pp. 39f.
37. *The Scots Brigade*, vol. iii, p. 396.
38. *Exercise for the Horfe, Dragoons and Foot Forces, etc.* (1740), pp. 9f.
39. Thomas Lediard, *The Life of John Duke of Marlborough* (1736), p. xx.
40. Blackader, *Diary*, p. 72.
41. *The Works of Lawrence Sterne* (1819), vol. ii, p. 16.
42. *Acts of the General Assembly*, 1710, Sess. 7, 3rd May.
43. ibid., 1712, Sess. 12; 1718, Sess. ult.; 1724, Sess. 14.
44. *The House of Commons Journals*, vol. xviii, pp. 708f.
45. McCormick, *State Papers and Letters*, p. 783.
46. *Scotch Presbyterian Eloquence Displayed, etc.* (1694), p. 89.
    An Account of the Persecution of the Church in Scotland in Several Letters, etc., Letter One (ascribed to Thomas Morer).
47. *An Account of the late Scotch Invasion, etc.* (1709).
48. *Fasti*, vol. iii, p. 236.
49. ibid., vol. iii, p. 114.
50. Charles Dalton, *George the First's Army* (1910), vol. i, p. 185.
    Scottish Church Rotterdam, p. 147 n.
51. *Fasti*, vol. i, p. 92.
52. *Miscellany of the Maitland Club* (1842), vol. iii, part I.
53. *Report from the Committee appointed to consider the State of H.M. Land Forces . . . 6th day of June, 1746*, pp. 39 and 170.
54. Dalton, *George I's Army*, vol. ii, p. iv.
55. *Fasti*, vol. ii, p. 569.
56. *Code Militaire ou Compilation des Ordonnances des Roys de France, Concernant les Gens de Guerre*, par le Sr. de Briquet (Paris, 1728), Tome, I, pp. 214ff.

IX

THE JACOBITE REBELLIONS

WHEN the Earl of Mar attempted to raise rebellion in Scotland in 1715 he had considerable clerical support. Robert Patten, himself a chaplain to the Rebels, says that

It is to be obſerved, That only two Preſbyterian ministers in all Scotland, complied to pray for the Pretender, and were afterwards turn'd out by the General Aſſembly; and only two Epiſcopal Miniſters Prayed for His Majeſty King George.[1]

Such a division of the sheep from the goats may be more neat than accurate, but it does broadly state the case. The bulk of the Presbyterian ministers remained loyal to King George, while the majority of the Episcopal clergy, who were still tolerated in many parishes in the dearth of more orthodox incumbents, favoured the Jacobite cause, and in some cases took an active part in the Rebellion.[2]

Such active support was given from the outset, for John Alexander, minister of Kildrummy, joined the Rebel standard when it was raised in Braemar. He was later associated with Andrew Livingstone of Keig, Andrew Jeffrey of Alford, Alexander Law of Kearn and John Robertson of Strathdon in charges of 'Abeting, encouraging and subsisting the late unnatural and wicked rebellion'.[3]

The Rebel army marched to Kirkmichael, where the minister, John Pearson, influenced his people to rebellion, pressed them to take arms against the reigning family, and mounted his horse himself with that in view.[4]

The records of the northern Presbyteries of Inverness, Forres and Elgin, all show much compliance and some active assistance by the ministers. These may have been opportunists, glad to fish in troubled waters, and to intrude into a charge under the protection of the Rebel army, but others were moved by a real sentiment of loyalty in their support for the Pretender.[5]

The Rebel army passed to Perth, by way of the indecisive Battle of Sherriffmuir, and here the Earl of Mar attended a service of Thanksgiving. One of the congregation has left his impressions of the sermon.

> What ſtruck me moſt, being intirelie neu, and ſurpaſſed all I ever heard, was a ſermon which was pronounced by one Barclay, a Scots-Irish priest of the Church of England, chaplain to Mar, if I'm not miſtakne, on a day of thankſ-giveing, or the firſt Sunday after our return to Pearth, i won't be poſitive; who, after raiſeying our hopes by the great advantages gain'd in our battle, turned to Mar, and took up the greateſt part of a longe ſermon in expoſtuleating, exorting, and begging and praying him, with ex-preſſions full of more zeale and paſſion than he addreſſed himſelf to God Almightie, not to hazard on another occaſion, as he had done ſo latelie, that ſo dear, ineſtimable, and invaluable perſon of his, the loſſ of which nothing could repair to his countrie.[6]

The author of the Memoirs from which this criticism is taken, is so plainly hostile to this chaplain, that we can hope that his account of Barclay's cowardice at Sherriffmuir is inaccurate. The preacher to whom he refers would be Mr Alexander Barclay, one time minister of Peterhead, who was deposed from that charge in 1695 and again in 1716.

Mr Barclay may have become one of the Episcopal chaplains attached to the Court of James III at Rome, mentioned in a letter of 1721.[7]

The Rebel army was now joined by the Pretender in person, who is said to have brought with him a Roman Catholic chaplain, a Father Innise. According to a News Letter:

> The Pretender continued to hear meſs all the time he was at Scoon. This disoblig'd many who flaterd themſelves and others that he was proteſtant.[8]

The Pretender soon 'disobliged' his followers even more by abandoning the whole enterprise, partly on clerical advice. The decision to escape being made,

> a French gentleman with a clergyman were secretly despatched to Dundee to direct three ships which lay there, or a little lower in the Firth of Tay, to put immediately off to sea and to come to an anchor about the height of Montrose.[9]

The Rebel army was now deserted by its leaders and quickly disbanded, the Day of Thanksgiving for the safe arrival of James in Scotland never having been celebrated. No comment on this sorry affair is needed, but we may note that fifteen or more ministers, who were nominally of the Church of Scotland, were deposed for their share in this futile Rebellion. Some of these clerics were made prisoners, and brought south for trial and a letter from one of these, Mr John Alexander, describes their journey. At Cupar in Fife their numbers were increased by

> other three Clergymen, viz—one Mr Elphinstone, chaplain to My Lady Strathmore at Longforgan, and one Mr Lindsay minister at Carriston, and one Mr Lyon, but he was kept behind, being libelled by the presbytrie of Dundee, and was to become a Sacrifice to yr rage. Mr Lindsay a minister, was pushed and driven here into a hole—the keeper of the prison who has served yr for 7 years protesting he had never seen man put yr before.[10]

No apology is required for turning now to the southern part of the Rebellion of 1715, for it was formed round a party of 1,500 Highlanders under Mackintosh, detached from the main body for this purpose, and the little army remained predominantly

Scottish to the end, for the prisoners after its defeat at Preston numbered 1,005 Scots and 463 English.[11]

This army of the Rebels had its chaplains, and one of the Articles of Impeachment exhibited against its leaders charged them with procuring such clerical support, thus:

> tho' many of the ſaid Conſpirators are vowed Profeſſors of the Popiſh Religion, yet the more effectually to cover and diſguiſe their moſt wicked and traiterous Deſigns, and to delude his Majesty's Subjects, they did prevail on and procure ſeveral Men in Holy Orders, Miniſters of the Church of England, and who had before time abjured the ſaid Pretender, to accompany, countenance and abet the ſaid moſt traiterous Enterpriſe, and in ſeveral Places in the Counties aforeſaid, where the ſaid Conſpirators, their Complices and Confederates then were, to pray for the ſaid Pretender in the publick Churches, as King of theſe Realms.[12]

One of the clergy here mentioned, Robert Patten, survived the attempt and wrote an account of the business, which is coloured by the fact that, to save himself, he turned 'evidence' against his friends and colleagues. His story does give considerable information concerning the chaplains who served this rebel force.

He says that the first clergyman to enlist with them was Mr Buxton of Derbyshire, who, by the order of the rebel leader, preached at Warkworth on 9th October. The sermon, according to Patten, was calculated to encourage the audience,

> being full of exhortations, flouriſhing arguments, and cunning inſinuations, to be hearty and zealous in the cauſe; for he was a man of a very comely perſonage, and could humour his diſcourſe to induce his hearers to believe what he preached, having very good natural parts, and being pretty well read.[13]

Mr Buxton also officiated at Hexham, where the incumbent modestly declined to pray for King James. He shared in the service at Kelso and dispensed the Sacrament privately to Mr Forster, the Rebel leader, at Hawick. Early in November Mr Buxton was sent off with letters to the gentlemen of Derbyshire, and was on this errand when the battle at Preston was lost. According to Patten, he was then ill of the smallpox and, being forced to flee in that condition, was never more heard of.[14]

Mr Patten, naturally, tends to enlarge upon the part he himself played in the rising, both as a preacher and a man at arms. It is only fair to state that, in the opinion of a fellow-prisoner, Patten was no coward:

> his intrepidity had been ſufficiently made appear in the Service of the French King and the attack at Preſton; and that he would have been faultleſs in his Character had he not made himſelf an Evidence.[15]

But this one blemish spoils the whole. Patten, the active agent and vigorous preacher, who had his horse shot under him in the battle, who struck up the pistol which threatened his leader, the hero of march and battle, was no sooner a prisoner with pinioned arms, with the quartering block preparing, than he bargained shamelessly for his life.

Patten's betrayal appears the darker in contrast to the fate of another chaplain to the rebels, Mr William Paul.

Mr Paul was vicar of Horton on the Hill, in Leicestershire, and only joined the Jacobite army when they had reached Lancaster. Patten says that the only duty Paul performed as a chaplain to the army, was to read prayers at Preston. He was then sent away from the force on a recruiting errand and so escaped the battle. He was later arrested in London, was tried, condemned and executed for high treason. From other sources we gather that Mr Paul played a larger part than his colleague ascribes to him.

One author declares that he was responsible for calling the people to prayers at Lancaster, having previously erased the name of Queen Anne from the Prayer Book and inserted that of King James. Patten gives the credit for this alteration to a Mr Guin, who was concerned to erase the name of King George. This last alteration would be chronologically correct, but Lancaster's Prayer Book may have been a little out of date.[16]

The trial and execution of Mr Paul must have been of considerable public interest, if one may judge by the crop of pamphlets it produced. Most of these agree that the victim was by nature 'Puſſillanimous', which makes the tragedy complete, for the coward went to the scaffold for the cause, and the hero lived to dedicate a book of recantation to King George.[17]

One Scot appears among the chaplains to the southern part of the Rebellion, William Irvine, who repeated at Kelso the sermon he had preached before Viscount Dundee. Mr Irvine seems to have continued with the rebel army and to have been among the prisoners taken at Preston. He survived, however, to become non-jurant Bishop of Edinburgh.[18]

Robert Patten says that there was also a Roman Catholic priest with them at Preston and that

> having a great deal of the Jeſuit, he contrived a moſt excellent Diſguiſe; for he put on a Blue Apron, and went behind an Apothecary's Counter, and paſſed for an Aſſiſtant or Journeyman to the Apothecary, and ſo took an opportunity of getting off. He took care of his own Tabernacle but left his Wafer Gods to be ridicul'd by the Soldiers.[19]

This priest, whose name was Littleton, may have been with the expedition for some time, for at Hawick

> the Roman Catholicks have had the Sacrament adminiſtered by a Prieſt; when opportunity ſerves, we will have all the Protestantſ ordered to Communicate.[20]

There is another hint of the presence of priests in the account of the debate which took place at Lancaster between two priests and the minister of the town.[21]

Some account must now be taken of those ministers who took the opportunity to demonstrate their loyalty to the reigning house by acting as chaplains to the troops that were raised to meet the emergency. The great reduction made in the size of the army of Britain after the peace of 1713 made the raising of new regiments imperative in the face of the Jacobite attempt. The authorities issued an order in pressing terms urging all Noblemen, Gentlemen and Ministers to assist in securing a sufficiency of recruits.[22] The ministers responded heartily and at least a dozen of them came to the rendezvous in person.

Their presence in the field is mentioned in a News Letter in connection with the raid of the rebels under Mackintosh upon Leith. The writer tells how

> we were formed to make the attack after Forfar's foot. We had 6 or ſeven miniſters under arms and Mr Semple from Liberton commanded a partie of his peritioners he brought with him. We drink now the health of these gentlemen under the name of the Church militant.[23]

On the other side of the country, the volunteers who came from Greenock were accompanied by Mr Turner, their minister, and when they were used to garrison the Castle of Touch he

> came and ſtaid three weeks, with his servant, who was armed with the reſt.[24]

In the south of Scotland the ministers were also active, and the inhabitants of Kelso prepared the town for defence under the direction of the local gentry and of Mr James Ramsay, the minister.[25] Mr Ramsay had held a commission as chaplain to Ker's Dragoons, now the 7th Hussars, from 1711 until the regiment was disbanded after the peace.

He then held the same office in the Royal Scots Greys, but was re-commissioned to the former corps when it was called into being once more in this emergency. Mr Ramsay became a Moderator of the Kirk in later years, but all that is known of his military career is a humourous story in *Fasti* of his attempt to attend a Presbytery meeting mounted on a mettlesome cavalry charger.[26]

The town of Dumfries was made aware of its danger by an intimation at a celebration of the Sacrament, and made great preparation for trouble.[27] The Provost of the town, however, failed to persuade a party of 300 Dissenters, under their minister, Mr John Hepburn, to join in the defence. These worthies declared that

> they had not freedom in their consciences to fight in defence of the constitution of church and state, as established since the sinful Union.

o

Mr Hepburn had been minister of Urr, in the Presbytery of Dumfries, since the Revolution, but had been in constant trouble with the courts of the Church, for a 'continuous tract of erroneous, seditious and divisive doctrines'.

He eventually formed an independent presbytery of himself and one other, and, as we have seen, refused to take sides in the troubles of 1715.[28]

The government forces had disciplinary troubles, and the ministers in attendance upon them were called upon to prepare prisoners for execution. One such case took place at Linlithgow, where the death penalty was decided by lot. Each prisoner handed in a white stick and these were given to the Preces of the Court,

> and he not knowing quhich is quhich breaks two and the whole stick escaps. So the broken sticks were instantly led out to execution after the chaplan had exhorted them and they had prayd.[29]

The News Letter does not name the chaplain who exhorted the condemned that day, but there was no scarcity of ministers with the Army. Among those present were several from the south of Scotland, including John McMurdo of Torthorwald, James Hunter of Dornock, Simon Riddell of Tynron, and John Pollock of Glencairn. From Govan came Charles Coote, and even from the Jacobite North there came Daniel McGilligan of Alness, whose house was burned by the rebels in reprisal for his loyalty.[30]

After the flight of the Pretender and the defeat of Preston, Scotland was swept by the government troops, and there was much burning of Prayer Books and even of Meeting Houses.

Many of the tolerated Episcopal clergy were deposed, the volunteer chaplains to the Royal Army returned to their parishes, and the Rebellion of 1715 passed into history.

Before we consider the chaplains who had a part in the much more alarming affair in 1745, mention might be made of the almost forgotten attempt made by the Jacobites in 1719. In that year a small force of Spanish troops landed on the north-west coast of Scotland, near Kyle of Lochalsh. They made Eileen

Donan Castle their base and ventured a few miles eastward into the parish of Kintail.

The clans were slow to rally round the invaders and English ships captured the Castle with the bulk of their supplies. One of these ships, the *Flamborough*, sailed up Loch Duich, and caused the destruction of another supply of ammunition near the present manse of Kintail, and a landing party burned the Church. The minister of the parish was Mr Donald McCra, two of whose sons had been killed at Sherriffmuir fighting for the Old Pretender His own sympathies lay with the Jacobites and it is surely possible that he acted as a chaplain to the little Rebel army during the brief period before it was crushed.[31]

The most dangerous of all the Jacobite attempts, that of Prince Charles Edward in 1745, was well supplied with chaplains from first to last. Setting aside the fact that the Prince himself passed as clergyman on board the ship which brought him to Scotland, we find that one of the little group that came with him was a cleric, George Kelly, who may have been more of the conspirator than chaplain.[32]

And when the last battle was lost, one of the band in attendance upon the fugitive Prince was a priest.

Before the Prince came ashore in Scotland he was visited by Bishop Hugh Macdonald, Vicar Apostolic of the Highlands, who begged him to abandon the attempt and to return to France. When this proved in vain, it is said that the Bishop blessed the Standard when it was raised in Glenfinnan, and that he appointed a number of his clergy to attend the Prince's army. Macdonald escaped to France after Culloden, but returned later to Scotland where he was allowed to live at home until his death in 1773.[33]

One of the most active agents in the recruiting of men for the Prince was John Gordon, priest and librarian at the house of Presholme, who marched with fifty men to join the rebels and who accompanied them to Edinburgh and beyond.

He was captured after Culloden but was released under the Act of Indemnity.[34]

The non-jurant ministers were also moved to assist the Pretender's Son, but three of them did not get beyond Stirling on their journey north, being arrested and held captive on suspicion until all was over. One of this party was Robert Forbes, after-wards Bishop of Ross, who made a careful collection of infor-mation concerning the Rising in which he had been unable to serve.[35]

The mysterious tactics of the commander of the Government troops in marching to Inverness permitted the Prince to take the town of Perth, and here, as in 1715, the Rebel army went to church.

> Prince Charles resolved, while at Perth, that he would publicly attend Scottish worship at St John's Church. He therefore appeared in the Middle Kirk on Sunday Septem-ber 8th, and, sitting in the King's seat, became the cynosure of all eyes. It was not to be expected that the Presbyterian Minister, Mr Black, would be allowed to fill the Pulpit on this occasion. Neither did the duty fall to Mr Lyon. The preacher was the Rev. Mr Armstrong of the Episcopal Church. He chose as his text, Isaiah xiv, 1 & 2.[36]

The Mr Lyon mentioned above was the Rev. Robert Lyon, Episcopal minister in Perth, who joined the rebels at this time and who marched with them as chaplain to the regiment of Lord Ogilvy. He was later tried and condemned for treason, on the accusation that he

> went from Perth with the Pretender and his Rebel Army, September, 1745 . . . and its informed that, when the Rebel Army were in England, the said Lyon was in Highland cloaths, bearing arms.[37]

Mr Lyon made a long speech from the scaffold which incidently gives his own conception of his duties as a chaplain. He said:

> while I accompanied my brave countrymen in their noble enterprise, I saw a decency and order maintained amongst them, equal if not superior to any regular or disciplined force . . . and for my own particular, I do solemnly affirm that during this Expedition I never bore arms, for this I thought inconsistent with my sacred character.

I never prayed in express terms for any King, (because for many years it has not been the practice of our Church, and to make such a change in her offices I thought incompetent for me without the appointment, or at least the permission of my superiors) and preached the plain truths of the Gospel without touching on political subjects.[38]

But that day of execution was still far ahead when the Rebel army marched from Perth toward Edinburgh. The Government troops under Sir John Cope were, literally, at sea, somewhere off the east coast of Scotland, and only a demoralised mob of dragoons protected the capital. As the rebels advanced the dragoons retired, the Highlanders surprised one of the city gates, and the Pretender's Son was established in the chief city of his northern kingdom.

Shortly after the fall of the city, the Government troops disembarked from their fruitless northern 'Tour'.

The Rebels wisely decided to put matters to the test of battle at once. According to a newspaper of the day:

Everything being now in readiness for advancing, the Highlanders took off their bonnets, and, placing themselves in an atitude of devotion, with upraised eyes uttered a short prayer.[39]

The charge with which they followed this prayer was decisive and the troops of Sir John Cope were swept from the field in disgraceful rout. If we can accept his own statement, the only Rebel chaplain who was present at this victory was John McLachlan. He wrote modestly to Robert Forbes in 1748:

If you'll make mention of any of our clergy that were in that army, I expect you'll not forget your writing friend who was the only clergyman at the battle of Gl[adsmuir], and who can get several gentlemen to attest that if his project and example had been follow'd neither Cope nor any of his horses had escap'd which would have made the victory still more compleat. He attended the Prince to Derby and back, and was at the battles of Falkirk and Culloden, acted chaplan to the Prince, and had a commission to be chaplain-general to all the loyal clans.[40]

McLachlan survived the Rising to become minister to the Episcopalians of Kilchoan.

This Rebel 'Chaplain General' may not have been so lonely in the field of Prestonpans as he says, for Mr David Brodie of Leadinton was later accused of being present and bearing arms.[41] Joseph Robertson of Haddington cannot have been far away, for he was quick to solicit the Prince for an order to take over the pulpit of the church of Haddington, but was gently snubbed for 'going on too fast'.[42] To these must be added the unnamed cleric of the Episcopal church who travelled so fast with the news of the victory, that he was able to announce it to his congregation, fifty miles away, at the usual time of worship the following day.[43]

The Rebels now had the whole of the Lowlands of Scotland at their mercy, with the exception of such strongholds as the Castle of Edinburgh, still held by its garrison for the King. Within the city of Edinburgh almost all of the Presbyterian ministers left their pulpits and refused all invitations to return. Alexander Carlyle declares that the Prince lost an opportunity for winning the allegiance of the people by not attending worship in the High Church of Edinburgh.[44] In the absence of the town's ministers, this policy would have involved Charles in serious controversy had he appointed any other to officiate. As in the case of Haddington, he was not willing to press on with such matters quite so fast. Robert Chambers says that Charles did attend worship in Holyrood, when the text of the sermon was from Joshua, xxii, 22, the same verse had served for the sermon Prince Rupert heard before the battle of Marston Moor.[45]

One of the Edinburgh newspapers, the *Evening Courant*, of October 1745, published an official statement concerning the religious views of the Rebel army which is of considerable interest. This was issued to refute an article which had appeared in the London newspapers,[46] telling of the success a certain Father Graham had had in converting some of the leading rebels to the Roman faith. The London letter was a palpable subterfuge aimed at alarming the Protestants of England for their faith and for their possession of the ancient estates of the Church, which, it said, must be restored on the Prince's victory. The Jacobites, however, thought it worth while to deny its authenticity, and proclaimed:

> It is therefore ſolemnly declared as well as notoriouſly
> known, that there neither is, nor ever was in the Army or
> Retinue of His Royal Highneſs, any ſuch Perſon as Father
> Graham, the pretended author of the Letter in queſtion . . .
> in fine the whole Series of the Letter is one continued and
> palpable lie, and notwithſtanding the pretended Converſion
> of the hopeful young Nobleman and the Highland Laird, it
> muſt be own'd that Religion is as little talked of in our
> Army (tho' we all believe in God) as in any other now in
> Europe.[47]

While the rebels continued in the city, the churches remained
empty, except for the West Parish where Mr McVicar, close
under the guns of the Castle, dared to pray for a Heavenly Crown
for the Young Man that has come amongst us.

One unexpected result of the cessation of public worship was
a sharp decline in the income of the Charity Workhouse, which
was compelled to solicit help through the Press.[48]

At length the Edinburgh newspapers were able to announce
on Monday 4th November that:

> Thurſday and Friday laſt the Highland Army marched from
> this place Southwards. . . . Yesterday there was Sermon in
> moſt of the Churches of this City.[49]

The Jacobite Army marched into England to terrify its enemies
and to enlist its friends. While it was amply successful in the first
of these it was much less so in the second, for many who had
noisily drunk the health of the 'King over the Water', were
reluctant to put their own health in jeopardy to bring him home.
Some recruits did come in, and with them came a few clergy,
both Episcopal and Roman.

At Manchester the Rev. Clayton celebrated their arrival with
a sermon of eulogy in the Collegiate Church, but the clerical
recruit who gained the greatest notoriety was Thomas Cappock.
He marched with the Manchester regiment to Derby, and there
conducted worship in the Great Church.

Cappock accompanied the retreating army to Carlisle, of which town it was alleged he had been made Bishop by the Prince. He remained with the Rebel garrison of Carlisle and was taken prisoner with them, being committed to Chester Castle.[50] He was tried and condemned for high treason, and his letter of appeal to the Archbishop of Canterbury is endorsed

> This Coppoch is in Deacon's Orders, and, for bringing a forged Testimonium, was removed from a Curacy in Kent.[51]

On hearing the savage sentence pronounced, Cappoch turned to his fellow-prisoners, with the salty comment:

> We shan't be tried by a Cumberland jury in the other world.

The *Scots Magazine* mentions other clergy being made prisoners about the same time as Cappoch:

> James Reiley, Samuel Newman and Martin Eades, were committed to Lancaſter gaol, and James Crane to that of Guilford. They were all Romiſh Prieſts.[52]

Another priest who is said to have accompanied the Prince into England was Gallus Leith. He appears to have been trained at St James's Seminary in Germany, and to have acted as confessor to the Young Pretender. After the battle of Culloden, where he was wounded, he escaped to the Continent.[53]

The long and difficult retreat from Derby was carried out with some degree of skill by the Rebel army. A study of the *Order Books* of the rebel regiments shows that very little was left to chance. For example, in the orders for the guard:

> The Capt. of the main Guards is to know where all the pipers are quartered in order to make Them play in case of an Alarm. He is likewise to have the key of the Church or Steeple where the Bells are & Cause them to be rung like-wise.[54]

When the Prince had got his army safely back into Scotland, he lost no time in calling together all those who had any zeal for his cause, and among these came more chaplains.

This clerical reinforcement was partly Roman and partly

Episcopal. Thus William Harper of Bothkiner, near Stirling, and Thomas Syme of Ardgarth in Perthshire, both of the Episcopal Church, joined the Prince at Falkirk.[55] Another of the same communion was George Law, from Aberdeen. He may have accompanied the march into England, but he later protested that he had only visited the rebel camp to persuade his son to come home.[56] From Carraldstone, near Montrose, came another Episcopalian, John Maitland. He had already been active as a tax collector for the Jacobites but now he marched with Ogilvy's regiment. He was at the battles of Falkirk and Culloden, and, at the latter, is said to have given the Sacrament to Lord Strathallan in oatcake and whisky, in default of the usual elements. Maitland was among those who escaped to France when all was lost.[57]

One of the priests involved in the last stages of the rebellion was John Tyrie, who accompanied the Glenlivet contingent. He is said to have cast lots with William Grant for the office of chaplain. Tyrie was wounded at Culloden but escaped from the field.[58] Alexander Gordon, another priest, was less fortunate, for, being taken prisoner, he died in captivity. He acted as chaplain to the French contingent, for his name appears in a list as 'Gordon, Aumonier'.[59] Mr Gordon was not the only priest to die as a prisoner, for Alexander Cameron, the brother of Lochiel, died on board the ship which carried him to London.[60] A fellow-prisoner has described the conditions under which the prisoners lived or died.

> At length by the indulgence of the Court every prisoner was allow'd half a pound weight of bread a day, and a quarter of an pound weight of cheese or butter for breakfast, and on flesh days half an pound boil'd beef for dinner, but no ale or beer. But by the avarice and villainy of the victualler, one Bonny, a broken taylor, they seldom or never receiv'd above three fourths of the said weights, and sometimes not so much.[61]

A priest who evaded capture until July 1746, was Allan MacDonald, who formed one of the little group who accompanied the Prince in his fugitive wanderings. When one of these was captured he was questioned whether the priest had prayed for the safety of the Prince when they were in fear of drowning, and he replied:

> If he prayed for himsell, he thought he did well enough. And had you been there, Sir, you would have thought you did well enough too, if you prayed for yoursell. Everyone of us was minding himsell then.[62]

Bishop Forbes seems to take a certain pleasure in belittling the part played by the priest in general, and by Allan MacDonald in particular. In addition to retelling the above tale, Mr Forbes himself questioned one of the fugitives concerning the relations between the priest and the Prince, and records the answer:

> Faith, I have reason to think that the Prince is not a great Papist, for he never gree'd well wi' the priest at all, and was very easy about his company.[63]

To sum up the services of the clergy with the Rebel army of 1745. At least ten non-jurant ministers were arrested for aiding or endeavouring to aid the Prince, of whom two, Lyon and Cappoch, were executed. Some seventeen priests were also made prisoners, of whom two, Alexander Gordon and Alexander Cameron, died as prisoners.

A few Presbyterian ministers found their loyalties divided by the Rebellion. John Cameron, the Presbyterian chaplain to Fort William, was drawn away by clan loyalty to forsake his duty to his Church and to the reigning House. He took an active part in the escape of the Prince and left a Journal of the adventures in which he shared.[64]

Another minister, Mr John Grant, of Urquhart, was tried in Edinburgh, for complicity in the Rising. In his defence he claimed that the Master of Lovat had sought to have him as a rebel chaplain,

> and promised to give him six and eight pence a day, if he would consent thereto, to which the Examnt. answered,

that if they would go to Inverness to serve His Majesty King George, he would be their chaplain with all his heart for one third of the money.

Local tradition says that Grant was certainly a Jacobite, but no serious attempt was made to convict him, and the case was allowed to drop.[65]

Only one minister of the Church of Scotland was brought before the General Assembly in connection with the Rebellion. This was Thomas Man, minister of Dunkeld, who was accused of praying for the Pretender, of drinking his health and similar disloyalties. He pleaded that the bulk of his parish were Jacobites and that his congregation included the rebel leader Tullibardine and his men. The plea was accepted in extenuation, and a nominal suspension from duty for five months was imposed.[66]

One Presbyterian student of Divinity joined the ranks of the rebels, and the *Diary* of the Rev. John Bisset, records the debate on his case before the Synod.

The Synod debated some time about a proper censure on Mr Whyte, who was on tryals before the presbitry of Deer, but since, a Captain among the rebels. Some moved summary excommunication; in my opinion a proper censure. Another moved to neglect him, alleging a rope and a tree would be his fitting reward. I frankly own, if I could not have obtained the first, I would have been for the last; but both were overruled; and in the depths of their wisdom and zeal, it was concluded to declare him for ever incapable of a license and that no presbytry might take him on tryals.[67]

One Elder of the Kirk appears as such in a list of persons concerned in the rebellion. He was Thomas Oliphant, 'late baillie and present elder in the church'. It was alleged that he had assisted

in carrying a Barrel of Gun Pouder to the Rebels & drank the Pretender's health.[68]

To round off this note of the few rebellious officers of the Kirk comes Robert Ross, a Beadle, whose lapse from grace may be explained, though not excused, by the statement that he had been 'imposed upon when drunk'.[69]

Turning now to the clerical assistance enjoyed by the Government forces in the suppression of the Rebellion, we find that the bulk of the ministers of the Church of Scotland gave all the help they could as recruiting agents and as 'intelligencers', from the moment Prince Charlie's ships were sighted until he was taken away again by ship.

The rebel leaders did what they could to win some measure of support from the younger ministers, 'but they were excessively baulked'.[70] An attempt was also made to secure the help of the Dissenters, but here again they had small success.[71] So far, indeed, was the Prince from winning the ministers to his side, that, as we have seen, the pulpits of Edinburgh were deserted on his approach.

This desertion preceded the actual arrival of the Jacobite army, for a correspondent of the *Scots Magazine* urged the resumption of public worship, and said:

> Ye know that ſome Sabbaths were ſspent before the late revolution in this city, both by miniſters and people in military maters; we then ſtood in defence of the government and of the city, now, when theſe reaſons exiſt not, ſhall we continue to deſpiſe or neglect the obligations of the Lord's day?[72]

The military matters which so engrossed both clergy and laity were offensive as well as defensive in intent. Debate waxed bitter between those who wished to defend the walls until Cope's forces could return, and those who advised that the volunteers of the city should co-operate with the dragoons to harass the march of the Highland army.

The inevitable result of such division was that the city fell to the rebels without a blow being struck in its defence.[73] Andrew Lang is scathing on the part played by the ministers in these days of doubt and debate, and says, 'it is a pity that the church should meddle with these matters', referring to the efforts of the clergy to keep the volunteers within the walls of the town.[74] Is it not barely possible that the ministers were in position to judge the outcome of a clash between the volunteers and the regiments of the Highland clans? The outcome of Prestonpans suggests that the volunteers were well advised when they handed back their newly acquired weapons and stayed at home. Mr Kinloch, one of the ministers, said that the proposed sally reminded him of a passage in Livy, when the Gens Fabia marched out of Rome against the Gauls, which ended ominously, 'Omnes ad unum periere'.[75] Some of the ministers and students of divinity who had been denied the opportunity of battle at this time were able to attach themselves to Sir John Cope's army shortly afterwards. Among the students were one or two who became well known in later years. One such was John Home who made an accurate count of the Rebel army and carried the information to Cope, who, characteristically, failed to profit by it. Mr Home became minister of Athelstaneford, but is remembered for his *History of the Rebellion* and for the writing of a stage play which caused grave offence in the Church.[76]

Another of these stalwarts was Alexander Carlyle, known to posterity as 'Jupiter', who became minister of Inveresk and a Moderator of the General Assembly. His service as a volunteer yields one incident which is amusing and a revelation of war as it was waged. Carlyle had been active as a scout for the Royal army, and, on the eve of the battle of Prestonpans, retired to rest in the house of a friend near by. In his own words, 'I directed the maid to wake me the moment the battle began.' The maid obeyed this order and Carlyle dressed without stopping to fasten any buckles, but the battle was lost before he got far from the door.[77]

But these student volunteers, though interesting, were not chaplains to the army, and there were ministers present to play that part. When Carlyle was seeking a bed before the battle, he found his father's manse at Preston full of such clerical aides. He says there were

some Merse clergymen, particularly Monteith and Laurie

and Pat. Simson. They were very noisy and boastful of their achievements.[78]

One of these braggarts was, Robert Monteith, minister of Long-formacus. He published a sermon on *The Rights of the Clergy to Appear in Defence of the Liberties of their Country*, but, if tradition speaks truth, he did not insist upon his 'Rights' on the day of Prestonpans. According to the *Ballad of Tranent-muir*, he

> wadna stand to bear a hand
> But aff fu' fast did scour, man,
> O'er Soutra Hill, ere he stood still,
> Before he tasted meat, man.
> Troth he may brag of his swift nag,
> That bore him aff sae fleet, man.[79]

Patrick Simson, minsiter of Fala, who was also in the manse of Preston that night, was made of sterner stuff.

He was among those made prisoner at the battle of Falkirk who escaped from the Castle of Doune, and he was in attendance upon Cumberland's army on its march north, as Ensign Mr Simson.[80]

Another minister who was present at the defeat of the Government troops was Alexander Webster, the popular preacher of the Tolbooth Kirk in Edinburgh. He is said to have pressed upon Cope the duty of fighting, and is, therefore, blamed by historians for the defeat. Mr Webster's career suggests that, whatever his advice on this occasion, his judgement was usually sound. He was a Moderator of the Assembly, was responsible for the actuarial basis of the Ministers' Widows Fund, drew up an authoritative account of the people of Scotland, and suggested the development of the New Town of Edinburgh.[81] The total rout of the Royal army brought a temporary halt to the activities of army chaplains, and, indeed, almost all clerical work came to a stand. We have seen one exception in the activities of Mr McVicar, a former chaplain at Fort William, as minister of the West Church. He was not quite alone in his witness, for Adam Gib, a minister of the Associate Presbytery, was preaching regularly at Dreghorn, under the noses of the Rebels stationed at Colinton. Some of the rebels are said to have attended his services and, on one occasion, to have interrupted the discourse with a shot.[82]

On the occasion of a military execution in the Rebel camp, however, the condemned men

> were attended in their laſt hours by Miniſters of the Eſtab-liſhed church.[83]

In contrast to the empty pulpits of Edinburgh, the ministers of Dundee

> preached as uſual, prayed for King George, and warmly exhorted their hearers to be ſteadfaſt in their loyalty, all without moleſtation, tho' ſome of the highlanders were preſent.[84]

When the rebels and the regular regiments were marching and counter-marching throughout England, resistance in Scotland began to appear again, and it was said that

> the Presbyterian preachers in Scotland were the best re-cruiting serjeants . . . that Cumberland and his father ever had.[85]

The *Scots Magazine* tells how the ministers and the people gathered together to resist the returning Rebel army.

> A ſmall corps of them accordingly came into town on the evening of the 30th [December] and a considerable number in a day or two after. Several miniſters marched with their pariſhioners, ſome of them in arms. The voluntiers of the Aſſociate congregations of Edinburgh and Dalkeith, ſece-ders from the eſtabliſhed church, kept in a body by them-ſelves, and had proper colours, with this inſcription, 'For religion, the covenants, King and Kingdom'. Their miniſter did not march with them.[86]

The *Evening Courant* supplements this information and tells that

> The Reverend Miniſters of the Preſbytery of Hamilton have raiſed at their own Expence, a Company of 60 Men, in Defence of his Majeſtys Perſon and Government; and are ready to march where his Majeſtys Service require.[87]

The town of Stirling found itself in particular danger, for it commanded the Rebels' line of communication with the north of Scotland. Volunteers mustered for the defence of the town but the usual division of opinion made their efforts of no avail. Among those who were urgent that an effort be made was Ebenezer Erskine, at the head of a body of his Seceders. The *Scots Magazine* mentions his vain effort:

> Mr Stevenſon, Conveener of the Trade, and Mr Erſkine, the Seceding Miniſter, took a proteſt againſt the capitulation, to which proteſt the greateſt part of the town adhered.[88]

It must not be presumed, however, that all the Dissenters were enthusiastic supporters of the House of Hanover.

Some of them professed that they could find little to admire in either of the claimants for the Throne, and one section of them issued a

> Declaration and Teſtimony againſt the Late Unjuſt Invaſion of Scotland by CHARLES pretended Prince of Wales, and WILLIAM pretended Duke of Cumberland and their Malignant Emiſſaries.[89]

While such an extreme of political exclusiveness is to be regretted, we need not endorse the judgement of Andrew Lang. He speaks rather strangely of

> the Persecuted remnant, who had learned nothing and forgotten nothing since Claverhouse broke their resistance to all power that was not 'from on High'.[90]

Mr Lang must surely have forgotten that the Persecuted remnant were capable of resisting a Highland army at Dunkeld after Claverhouse had done his best to crush them.

The Rebel army, now returned from England and augmented by many sympathisers, was able to inflict a smart defeat upon the Government troops, regular and volunteer, at Falkirk. According to an English officer, some Scottish ministers were killed in the battle or the pursuit,[91] having quitted their Bibles and taken to their swords. It is not apparent that any of the ministers were killed but a number of them were captured by the rebels and imprisoned in Doune Castle. Among these prisoners were John Home and Patrick Simson, who had been at Prestonpans, James Smith of Garvock and Andrew McVey of Dreghorn.[92] Another chaplain-captive was John Witherspoon of Beith. He became minister of Paisley, and was called from that charge to be President of Princeton College in North America. He took a prominent part in the movement for American Independence, and was the only clergyman to sign the Declaration.[93]

Although they had been victorious at Falkirk, the Rebels continued their withdrawal to the north, and, on their way, they surprised certain Campbell garrisons. In one of these posts, Kirkton of Struan, they captured Mr Alexander Stewart, minister of Blair Atholl.[94]

The Royal army, under the Duke of Cumberland, followed this movement, and it was accompanied by certain of the more adventurous clergy. Other ministers assisted the expedition in various ways. Mr Bryce of Kirknewton, for example, was able to advise their choice of route from his extensive geographical knowledge.[95]

The minister of Kintore was taken by the rebels in an attempt to carry information to the loyal McLeods, and his colleague of Rayne, avoiding capture by a detour, was too late to affect the skirmish at Inverurie.[96]

An officer of the army pays this tribute to the clergy when engaged on an expedition into the hills:

I do assure you the Clergy, who have everywhere in Scotland much distinguished themselves for our religion and happy constitution, behaved very kindly to us, were our guides and intelligencers everywhere . . . and three of them went quite up to the Castle of Corgarff with us.[97]

The zealous support of the ministers was to be found even in the skirmishings of the rebels and the loyalists in Sutherlandshire, where Aeneas Sage was with the loyal army. It was said of him, in later days, that, in a ministry of fifty years, he had brought his parishioners 'to a state of comparative civilisation'.[98] In this northern sector of the war, the minister of Dornoch, Mr Robert

Kirk, dared to pray for King George, even when threatened with Rebel violence.[99]

It may, however, have been curiosity rather than courage or a desire to serve, which took Alexander Macbean, of Inverness, to the field of Culloden. He had, it is said, a narrow escape from death at the hands of a fleeing clansman.[100]

The Rebellion broken at Culloden, the work of the volunteer clergy with the army came to an end. We can but hope that some ministers did their duty by the sick and the wounded of the Royal army. These troops suffered more severely in the campaign than is usually realised, for, although there were only 270 wounded at Culloden, there were, in all, two thousand in hospital, of whom three hundred died.[101]

The Rebel wounded died of exposure or were slain in cold blood, and so, in mutual suffering, the last attempt to restore the ancient Scottish line came to its end.

The rights and the wrongs of the Jacobite cause are for others to debate, we have tried to show that the clergy, torn by conflicting loyalties, were faithful in their service on either side in the strife, giving new meaning to the Jacobite song:

> On whatever sod we kneel,
> Be ye sure we ever feel,
> For the Honour and the Weel,
> O' oor ain Countree.

REFERENCES

1. *The History of the Late Rebellion with Original Papers, etc. by the Rev. Mr Robert Patten, formerly Chaplain to Mr Forfter* (1717), p. 71.

2. *Historical Papers Relating to the Jacobite Period, 1699-1750*, New Spalding Club, vol. i, pp. 63, 65, 83, 93, etc.
   G. D. Henderson, *Mystics of the North-East*, Third Spalding Club (1934), p. 29.

3. *Fasti*, vol. iii, pp. 559, 556, 547, 550, 564.

4. ibid., vol. ii, p. 803.

5. *Papers relating to the Jacobites*, vol. i, pp. 33-35.

6. *Memoirs of the Insurrection in Scotland in 1715*, Abbotsford Club (1858), p. 262.

7. Andrew Lang, *Prince Charles Edward Stuart* (1903), p. 14.

8. *News Letters of 1715 and 1716*, ed. A. Francis Steuart (1910).

9. *A True Account of the Proceedings at Perth, by a Rebel* (1716), pp. 26 and 65f.

10. *Papers Relating to the Jacobites*, vol. i, pp. 124f.

11. *Annals of King George Year the Second, being a Faithful History of the Affairs of Great Britain for the year MDCCXVI* (1717), p. 46.

12. ibid., p. 77.

13. *The History of the Late Rebellion*, p. 29.

14. ibid., pp. 33, 39, 70, 96.

15. *The Case of William Paul, a Clergyman, and John Hall*, etc. (1716), p. 7.

16. *The History of the Late Rebellion*, pp. 107ff and 90.
    Papers about the Rebellions of 1715 and 1745, ed. Henry Paton, Scottish History Society (1893), p. 519.

17. Cf. *The Epistle of Paul the Parson*, etc. (1716),
    The Case of William Paul, a Clergyman (1716),
    Matter of Fact, being a Short Account, etc. (1716).
    Rebel Convinc'd and Liberty Maintain'd, etc., by Robert Patten, one of the Chaplains concerned in the late Rebellion (1718).

18. *The History of the Late Rebellion*, pp. 39f.
    Fasti, vol. ii, p. 119.

19. *The History of the Late Rebellion*, p. 132.

20. ibid., p. 70.

21. *Papers about the Rebellions*, pp. 519f.

22. *Annals of King George*, p. 58.

23. *News Letters*, Steuart, pp. 44f.

24. George Charles, *History of the Transactions in Scotland* (1817), vol. i, pp. 289f.

25. Peter Rae, *The History of the Late Rebellion* (1718), p. 185.

26. C. R. B. Barrett, *The 7th Hussars* (1914).
    Dalton, *George I's Army*, vol. i, p. 107.
    Fasti, vol. i, p. 457.

27. C. S. Terry, *The Chevalier de St George*, p. 276.

28. Charles, *Transactions*, vol. i, pp. 307f.
    Fasti, vol. i, p. 607.

29. *News Letters*, Steuart, pp. 128f.

30. *Fasti*, i.602, 617, 685, 676; ii.69; iii.291.

31. *The Historical Register for 1719*, vol. iv, pp. 279-85.
    The Jacobite Attempt of 1719, Scottish History Society.
    Fasti, vol. iii, p. 103.

32. Robert Forbes, *The Lyon in Mourning*, Scottish History Society, vol. iii, p. 50; vol. i, pp. 282-4.

33. Alphons Bellesheim, *History of the Catholic Church in Scotland* (1890), vol. iv, p. 191.

W. B. Blaikie, *The Origins of the 'Forty-Five*, Scottish History Society, p. 82 n.

34. *List of Persons Concerned in the Rebellion*, Scottish History Society, p. 28; *Lyon in Mourning*, vo.l iii, p. 164.
35. J. B. Craven, *Bishop Forbes Journals* (1886), p. 12.
    The Scots Magazine, vol. viii, p. 399.
36. G. T. S. Farquar, *The Episcopal History of Perth* (1894), p. 166.
37. ibid., p. 172.
38. *Lyon in Mourning*, passim.
    Alexander Mackintosh, *Forfarshire or Lord Ogilvy's Regiment, 1745/6* (1914), passim.
39. *Caledonian Mercury*, 23rd September 1745.
40. *Lyon in Mourning*, vol. ii, p. 85 and n.
41. *List of Persons*, p. 134.
42. ibid., p. 138.
43. Robert Chambers, *History of the Rebellion* (1869), p. 140.
44. *Autobiography of Dr Alexander Carlyle* (1910), p. 168.
45. Chambers, *History*, p. 141 n.
46. *General Evening Post*, 22nd September.
    St James Post, 24th September.
    'A Genuine Intercepted Letter, from Father Patrick Graham, Almoner and Confeſſor to the Pretender's Son in Scotland, to Father Benedick Yorke, Titular Bishop of St David's, etc.'
47. *Edinburgh Evening Courant*, 4th October 1745.
48. ibid., 18th October 1745.
49. ibid., 4th November 1745.
50. Chambers, *History*, p. 186.
    Papers relating to the Jacobites, vol. i, p. 290.
    The Scots Magazine, vol. viii, p. 94.
51. *Prisoners of the 'Forty-Five*, vol. i, p. 223.
52. *The Scots Magazine*, vol. viii, p. 94.
53. Fischer, *The Scots in Germany*, p. 149.
54. MSS. *Order Book of the Stewart of Appin, Clan Regiment*, 4th December 1745, Military Library, Edinburgh Castle.
55. *List of Persons*, pp. 56 and 236.
56. D. M. Rose, *Prince Charlie's Friends or Jacobite Indictments* (1896), p. 70.
57. *List of Persons*, pp. 180f.
    Craven, *Bishop Forbes Journals*, p. 182.
58. *List of Persons*, p. 130.
    A. and H. Tayler, *Jacobites of Aberdeenshire* (1928), pp. 409f.
59. ibid., pp. 202f.
    Prisoners of the 'Forty-Five, vol. i, p. 224.
60. *Origins of the 'Forty-Five*, p. 87 n.

61. *Lyon in Mourning*, vol. iii, p. 31.
62. ibid., vol. i, p. 180.
63. ibid., vol. i, p. 199.
64. ibid., vol. i, pp. 83-101.
65. *Origins of the 'Forty-Five*, pp. 320 and lxxvii.
    Fasti, vol. iii, p. 120.
66. *The Scots Magazine*, vol. ix, pp. 246f.
67. *Jacobites of Aberdeenshire*, pp. 414f.
68. *List of Persons*, p. 66.
69. ibid., p. 126.
70. *Origins of the 'Forty-Five*, p. 125.
71. *Memorials of John Murray of Broughton*, Scottish History Society, pp.
    52f.
72. *The Scots Magazine*, vol. vii, p. 462.
73. John Home, *The History of the Rebellion* (1802), pp. 79ff.
74. Lang, *Prince Charles Edward*, p. 141.
75. ibid., p. 142.
76. *Fasti*, vol. i, pp. 320f; cf. his *History*.
77. ibid., vol. i, pp. 287f; cf. *Autobiography*.
78. *Autobiography*, p. 150.
79. *Fasti*, vol. i, p. 421.
    James Hogg, *Jacobite Relics of Scotland*, Second Series (1821), p. 122.
80. *Fasti*, vol. i, p. 279.
    Origins of the 'Forty-Five, pp. 158f.
81. *Fasti*, vol. i, p. 51.
82. John McKerrow, *History of the Secession Church* (1841), pp. 200-6.
83. *The Scots Magazine*, vol. vii, p. 491.
84. ibid., vol. vii, p. 399.
85. *Lyon in Mourning*, vol. ii, p. 108.
86. *The Scots Magazine*, vol. viii, p. 32.
87. *Edinburgh Evening Courant*, Thursday 19th December 1745.
88. *Fasti*, vol. ii, pp. 682f.
    The Scots Magazine, vol. viii, p. 73.
    McKerrow, *Secession Church*, pp. 200-6.
89. *An Active Teſtimony of the True Preſbyterians* (1749).
90. Lang. *Prince Charles Edward*, p. 208.
91. *Origins of the 'Forty-Five*, John Daniel's Progress, p. 198 and n.
92. *Fasti*, i, p. 320; i, p. 279; iii, p. 871, ii, p. 164.
93. ibid., vol. ii, p. 160.
    Trinterud, *American Tradition*, p. 218.
94. *Fasti*, vol. ii, p. 793.
    Lyon in Mourning, vol. i, p. 316.
95. *Fasti*, vol. i, p. 143.
96. *Origins of the 'Forty-Five*, pp. 141f.

97. *Papers relating to the Jacobites*, vol. i, p. 311.
98. *Fasti*, vol. iii, pp. 94f.
    The Book of Mackay, p. 180.
99. Andrew Lang, *Companions of Pickle* (1898), p. 109.
    Fasti, vol. iii, p. 328.
100. ibid., vol. iii, p. 258.
    Origins of the 'Forty-Five, p. liv.
101. John Pringle, *Obſervations on the Diſeaſes of the Army* (1765), pp. 44, 52, and passim.

X

THE HOUSE OF HANOVER

THE fifty years which followed the Jacobite Rebellion of 1745 saw the decline and fall of the office of Regimental Chaplain in the British Army. But the story of these years is not of unrelieved failure, for many chaplains of this period were worthy of the highest praise and others were at least adequate to their duty.

The official position of the army Chaplain under the Hanoverian kings did not differ in essentials from that enjoyed in the preceding reigns. The *Articles for War* show the same insistence upon church attendance, for regiments at home and abroad, the same regard for the outward forms of religion. There is a letter from General Wolfe, when he was commanding the 20th Regiment in Glasgow in 1749, which illustrates the reality of this church-going, and reveals a common attitude toward it.

He wrote to his mother:

> I do several things in my character of commanding officer which I would never think of in any other, for instance, I'm every Sunday at the Kirk, an example justly to be admired. I would not lose two hours of a day if it did not answer some end. When I say, 'lose two hours', I must explain to you that the generality of Scotch preachers are excessive blockheads, so truly and obstinately dull that they seem to shut out knowledge at every entrance. They are not like our good folks. Ours are priests, and though friends to venaison, they are friends to sense.[1]

In another letter he is able to reassure his mother that their own chaplain has come, and that he is now 'back to the old faith, and stick close to our communion'.[2]

This zealous attendance, even in the House of Rimmon, may have been due in part to the re-publication in 1747 of the *Articles for War* of 1717, with their insistence on church attendance. The Orders issued by the Duke of Cumberland for the troops employed in Scotland emphasise this:

> Divine service to be regularly performed in Camp, which Officers and Soldiers are to attend to.[3]

The reading of Daily Prayers is also enjoined, as in a *System of Camp Discipline*, published in 1757, in which it is laid down that Prayers

> be read every morning at the head of each Brigade at nine; the Chaplains of each Brigade to take it in turns, beginning with the Eldeſt.[4]

The *Order Books* of the Scottish regiments show that such regulations were much more than a polite fiction. The newly formed Highland regiment, the Black Watch, for example, provides evidence that prayers were held as regularly as was possible, by such entries as, 'Prayers tomorrow at nine o'clock, and, 'Prayers in the Barracks on Tuesday at eight o'clock.'[5]

Another illustration comes from the Orders of the Edinburgh or Queen's Regiment, when in Ireland in 1779, 'Church tomorrow as usual, the men well drest and powdered.'[6]

In addition to this insistence upon public worship and prayers, the laws against cursing and swearing were re-enacted, as is shown in the *Scots Magazine* for June 1746.

The same authority demonstrates that these laws were enforced, for

> a ſoldier rode the mare there [Glasgow] with a paper on his breaſt denoting his crime, for tranſgreſſing the laws againſt curſing and ſwearing.[7]

The *Order Books* also show that the Army had strong views on the subject of marriage, and in 1798 one of them declares that soldiers ought to be particularly careful not to contract raſh or improper marriages, which tend to encumber them for life, to break their ſpirit, and damp every hope of promotion. ... When a chaplain is appointed to the regiment, he is the proper perſon to be employed; and no one is to have recourſs to a prieſt, in order to evade the regimental ſtanding orders.[8]

The decent conduct of military funerals was also provided for in the rules and regulations which affected the work of the military chaplains. These included a careful gradation of the escort and the volley firing, ranging from an escort of six battalions and eight squadrons, with a salute of three rounds from fifteen cannon, for a field marshal, to an escort of one sergeant and thirteen rank and file, who were to fire three rounds of small arms, for a private soldier. An estimate of the cost of burying one of the 'private men', in 1776, is as follows.[9]

	s.	d.
To the parſon	2.	6.
To the ſexton	1.	0.
To the grave digger	1.	0.
For a pall	1.	6.
For a coffin	8.	6.
	14.	6.

A commissioned chaplain was paid 6s. 8d. per day, and a chaplain's widow was entitled to a pension of £16 per annum.[10] If the Chaplain was with a Foot Regiment, he received an extra allowance, on campaign, of £3 15s. to provide a 'bat-horse' to carry his baggage. This allowance was held to be too small in the case of other officers, so the chaplain may also have found it inadequate.[11]

In India, in the service of the Company, the Madras Presidency General Orders for 1788 declare that

Regimental chaplains in the Company's Service are to receive the same rate of pay and allowances as Captains but Batta only at the stations where the Corps or Troops they are attached to are in receipt of that allowance.[12]

The conditions under which the chaplains worked among the troops and their families in home stations are described at some length by William Agar, chaplain to the 20th Regiment and a rector in Lincolnshire. He wrote:

That we ſhould be deemed leſs devout than other nations is not ſurpriſing, if we only conſider that our Children born in Camps or among our private Centinels, are brought up in a total ignorance of moral duty to God or Man. I reckon at leaſt, about two hundred women to each Battalion. I know that ours had but one hundred and fifty at the Camp near Blandford. Some regiments had three hundred after them; and it might be heartily wiſhed, that all, unleſs proved lawfully marry'd had been ſent off, for the better ſupport of the honeſt and induſtrious. . . . I have reckoned in my own regiment, between forty and fifty children born each year; among thoſe at age to be called to their Catechiſm, ſome few repeated pretty well, and remarking their parents I always found them clean, ſober and in good repute; but the greateſt part at the years of ten or twelve, were totally ignorant (to my own ſhame I ſpeak it) of the God that made them; nor could I do juſtice to my Office, for want of one on leiſure days to ſend through the Lines for thoſe Children who were (knowing their inſufficiency) backward of coming to me.[13]

In Mr Agar we have a chaplain who was conscious of the responsibilities of his office, but there were others of his brethren who were less worthy.

Among such were the growing numbers of those who purchased a commission as a chaplain, as an investment which would yield a steady income of 6s 8d. per day, less a small sum for the payment of a deputy. Such gentlemen had no intention of actually joining the regiment to which they had been commissioned. For example, Mr Miles Beevor, chaplain to the Royal

Scots, is mentioned in their Records of 1795 as 'Absent since 14.2.1786', that is, from the date his commission was granted.

Nor was absenteeism the only charge levelled against the chaplains as a class, for the satiric *Advice to the Officers and Soldiers* gives this guidance to the clergy with the Army.

The Chaplain is a character of small importance in a regiment, though many gentlemen of the Army think otherwise. Yet if you are not more successful in the cure of the soul than the surgeon is in that of the body, I would confess your 6s 8d. a day would be a judicious saving. You have such hardened sinners to deal with that your office is rather an ungracious one; but though the officers and soldiers are in general irreclaimable, the women of the regiment may perhaps be worked on with better effect. If you are ambitious of being thought a good preacher by your scarlet flock, you must take care to keep your sermons short. That is their first virtue in the idea of a soldier. Never preach any practical morality to the regiment. That would be only throwing away your time. . . . You may indulge yourself in swearing or talking bawdy as much as you please; this will only show you are not a stiff high priest. Moreover, example being more effectual than precept, it will point out to the young officers the ugly and ungentlemanlike appearance of the practice and thereby deter them.[14]

Robert Burns, in *The Jolly Beggars*, endorses the same criticism in the pungent phrase, 'sanctified sot', and William Wordsworth echoes it more gently in *The Excursion*. He tells of a 'lad o' pairts' for whom every sacrifice was made,

>   that he
> By due scholastic discipline prepared,
> Might to the ministry be called; which done
> Partly through lack of better hopes—and part
> Perhaps, moved by a curious mind,
> In early life he undertook the charge
> Of chaplain to a military troop
> Cheered by the Highland bagpipe, as they marched

In plaided vest—his fellow countrymen.
This office filling, and by native power,
And force of native inclination, made
An intellectual ruler in the haunts
Of social vanity, he walked the world,
Gay, and affecting graceful gaiety;
Lax, buoyant—less a pastor with his flock
Than a soldier among soldiers—lived and roamed
where fortune led . . .[15]

That there was a basis for such charges against the chaplains is made plain by the insertion of the following clauses in the *Articles for War* as published in 1748.

5. No chaplain who is commissioned to a Regiment, company, Troop or Garrison, shall absent himself from the said Regiment, Company, Troop or Garrison (excepting in the case of sickness or leave of absence) upon pain of being brought to a Court Martial, and punished as their judgement and the circumstances of the case may require.

6. Whatever chaplain to a Regiment, Troop or Garrison shall be guilty of drunken-ness. or of other scandalous or vicious behaviour derogating from the sacred character with which he is invested, shall, upon due proofs before a Court Martial, be discharged from his sacred office.[16]

Such an attempt to control the wayward and the unworthy was made of little avail by the exemptions for sickness and leave of absence. For example, Peter Vatass, chaplain of the 14th Hussars, was alternately sick or on leave for fifty years.[17] Such subterfuge was impossible without the connivance of the commanding officers, many of whom profited financially from the sale of the commission and also pocketed the moiety of the pay which was supposed to reimburse the deputy chaplain.

Having shown the dark side of the picture as regards the chaplains of the British army in the latter half of the eighteenth century, we may now consider the narrower field of those ministers who were attached to the Scottish regiments, both Fencible and of the Line.

During that period the appointments of 106 chaplains can be traced in the history of such Scottish units. Among them there were 45 who were also parish ministers in Scotland, and 24 who have no traceable history in the Scottish Church and who were probably Episcopalian. The remainder were commissioned as chaplains before they became ministers of Scottish parishes. A reasonable deduction from these figures would suggest that 37 Presbyterian ministers and an unknown proportion of the Episcopalians did serve as chaplains with the Scottish regiments.

It will be noticed that the practice of commissioning other than Presbyterian chaplains continued, and this was particularly true of the older regiments, whose existence was not threatened by every wave of financial retrenchment, and in which a commission was a sound investment. Thus the chaplains of the Royal Scots rejoiced in such southern names as, Loveday, Herbert, Groves and Best, while the Scottish Borderers were served by DeLamillier, Cheap, Ford and Williams.

The Presbytery of Perth objected to this practice, when it permitted Episcopalian clergy to become chaplains to Scottish regiments. In 1762 that Presbytery presented an Overture to the General Assembly, craving

> that the Assembly should address the King, that His Majesty would be graciously pleased to order, that such regiments as are levied in North Britain may have Presbyterian chaplains.

The Assembly referred this to its Committee on Kirks and Manses, who reported that, in their opinion, it would be improper to address the King on this subject, but that other means might be thought of to obtain the end in view, and this the Assembly unanimously approved.[18] It does not appear what other means, if any, were used, but the abuse continued unchecked by any official act of the Church of Scotland.

A number of the younger sons of Scottish noble families were provided for by being commissioned as chaplains to Scottish regiments. Thus the Hon. Gideon Murray, the brother of Lord Elibank, became chaplain to the Black Watch in 1739, and Henry Hay Drummond, second son of the Earl of Kinnoul, was

with the army at Dettingen. The Hon. James Bruce, second son
of the Earl of Kincardine, became chaplain to the 105th Regiment
of Foot, in 1761, and the Hon. Archibald Cathcart, third son of
Lord Cathcart, was chaplain to the 90th Regiment, in 1794.
One of the younger sons succeeded to the title while commissioned as a chaplain, and appears in the *Army Lists* for 1761, as,
'Alexander, *Earl* Home', chaplain to the 25th Regiment, now
the King's Own Scottish Borderers.

It is not easy to show to what extent the purchase of commissions prevailed in the Scottish regimental chaplaincies.

It seems clear that in the older regiments purchase was the rule
rather than the exception, but, among the regiments raised to
meet an emergency there was no uniformity of practice. In the
case of the Highland Regiments there was the additional complication of language, for a sound knowledge of Gaelic was essential
for any chaplain who attempted to perform his duties. There is a
MS. *Record of Officers' Service* preserved at the Regimental Depot
of the Gordon Highlanders, which notes against the name of
their only regimental chaplain, William Gordon, 'Not by purchase'. It may be concluded, therefore, that many of the chaplains purchased their commissions, but that an unknown proportion were nominated by the Colonels concerned without any
cash transaction.

It must now be determined if any of the chaplains did serve
with the units to which they were commissioned.

If we consider, in the first place, those regiments stationed overseas, there is evidence of the attendance of some of their chaplains.
Thus when George II achieved the distinction of being the last
British sovereign to command his army in battle, at Dettingen,
his personal Chaplain was Henry Hay Drummond. To this Scot,
in Episcopal orders, fell the honour of preaching the sermon of
Thanksgiving before the King, at Hanover, on 7th July 1743.
Mr Drummond rose steadily in the service of his Church and became Archibshop of York in 1781.[19] Another chaplain who was
present at the battle has left us an account of the campaign.[20]
He mentions that 'our wounded were neglected, and a very
heavy rain falling increaſed their miſeries', but tells us nothing of

chaplaincy duty except that Te Deum was sung and the guns fired in triumph.

The battle of Fontenoy was attended by two Scots chaplains who were to become famous in later years, John Douglas and Adam Ferguson.

Mr Douglas was appointed to the Scots Guards in 1744, and joined the regiment in Flanders. It is said that he spent much of his time in the study of foreign languages, but he was present at the battle, and even acted as an emergency aide-de-camp. He returned to England with the troops sent there to quell the Rebellion of 1745, and began a long career of distinction in the literary world and of preferment in the Church of England.[21]

His colleague, Adam Ferguson, was chaplain to the Black Watch, and is said to have been carried away by the heat of the battle, and taken part in it sword in hand. David Stewart, who was himself an officer in the Black Watch, has another account of the chaplain's conduct that day, which redounds rather more to his credit. Stewart says that when Ferguson was advised to withdraw to a place of greater safety, he said that he had a duty to perform:

> Accordingly he continued with the regiment during the whole of the action in the hottest of the fire, praying with the dying, attending to the wounded and directing them to be carried to a place of safety.[22]

There is a painting by W. Skeoch Cumming of Adam Ferguson on the battlefield, which neatly combines these two versions of his conduct, for it shows him, girt about with a sword, and kneeling beside a wounded man.

Mr Ferguson continued to serve with his regiment until 1757, and then, after two years as a tutor, he became Professor of Natural Philosophy in the University of Edinburgh. He later surrendered this Chair for that of Moral Philosophy. It is possible that his published works of history owe something to his experience as a chaplain.

There is a contemporary poem which seems to pay tribute to the chaplains at Fontenoy.

But let me ſtill the Same purſue
When all the Troops for certain knew
  Next day the Fight begins;
In the calm night, a Preacher ſtood
And ſpoke the Love, the Truth of God
  Who bore our many Sins.

What charming News he told to those
Who Christ the better Part had choose;
  Methinks I hear the Sound
Boldly you may to battle go,
Nor fear the Number of the Foe.
  Nor fear the Mortal Wound.

The Preacher, who his work had done
The night before the Fight begun;
  Was kindly called away
A cannon Ball cut off his Thighs,
And yet before he reached the Skies
  He made a little stay.

And cheerful ſpoke his Joy of Heart,
Forgot his wounds, ſcarce felt the Smart,
  While talking of his God;
And thus in Joy, reſign'd his Breath
A Conqu'ror over Hell and Death
  Through Jesus precious Blood.[23]

There were other fields for the service of Scottish soldiers and for
their attendant chaplains. Thus, Mr James Gordon was ordained
by the Presbytery of Edinburgh as Chaplain to the 21st Regiment,
The Royal Scots Fusiliers, in 1753. The Regiment was then part
of the garrison of Gibraltar, and Mr Gordon appears to have
served with them until he was presented to the Parish of Bellie,
in 1769.[24]

On the other side of the Atlantic, the 78th Regiment, or
Fraser's Highlanders, were engaged in the conquest of Canada.
They earned this tribute:

On all occasions this brave body of men sustained a uniform character for unshaken firmness, incorruptible probity, and a strict regard both to military and moral duties. Their religious discipline was strictly attended to by their very respectable chaplain, the Reverend Robert Macpherson, who followed every movement, and was indefatigable in the discharge of his clerical duties. The men of the regiment were always anxious to conceal their misdemeanours from the Caipal Mor, as they called the chaplain from his large size.

Mr Macpherson continued with the regiment until it was disbanded in 1763, and was on half-pay for many years.[25]

A somewhat similar tribute was paid to Mr Macaulay, who was commissioned as chaplain to the linked 87th and 88th regiments (Keith's and Campbell's) in 1760.[26] Equally active and worthy chaplains are to be found in the later years of the century. For instance, when the Second Battalion of the Black Watch went out to India in 1781, they had a bad journey, lasting more than a year, and many officers and men died on the voyage. Among these was the chaplain, Mr John Stewart.[27] A Mr Dennis was appointed to fill the vacancy and he was killed on the ramparts at the siege of Mangalore.[28]

Yet another chaplain to serve with this corps in India was Mr Donald Bayne, who was commissioned in 1784, and who survived to become minister of Elgin and to receive the degree of D.D. from the University and King's College, Aberdeen.[29]

Supporting evidence for the quality of the chaplains attached to the Black Watch may be found in the proud boast of that corps, that

In the course of 79 years service [i.e. from their formation] no individual has ever been brought to a General Court Martial for theft or any crime showing moral turpitude or depravity.[30]

This claim is itself supported by John Wesley, who said of some sixty of their number that they were 'fit to appear before Princes'. Let some credit be given for this remarkable record to the chaplains, Adam Ferguson, Lachlan Johnstone and James

Q

Maclagan, and to those named above who served the Second Battalion.

It may not be wholly relevant, but justice demands that mention be made of the good work done by laymen to supplement the efforts of the chaplains for the troops in foreign stations. A little-known instance of such assistance was originated by Thomas Mitchell, a Scottish gipsy. He had been converted by a sermon by Mr Robert Jack, minister of Biggar. As a soldier of the Royal Scots Fusiliers he was sent to Gibraltar and formed there a small religious society, teaching sobriety by precept and example and distributing Christian literature. This society flourished in 1756, and it, or a successor, was mentioned in an Order by Lord Cornwallis in 1769 as follows[31] :

> Whereas divers soldiers and inhabitants assemble themselves every evening to prayer, it is the Governor's positive order that no person whatever presume to molest them, nor go into their meeting to behave indecently there.[32]

Similar societies flourished in other garrisons as the result of the Wesleyan revival but these do not concern us here.

In the absence of a chaplain it was not unusual for an officer to read prayers. General Dyott notes in his Diary that when on a troopship in 1796

> I read prayers to all the people, which indeed I never failed to do on a Sunday morning when the weather would permit.[33]

Having made certain that some of the chaplains served with Scottish regiments abroad, we may now consider their colleagues who were commissioned to the troops stationed at home. The home sphere can be divided conveniently in two parts, first the garrisons, large and small, throughout Scotland, and, second, the fencible regiments. These regiments consisted of full-time soldiers whose liability for service was limited by the duration of the war and by the coasts of Britain.

The chaplains of the garrisons were normally recruited from among the ministers of neighbouring parishes, who were only expected to give part-time service, since the salary paid was not usually large. Many of these clergy gave good and diligent attention to their military duties, although the teaching which they gave to their 'scarlet flock' sounds strange today. There is a sermon by Mr Agar, from whom we have quoted above, which is at once a revelation of the preacher and of his people. His text was, 'Be content with your wages', and he urges the soldiers:

> think with yourſelves, how many of you, by your In-diſcretion and youthful folly, had rendered yourſelves unfit for the Buſineſs your Friends intended you; think how many of you, out of Idleneſs and Sloth, Lewdneſs and Intemperance, would not earn your Bread by the Sweat of your Brows; nay, I fear that many were drawn to this laſt Shift to ſerve your Prince or almost ſtarve. How then can you be too faithful to that generous Sovereign, who when you was hungry Fed you, when you was naked cloathed you, when you was ſick viſited you, when you was deſtitute of Friend or Fortune, took you into his Protection, as the Father took the Prodigal Son, or as your Creator receives the repenting Sinner. . . . Keep up then, my Fellow Soldiers, the Spirit of your Calling; be good, yet brave; be honest, yet obedient; be humble and yet bold, let nothing daunt you. . . .[34]

To the modern ear this borders upon blasphemy, but it was preached by a conscientious chaplain to the soldiers of Britain in 1756.

If we turn from the type of teaching to consider how the garrisons of Scotland were staffed with chaplains, the Castle of Edinburgh is the obvious starting-point. As we have seen, the Castle Kirk, a very ancient building, had its own minister, who had a seat in the Presbytery, but a peculiar status, for, he was not allowed to share in the benefits of the Widows' Fund when that was established in 1744.

Mr James Glasgow, then minister of the Castle, failed to secure this right,[35] and the matter remained unsettled for seven years. Then Mr John Johnstone pressed the matter again before the Assembly of 1751, by whom it was referred to the Presbytery for consideration. At the next Assembly it was reported that a majority of the Presbytery were in favour of granting Mr Johnstone's application, but that an influential minority were opposed. The Assembly accepted the majority view and admitted the minister of the Castle to become a contributor to the Widows' Fund. Two years later Mr Johnstone became minister of Biggar by an exchange with William Haig, an unpopular presentee to that charge. Mr Haig, however, was not regarded as the minister of the Castle, but as merely the chaplain to the garrison. This is confirmed by a statement made in the Assembly of 1764, in connection with the appointment of Mr Haig's successor. The matter is explained in the *Annals of the Assembly* as follows:

A minister who lived at a distance from Edinburgh and had but a small stipend, having been appointed to succeed Mr Haig as minister to the Castle of Edinburgh, divine service was not now performed there regularly.

This moved the Presbytery of Haddington to overture concerning that ministerial charge, 'That the Assembly should make a representation to His Majesty's secretary of state for the northern department, of the circumstances of the inhabitants of the said garrison, as totally destitute of the benefits of public worship in the church there, by reason of the want of a fixed minister of the Gospel residing in the Castle, a privilege they have enjoyed ever since the happy Revolution'.

The opinion of the Committee of Overtures on this was, 'That whereas the alleged ministeriall charge appears to be constituted by a commission in common form, from the secretary at war's office, to one to be chaplain to a company of foot in the said Castle, and who is consequently subject as such, not to the judicatures of this Church, but to the War Department; and finding also that the last General Assembly thought meet to dismiss a similar overture that came before it from the Synod of Perth and Stirling, therefore the present General Assembly should dismiss the said overture.'[36]

The ministry of ninety years thus comes to an end, and it

would seem that the 'influential minority', who had vainly opposed Mr Johnstone, had found other means to their end. The chaplaincy continued, but it became the sinecure of one family until it ceases to appear in the *Army Lists* in 1810. These annual Lists show that the successor of Mr Haig, from 1762, was '—— Home'. The name is repeated in this form every year to 1779, when it becomes 'Robert Home', and so continues to 1810.

In the Appendix to the *Seventh Report of the Military Inquiry Commission* (1809) it is said that Robert Home was commissioned to the Castle in 1762. This does not seem probable, for Robert Home, minister of Polwarth, was not ordained until 1769. According to *Fasti*, Mr William Home, father of the aforesaid Robert, became chaplain of the Castle in 1778, but this is certainly wrong. It seems possible that Mr William Home was appointed to the Castle in 1762, and that he was succeeded by Robert in 1778.[37]

An additional complication is introduced by the statement by James Grant, in his history of the Castle, that John Home, one time minister of Athelstanford, and author of the tragedy *Douglas*, was chaplain to the Castle for many years. Mr John Home, having demitted his charge, was in receipt of a Royal pension of £300 per annum, and was living in London in 1761. It is possible that he had some influence in securing the chaplaincy for William Home, who became his father-in-law.[38]

The chaplaincy of the Castle of Stirling also degenerated and became a source of extra income for ministers who might live far from their military charge. According to the *Army Lists*, the chaplain for 1754 was Mr William Campbell. He was minister of Alva in the Presbytery of Stirling, and could perform some military duty,[39] but his successors were certainly unable to serve the Castle in person. The first of these sinecurists was William Robertson of Lady Yester's Church, Edinburgh. He became Moderator of the General Assembly and Historiographer to the King.[40] The *Army Lists* show that he held the chaplaincy until 1761, when he was succeeded by George Kay, minister of the Second Charge of Old Greyfriars, Edinburgh, who had been a Moderator of the Church.[41] After the death of Mr Kay in 1766,

John Gibson of St Cuthbert's, Edinburgh, was appointed Chaplain and continued in the post until 1785.[42] The line of Edinburgh ministers as chaplains of Stirling Castle closed with William Martin of New Greyfriars, who was chaplain until 1788.[43]

Mr Martin's successor was John Muschet, minister of Stirling,[44] and he was followed by William Innes, minister of the Second Charge of Stirling, in 1793. Mr Innes was deposed from the ministry for Independency in 1799, and lost the chaplaincy at the same time.[45] Robert Moodie, who received the appointment in that year, was minister of Clackmannan, and continued in the post until 1811, when the *Army Lists* cease to mention the chaplaincy.[46]

There were other garrisons throughout Scotland of various degrees of importance, which did not normally have commissioned chaplains except when occupied by a regiment, when the regimental chaplain became responsible for the garrison.

In the absence of such military supply the inhabitants of the station were dependent upon the good offices of a neighbouring minister, who rarely received payment from Army funds.

One of the most important of these posts was Fort George, which was established in the middle years of the century.

The Fort had accommodation for two thousand men, and was equipped with a handsome chapel. But the garrison was rarely very large and the minister of Ardersier usually acted as the chaplain. The first to hold these two appointments was Harry or Henry Gordon, who was ordained to the parish in 1757. He was compelled to petition the General Assembly at the outset of his ministry for some augmentation of his stipend, on the grounds that the building of the Fort had taken away more than one third of the lands from which his stipend was drawn.[47] In 1758 his petition came before the Church's Committee for the Management of the Royal Bounty, and that Committee proposed to augment by £5 the allowance which he received for officiating at Fort George. In August of that year the Committee were compelled, for reasons of economy, to cancel all such augmentations, so it is unlikely that it was ever paid.[48]

The case was again before the Assembly in 1760, when the

Bounty Committee were instructed to pay Mr Gordon the sum of £25 for that year. According to *Fasti*, Mr Gordon was paid 15s per week for his services as chaplain to the Fort, presumably from the funds of the Bounty Committee.

This presumption is strengthened by a petition of the time of his successor in the parish and in the Fort, Mr Walter Morrison. This petition, which reached the Committee in 1776, refers to the considerable salary which they had allowed to Mr Gordon, and states that

> Fort George had no chaplain paid by the Government nor could it have any benefit from a Regimental Chaplain it not being as formerly the head quarters of a Regiment, but Garrisoned by Independent Companys.[49]

Mr Morrison died in 1780, and he was succeeded in the parish by Pryse Campbell. The chaplaincy did not continue as the undisputed right of the minister of Ardersier, for, in 1788, the Fort was given a commissioned though absentee chaplain. This was Mr James Gordon, ex-chaplain to the Royal Scots Fusiliers, and minister of the parish of Bellie.

According to the *Army Lists* he received a salary of £105 5s. per annum. Mr James Gordon continued as chaplain until 1797, when he resigned in favour of his son Alexander. On the early death of the latter, in January 1800, Mr James was re-appointed on the suit of the Duchess of Gordon,[50] and continued until 1804. He was followed in the chaplaincy by George Gordon, possibly the minister of Loth, in the Presbytery of Dornoch, who continued until the post ceases to be mentioned in the *Army Lists*.[51] The work of these chaplains must have been done by deputy, possibly by Mr James Stalker, who was ordained to assist the chaplain of Fort George in 1785, by the Presbytery of Chanonry, and who did not obtain a charge until 1804.[52]

When the official chaplains were withdrawn, recourse was made once more to the minister of Ardersier, and Mr Pryse Campbell was acting as chaplain to the Fort in 1835, when he was over eighty years of age.[53]

The other military posts in the Highlands were largely dependent upon the Royal Bounty Committee for the payment of their chaplains. This Committee of the Church had the management of an annual grant from the Crown, which was intended for the evangelising of the Highlands and Islands of Scotland. The Minutes of their meetings show that they had a care for the soldiers stationed within the area of their brief. For example, as early as 1720, Mr Murdo McLeod, one of their missionaries, reported to the Committee that he

> preaches frequently in Englijh to the military in the garrijon at Glenelg, that he vijits their Sick.[54]

The Committee made grants from their funds to parish ministers whose work had been increased by the care of a military post. Thus, in 1757, James Richardson, minister of Aberfoyle, petitioned the Committee for consideration of the expense he is put to in entertaining the army officers travelling between Stirling and Inversnaid, and

> the troubles he is at in officiating to the Barracks of Glendow and craving some allowance may be given him out of the Royal Bounty.

This petition was repeated in the following year, when it was supported by a certificate from the Commanding Officer at Inversnaid, to the effect that Mr Richardson had cared for the troops stationed at Glendow, Stronachlachar and Achray. The Committee made a grant of £10 in 1757, and increased this slightly in the following year.[55] They continued an allowance to Mr Alexander McFarlane, minister of Tarbet, for officiating to the garrison of Inversnaid and adjacent places.[56]

The church's care for these groups of soldiers sprang, in part, from the fear that the heathen ways of the redcoats might prove to be contagious. Such a fear caused the Presbytery of Mull to approach the Committee in 1755. They wrote

> that the Soldiers garrijoned at Dowart Cajtle in Mull being always dejtitute of Gojpel Ordinances do generally Straggle on the Sabbath Days which is not only offenjive to the more Serious Sort of the People but pernitious in its Conjequences

to the more inconſiderate who catch the Example and are led away from minding the Concerns of that Day. For remedying which the Preſbytery propoſe that the Miniſter of the bounds have Some allowance out of this Royal Bounty for attending in the afternoons every Second or third Sabbath at Dowart and preaching there which he can perform without any great Difficulty as he lives within two or three Miles of this Garriſon.

The Committee replied that this application was too late for that year, but eventually an allowance was given to the minister of Torosay for serving the soldiers at Dowart.[57]

The Committee was watchful of any changes in the military posts, and regulated their grants accordingly. Thus, in the case of Ruthven, in 1758, they noted that the post was now held by only twelve men, and they therefore recommended that Mr Blair of Kingussie, be struck off the scheme.[58]

Even the more important stations of Fort William and Fort Augustus were dependent to some extent upon the Bounty Fund for the provision of preachers. The general policy was to make use of the local ministers, for Mr James Gilchrist of Kilmallie was instructed by the General Assembly of 1726 to preach to the soldiers of Fort William,[59] as often as possible. But it was chronically difficult to fill the pulpits of some of these Highland charges, and the Bounty Committee had, on occasion, to appoint a minister to the Fort who would also serve the neighbourhood. They did appoint George Anderson, formerly a chaplain to the Scots troops in Holland, as missionary at Abertarff or chaplain at Fort William, in 1733.[60] In 1744 they appointed Malcolm MacCaskill, who was later minister of Kilmallie, to attend to the Fort.[61]

There is a Minute of the Bounty Committee in 1759, which illustrates their methods and, indeed, their powers in the filling of such difficult charges. It reads as follows:

the Committee finding that both the Stations at Fort William and Fort Augustus are preſently vacant, Agreed that the ſaid Mr Alexander Fraſer be employed as Itinerant Preacher at the

Garri∫on of Fort William with £27 of Salary . . . and that
he preach by turns in the Church of Kilmalie during the
vacancy in that Pari∫h and the Pre∫bytery are hereby author-
i∫ed to ordain him a mini∫ter of the Go∫pel and to look out
for a proper per∫on to be employed as Mi∫∫ionary at Fort
Augustu∫.

In the event, Mr Fraser was appointed to the charge of Kilmallie,
and continued there until his death in 1812.[62]

Fort Augustus was similarly assisted by the Committee; for
example, they appointed James Grant, later minister of Laggan,
as missionary to that Fort in 1769.[63]

To sum up the situation of the garrison chaplaincies of Scotland, it must be admitted that the ancient fortresses of Edinburgh
and Stirling were very badly served, and were normally supplied
by deputy chaplains, if at all. The Highland posts were, on the
whole, in a better case, for they were attended by ministers or
missionaries, whose extra stipend could only be secured by
attention to their military duty.

The second, and numerically the greater, part of the Army at
home, was composed of the Fencible Regiments. Several
attempts were made during the eighteenth century to introduce
a Militia Bill for Scotland, but these had little success.

The hasty levies of 1715 and 1745 were called in official documents 'Fencible or Militia', the former title recalling an ancient
name for the defencive forces of Scotland. In 1759, when extra
troops were urgently required, this old title was remembered
and used. Two regiments of Fencible Men were easily raised for
home duties and for a limited period of service, and the same
name and method proved useful on later occasions.[64]

The official establishment of these regiments included a
chaplain, who was paid 6s. 8d. per day. In common with the other
officers, the chaplain was expected to find a certain number of
recruits, the requirement varying according to the rank of the
officer, the chaplain having to provide ten men. This provision
presented no great difficulty for the ministers were valued recruiting agents for the many regiments raised in Scotland during

the century.[65] For example, John Grant, minister of Abernethy and chaplain to the 97th Regiment or Inverness-shire Highlanders, enlisted twelve men, and Alexander Cameron, minister of Findron, boasted that, from his small congregation, sixteen or seventeen had enlisted, 'which in my narrow sphere, I did all in my power to promote'.[66]

Nor were the ministers backward in the offer of their own services as chaplains to the new regiments, though few can have been so naive as Robert Gordon. His letter of application for the chaplaincy of the Northern Fencibles in 1778 was as follows:

> Your memorialist has been for some years a Preacher of the Gospel and for many years Schoolmaster at Rhynie, a laborious and painful occupation of which he feels himself very weary.
>
> That he would be extremely happy to accept of the honour of any employment under your Grace in the Regiment now raising and of which your Grace has the command, as he has but a very remote prospect of any provision in the line of life in which he was educated.[67]

This poor tired Dominie was not successful in his application, although he might well have made a better chaplain than some of the ministers who were appointed to the Fencible chaplaincies. It became almost customary to select parish ministers for these appointments, as a token of the Colonel's friendship, or as a reward for recruiting zeal, the duty being done by deputy for a moiety of the salary. The case of James Grant sufficiently illustrates the system in operation. Mr Grant, minister of Urquhart and Glenmoriston, was commissioned on 1st March 1793 as chaplain to the newly embodied Strathspey Fencibles. He may have seen something of the corps during the months when it was being brought to strength, but from October 1793 to his death in 1798 he was only with the regiment for one period of three weeks, in July 1795.[68] His one burst of military activity seems to have been due to a military execution which he then attended. This incident was reported in the newspapers of Edinburgh, as follows

On the 17th. the five prisoners were conveyed from Mussel-
burgh Jail about six o'clock in the morning . . . in two
mourning coaches, accompanied in the first by Rev. Robertson McGregor, minister of the Gaelic Chapel, Edinburgh,
and in the second by the Rev. James Grant, Chaplain of the
Regiment, to the Links of Gullane. . . . They arrived at the
Links about twelve o'clock . . . the prisoners then walked to
the ground accompanied by the two clergymen . . . the
sentence was read . . . after which the Rev. James Grant
sung psalms and prayed.[69]

Mr Grant then returned to his parish, but his name appears in all
the Muster Rolls of the regiment, and his widow drew a military
pension. To complete the picture, something is known of his
Deputy Chaplain, Alexander McGregor. Mr McGregor had
been Deputy Chaplain to the 97th Regiment of Foot, then
stationed in the Channel Islands, where he received four shillings
per day from the Chaplain, augmented by another shilling from
the Colonel. This regiment was soon disbanded, being drafted
into other units, and Mr McGregor was transferred to the
Strathspey Fencibles. He continued in this position for some years
after the abolition of the regimental chaplaincies, and his Colonel
was able to certify that he had never been absent from his duty.[70]

Although many of the chaplains to the Fencible regiments were
pluralists, whose first duty was to their civil charge, there were
other ministers who were ordained as chaplains or as deputy
chaplains, who may be presumed to have attended to their
military and sole task. The number of such 'whole-time' chaplains is surprisingly large and goes some way to rebut the sweep-
ing charge that all chaplains were sinecurists. If we consider all
the regiments of Scotland, both those of the Line and the Fencibles
we find at least thirty-seven Scottish ministers who were army
chaplains before being called to a civil congregation, and this
figure does not include the deputy chaplains, who do not appear
in the *Army Lists*, but whose ordination to that task is frequently
mentioned in Presbyterial records.

The most distinguished of the deputy-chaplain-ordinands was

Adam Ferguson, who was not only ordained as Deputy Chaplain to the Black Watch, but had a large part of his college course waived in order that he might join his regiment at once. His case was dealt with by the General Assembly of 1745, as follows:

> Upon a representation, that Lord John Murray, Colonel of the Highland Regiment in His Majesty's service, inclines to have a chaplain of the communion of this church, having the Irish language, who must soon be ordained to that office; and that Mr Adam Ferguson, student in Divinity, son to the minister of Logierait, in the Presbytery of Dunkeld, is pitched upon for that purpose; the General Assembly, in respect of the ample certificates given of the said Mr Ferguson's capacity and good character, and of the peculiar circumstances of the case, remitted to, and appointed the Presbytery of Dunkeld to take him upon trials; and, in case they find him qualified, to ordain him on his passing his first trials; and Mr Mac-Laggan is ordered to return thanks to Lord John Murray for his good disposition towards this church and the interest of religion.[71]

Mr Ferguson was duly ordained and joined his regiment, and did not have to wait long for promotion, for his commission as Chaplain to the Black Watch was dated 30th April 1746.

Another Black Watch chaplain who was ordained to the task was James Stewart, later minister of Dull. He was ordained to the Second Battalion of the regiment by the Presbytery of Duns in December 1757, but he did not remain long with the army, being presented to his parish in 1759.[72]

Yet another chaplain was ordained to this regiment, Mr Alexander Stuart, by the Presbytery of Isla and Jura, in April 1782. Mr Stuart became minister of Jura and Colonsay in 1786.[73]

The Royal Scots Fusiliers also had chaplains ordained to their service. Mr James Gordon was so appointed by the Presbytery of Edinburgh in 1754, and he was followed in the regiment by Mr Andrew Brown, who was ordained by the Presbytery of Hadding-ton in 1777. Mr Gordon became minister of Bellie in 1770, and Mr Brown of Falkland in 1784.[74]

The Scottish regiments in Dutch service also called Scottish probationers, and Mr Robert Douglas was ordained by the Presbytery of Ayr as chaplain to Lord Drumlanrig's regiment in Holland in 1747. He did not become minister of Bonkle until 1765.[75] Francis Sherriff was ordained as Deputy Chaplain to General Houston's regiment in the Dutch service in 1775 by the Presbytery of Haddington. He did not remain long with them, however, for he became minister of Lady Glenorchy's chapel in Edinburgh in 1777.[76]

Some of the younger regiments also called for the ordination of chaplains and deputy chaplains. James Mylne, who became Professor of Moral Philosophy at Glasgow University, was ordained as Deputy Chaplain to the 83rd Foot,[77] by the Presbytery of Dundee in 1779. He was followed as Deputy by James Playfair, ordained by the Presbytery of Meigle in 1781. Mr Playfair became Chaplain to the regiment in December 1782 and retired on half-pay when they were disbanded. He became minister of Bendochy in 1785.[78]

The ordination of George McKenzie in 1778, of Donald McNicol in 1781, of John Ferguson in 1788, of Morris Forsyth in 1795 and of Samuel Peat in 1796, show that the practice of ordaining chaplains and deputy chaplains continued until the abolition of the regimental chaplaincies.[79]

Two of these ordinations are remarkable for they involved Scottish ministers appointed to English regiments. Morris Forsyth was educated at Aberdeen, and was ordained by that Presbytery as Chaplain to the 69th Regiment (South Lincolnshire). He became minister of Mortlach in 1805.[80]

Mr Samuel Peat almost became minister of Gigha but was found to be ignorant of Gaelic and therefore unfit for that charge. He was then ordained by the Presbytery of Hamilton in August 1796 as 'Chaplain of a Regiment'. The *Army Lists* show that the regiment was, in fact, the York Rangers, composed of French émigrés, and disbanded in the following year. Mr Peat has no further history in the Church of Scotland, but he would, presumably, retire on a pension from the office of chaplain when that was abolished by Royal Warrant in September 1796.[81]

We have established that the Regiments of the Line called for the ordination of their chaplains, and can show that the same was true of the Fencible corps. Thus Mr Robert Lorimer was ordained to the Seventh Fencibles in 1793, and did not become minister of Haddington until three years later.

He was followed in the regiment by Thomas Hardie, who was ordained by the Presbytery of Edinburgh. Mr Hardie became minister of Ashkirk in 1798.[82]

Mr James Hunter, who was to be Professor of Logic and Rhetoric at St Andrews University, was ordained by the Presbytery of St Andrews, as Deputy Chaplain to the 4th Fencible Regiment, in 1795.[83]

The Presbytery of Penpont ordained James Keyden as chaplain to Drummond of Perth's Fencible Regiment in April 1795, but he had been commissioned to that regiment, as Lord Elgin's, in November of the previous year. Mr Keyden became minister of Keir in September 1795.[84]

This slight discrepancy between the dates of commission and of ordination, and the confusion of the names of units, occurs quite frequently. For example, according to *Fasti* Thomas Adamson was ordained in 1797, as chaplain to the St Andrews Volunteers, but, according to the *Army Lists*, a chaplain of the same name was commissioned to the Second Battalion of the Breadalbane Fencibles in March 1793.

This might easily be the same person, licensed in 1785 and minister of Cameron Church in 1798.[85]

Similarly, John Stewart is said to have been ordained as Chaplain to the Fifeshire Fencible Cavalry in January 1797, but the *Army Lists* show that this corps was served by a James Stewart, whose commission was dated 8th May 1795.[86]

To close this note of discrepancies comes the name of David Ritchie, Moderator of the General Assembly of 1814.

According to *Fasti*, Mr Ritchie was licensed in 1789 and ordained by the Presbytery of Edinburgh, as chaplain to the 1st Battalion of the Second Regiment of Edinburgh Volunteers, in April 1797. The *Army Lists*, however, show that a David Ritchie was commissioned as chaplain to the Royal Scots Fusiliers, 31st

July 1787, and to the 94th Regiment (Scots Brigade), 5th July 1793. It is just possible that the future Moderator held these army posts before he ever joined the Edinburgh Volunteers.[87]

When everything possible has been said in favour of the army chaplains of the latter part of the eighteenth century, when every allowance has been made for those who did give good service and for those who may have done so, it is quite clear that there was a progressive deterioration throughout the period which made reform imperative.

The state of the Scottish regimental chaplaincies in 1796, the last year of their existence, was bad and tending to get worse. There were then twenty-three commissioned chaplains of Scottish Line regiments. Thirteen of these had no connection with the Church of Scotland, and were, by inference, Episcopalian. Five of the remainder were parish ministers and the remaining five had no other charge.

These last and a proportion of the Episcopalian clergy may have attended to their military duties. With the Fencible regiments in the same year there were twenty-five chaplains, of whom no fewer than eighteen were parish ministers, three were presumably Episcopal, and four had no other charge. There were, in addition, an unknown number of deputy chaplains, who were sometimes the sole spiritual guides of the British soldier.

The situation of the Scottish regiments was not unique, the chaplaincy services of the whole army were at a very low ebb. Expedition after expedition left Britain with too few chaplains, until the nadir of 1795, when not one regimental chaplain could be induced to accompany the army to America.

Change was now inevitable, and, in 1796, change took place.

REFERENCES

1. J. T. Findlay, *Wolfe in Scotland* (1928), p. 165.
2. ibid.
3. *Rules and Orders for the better Government of His Majesty's Forces Employed in Foreign Parts* (1747).
   Orders for the Troops in Scotland, 1753-57, Military Library, Edinburgh Castle.

4. *A System of Camp Discipline* (1757), Part II, p. 11.
5. David Stewart, *Sketches of the Highlanders* (1822), vol. i, p. 292 and n.
6. R. C. Dudgeon, *History of the Edinburgh or Queen's Regiment* (1882), p. 17.
7. *The Scots Magazine*, vol. viii, pp. 347 and 545.
8. *Standing Rules . . . of the Fraser Fencibles* (1798).
9. Thomas Simes, *A Military Guide*, etc. (1776), pp. 301f. and 304.
10. Grose, *Military Antiquities*, vol. i, pp. 313-15.
11. Simes, *Military Guide*, pp. 359f.
12. *MSS. General Orders of Madras Presidency, 7th April 1786—25th November 1794*, Military Library, Edinburgh Castle.
13. Wm. Agar, *Military Devotion . . . Fourteen Sermons preached at the Camps near Blandford*, etc. (1756).
14. F. Grose, *Advice to the Officers and Soldiers of the British Army* (1946), chapter lx.
15. William Wordsworth, *The Excursion*, Book II, lines 179ff.
16. Clode, *Military Forces*, vol. ii, p. 368.
17. *Army Lists*, passim.
18. Nathaniel Morren, *Annals of the General Assembly* (1840), vol. ii, pp. 255 and 256.
19. *Dictionary of National Biography*.
20. *Operations of the Campaign of 1743, by James Taylor, Rector of Broadway in the County of Dorset and Chaplain to His Majesty's Own Regiment of Horse*, pp. 324 and 331.
21. *Dictionary of National Biography*.
22. *Fraser's Magazine*, September 1834.
    Stewart, *Highlanders*, vol. ii, Appendix, p. lvii.
    Dictionary of National Biography.
23. E. Godwin, *A Brief Account of the Late Work of God in the British Army in Flanders* (1746).
24. *Army Lists*; *Fasti*, vol. iii, p. 192.
25. *Army Lists*; Stewart, *Highlanders*, vol. ii, p. 22.
26. *Army Lists*; Stewart, *Highlanders*, vol. ii, p. 30.
27. *Army Lists*; Stewart, *Highlanders*, vol. ii, p. 149.
28. Stewart, *Highlanders*, vol. ii, p. 157 n.
29. *Army Lists*; *Fasti*, vol. iii, pp. 481, 156, 259, 264.
30. Stewart, *Highlanders*, vol. i, p. 591.
31. *The History of Thomas Mitchell, born and educated among the Gipsies of Scotland, afterwards a Soldier in the 21st Regiment of Foot* (1826).
32. William Harris Rule, *Wesleyan Methodism in the British Army* (1883), p. 14.
33. *A Selection from the Journal of William Dyott, sometime General in the British Army*, ed. R. W. Jeffrey (1907), Jan. 1796.
34. Agar, *Military Devotion*, pp. 114f.
35. *Fasti*, vol. i, p. 92.
36. Morren, *Annals of the Assembly*, vol. ii, pp. 288f.

R

37. *Fasti*, vol. i, pp. 415 and 424.
38. ibid., vol. i, p. 320.
39. ibid., vol. ii, p. 692.
40. ibid., vol. i, p. 43.
41. ibid., vol. i, p. 47.
42. ibid., vol. i, p. 126.
43. ibid., vol. i, p. 71.
44. ibid., vol. ii, p. 676.
45. ibid., vol. ii, p. 679.
46. ibid., vol. ii, p. 697.
47. ibid., vol. iii, p. 245.
48. *MSS. Minutes of the Committee for the Management of the Royal Bounty* 8th June and 10th Aug. 1758, Library of the General Assembly, Edinburgh.
49. ibid., 5th June 1776.
50. *Army Lists.*
    Fasti, vol. iii, p. 192.
    The Gentleman's Magazine, vol. 70, p. 275.
51. *Fasti*, vol. iii, p. 341.
52. ibid., vol. i, p. 555.
53. ibid., vol. iii, p. 245.
54. *Minutes of the Bounty Committee*, vol. i, p. 50.
55. ibid., 2nd June 1757 and 8th June 1758.
56. ibid., 2nd June 1757.
    Fasti, vol. ii, p. 341.
57. *Minutes of the Bounty Committee*, 20th Nov. 1755.
58. ibid., 8th June 1758.
59. *Fasti*, vol. iii, p. 112.
60. ibid., vol. iii, p. 114.
61. ibid., vol. iii, p. 113.
62. ibid., vol. iii, p. 112.
    Minutes of the Bounty Committee, 25th June 1759.
63. *Fasti*, vol. iii, p. 118.
64. H. B. Mackintosh, *The Grant, Strathspey or First Highland Fencible Regiment* (1934), pp. 13f.
65. H. B. Mackintosh, *The Northern or Gordon Fencibles* (1929), p. 91.
    Mackintosh, *The Grant Fencibles*, p. 28.
66. H. B. Mackintosh, *The Inverness-shire Highlanders or 97th Regiment of Foot* (1926), p. 21 n.
    J. M. Bulloch, *Territorial Soldiering in the North East of Scotland*, Spalding Club (1914), p. 98.
67. ibid., p. 79.
68. *Fasti*, vol. iii, p. 120.
    Mackintosh, *The Grant Fencibles*, pp. 94f.

69. *The Scots Magazine*, July 1795, p. 475.
Edinburgh Advertiser, 21st July 1795.
70. Mackintosh, *97th Regiment*, p. 60 n.
Mackintosh, *The Grant Fencibles*, p. 78.
71. Morren, *Annals of the Assembly*, vol. i, pp. 73f.
72. *Fasti*, vol. ii, p. 819.
73. ibid., vol. iii, p. 46.
74. ibid., vol. iii, p. 192; vol. ii, p. 492.
75. ibid., vol. i, p. 409.
76. ibid., vol. i, p. 79.
77. ibid., vol. ii, p. 201.
78. ibid., vol. iii, p. 742.
79. ibid., vol. iii, p. 366; iii, p. 53; i, p. 207; iii, p. 211; iii, p. 40.
80. ibid., vol. iii, p. 211; *Army Lists*.
81. ibid., vol. iii, p. 40.
82. ibid., vol. i, pp. 313 and 543.
83. ibid., vol. ii, p. 424.
84. ibid., vol. i, p. 678.
85. ibid., vol. ii, p. 411.
86. ibid., vol. i, p. 417.
87. ibid., vol. i, p. 306; ii, p. 174; i, p. 74.
Army Lists.

XI

AFTER 1796

ON 23rd September 1796 a Royal Warrant was published which ended the old system of Regimental Chaplaincies in the British army, and established a new plan for the spiritual care of the troops at home and abroad. This document explains its own purpose with sufficient clarity, and is, therefore, repeated here in full.

GEORGE R.

Whereas We have taken into Our moſt ſerious Conſideration the nearly univerſal Want of Perſonal Attendance among the Chaplains of Regiments, and of Care in providing proper Deputies; as well as the Difficulty of finding Clergymen to attend Corps ſerving abroad upon ſuch a Stipend as is uſually ſtopped from the Pay of the Chaplains for that Purpose, and left to the Management of Commanding Officers; and it appearing to Us, that by aboliſhing the office of Regimental Chaplain, as ſoon as the ſame may be practicable, and aſſigning an adequate Pay to ſuch Clergymen as ſhall attend Our Forces on foreign Service, more effectual Proviſion may be made for the regular Performance of Religious Duties throughout Our Army, without bringing any aditional Charge upon the Public. We have Therefore thought fit hereby to ſignify OUR WILL AND PLEASURE, that all Regimental Chaplains, who do not join their reſpective Corps on or before the 25th of December next, ſhall retire from Our Service on a reduced Subſiſtence of Four Shillings *per Diem*, to commence from that Day incluſive, and to be continued to them during the Term of their natural Lives; and that all future Savings from the Pay of Regimental Chaplains, as now borne on the Eſtabliſhment, ſhall be applied to the Purpoſe of compenſating ſuch Perſons as may from Time to Time be employed in the actual Performance of Divine Service to Our Forces, in the Manner herinafter directed:

On the 25th of June, 1797, and at the End of every ſubſequent Half-year, a Certificate (according to the Form annexed, No. I.) ſhall be tranſmitted to the office of Our Secretary at War by the Commanding Officer of each Corps whoſe Chaplain ſhall have joined, ſtating that ſuch Chaplain continues in the perſonal Discharge of his Duty; without which Certificate the Chaplain's Pay ſhall be reſpited on the Settlement of the Accompts of the Regiment to which he belongs; unleſs it ſhall appear that ſuch Chaplain has ſignified his Deſire of being placed on the retired Liſt; but any Chaplain failing in his Perſonal Attendance, and not having made ſuch Application ſhall be ſuperſeded.

No Chaplain ſhall hereafter be allowed to appoint a Deputy; no Chaplaincy which may become vacant by Death, or Reſignation, ſhall be again filled up; no Sale, Exchange or Transfer of Commiſſions by the preſent Chaplains ſhall be permitted after the 25th of December 1796, unleſs the Application for that Purpoſe ſhall have been made previous to that Day; and in the Interval preceeding it, no Chaplaincy ſhall be ſold for more than was given for it by its preſent Poſſeſſor; nor ſhall the Purchaſer have any claim to ſell the ſame again.

And in order to provide for the regular Performance of Religious Duties in future among the Regiments whoſe Chaplains may retire in Conſequence of theſe Our Regula- tions.

OUR FURTHER WILL AND PLEASURE IS, that wherever an Army is formed or a body of Troops ordered to be aſſembled for Service abroad, and in all Garriſons or Stations where ſeveral

Regiments are near together, Chaplains ſhall be appointed according to the Number of Corps in the Proportion of One to each Brigade, or to every Three or Four Regiments; which Chaplains ſhall receive Ten Shillings *per Diem* each during the Time of their actual Continuance on foreign Service, whether in the Field or Garrison; and that, after Twelve Years of real foreign Service, every ſuch Chaplain ſhall be permitted to retire on an Allowance of Four Shillings *per Diem*, payable in the ſame Manner and ſubject to the ſame Regulations as the Half-pay.

For ſuch Regiments on foreign Service as are in ſeparate Stations, or not more than two in one Place or near together, an efficient Chaplain ſhall be appointed at each Station, with an Allowance of Seven Shillings *per* Day; ſuch Chaplains to be promoted to Brigades, with Ten Shillings *per* Day, as Opportunity may offer, and as they ſhall be found deſerving; and likewiſe, after Twelve Years actual and foreign Service, to be permitted to retire, with an Allowance of Four Shillings *per Diem*, ſubject to the ſame Regulations as are obſerved in regard to the Receipt of Half-pay.

The neceſſary Number of Chaplains for foreign Service ſhall be borne on the Staff of the different Armies and Garriſons at the Rates above ſpecified, and their Pay ſhall be drawn by them Monthly from the Agents of the reſpective Commanders in Chief, and Governors.

For every Barrack in the British Dominions a neighbouring Clergyman is to be employed as the Curate to perform Divine Service every Sunday, and to be paid Twenty-five Pounds *per Annum*.

The Commanding Officer of every ſeparate Regiment in Quarters will attend with his Regiment at ſome Pariſh Church; or employ a neighbouring Clergyman to perform Divine Service to the Men; and he will empower the Clergyman whose Pariſh Church he may attend, or who has done the Duty of the Regiment, to draw on the Agent of the Regiment for ſuch Sum as he may think a juſt Compen-

ſation, provided that for any ſingle Regiment the Sum ſo
drawn does not exceed Ten Shillings *per* Week for the actual
Time of Service performed; the Clergyman's Draft to be
accompanied by a Certificate agreable to the annexed form,
No. II.

Lastly, We do hereby subject all Regular Chaplains, de-
ſiring to be continued in Our Service, to the orders of the
Perſon whom We ſhall hereafter appoint to be Chaplain-
General of Our Army, and who is to govern himself by
ſuch Inſtructions as We ſhall from Time to Time think fit
to give him through Our Secretary at War. Given at Our
Court of St James's, etc.[1]

The reactions of the clergy concerned to this royal bombshell are
poignantly expressed by one of their number in a letter to the
Editor of the *Gentleman's Magazine*, in October 1796. He wrote:

Mr URBAN,
    I am almoſt annihilated, ſpiritually and corporally, and
that by an *ex poſt facto* law (for law and ordinances are the
ſame). From a ſituation I deemed in ſunſhine, I am as
ſuddenly covered with gloom and darkneſs as a candle under
an extinguiſher. Sir, I am a chaplain to a regiment. Four or
five years ago I expended my inheritance and oeconomical
accumulation, amounting to £900, in purchaſing a chaplaincy in an old regiment, then returning home from abroad,
enjoying in anticipation an income of 6s. 8d. a day, the full
pay of a chaplain. But what was my diſmay when I found by
the public papers, my regiment was immediately ordered to
the Weſt Indies, and 2s. 6d. withdrawn from my pay for a
deputy, nominally ſo only, for no duty was done!
    I quieted my mind, in daily hopes of peace, of my regiment
returning home, and my enjoyment of full pay. But a few
weeks ſince, an official communication told me I muſt join
my regiment in perſon, muſt conſtantly perſonally attend
it, or accept an annuity for my own life of 4s. a day, or the
alternative of forfeiture and extinction.
    Alas Sir, what a privation of property, purchaſed under

the ſanction of 50 years uſage, with the right of ſelling again!

I hope ſome liberal military man in power will, at his hour of amuſement, catch your general Publication, and, in compaſſion and benevolence, obtain for us our original full-pay of 6s. 8d. a day for life. We then ſuffer enough from parting with it; a privilege and condition ever before granted and conſidered annexed. Such a benevolent act to us will be a ſhield and buckler of defence in the day of battle and the hour of danger, to the promoters of it.

A Chaplain of a Regiment.[2]

This ingenuous plea went unanswered, and its author, and almost all the regimental chaplains, retired on the promised 4s. per diem. The same issue of the *Gentleman's Magazine* notes the appointment of Mr John Gamble as the Chaplain General charged with the organisation of the new dispensation in chaplaincy affairs. His task proved most onerous, since he had, without assistance, to adjust the many grievances among the old school of chaplains and, also, to find suitable clerics to fill the many vacancies.

The grievances were met by financial concessions, for example, compensation was promised to the colonels in the event of the death of the regimental chaplain. As the commission could no longer be sold, the colonel was to receive £500 if in command of an infantry unit and £700 in the case of the cavalry, a piece of economic policy which a foreign critic calls 'folly'.[3]

The establishment of the new scheme was not so readily managed, and many explanatory letters went out during 1797 and 1798, especially in connection with the payments to parochial clergy for their attendance upon troops quartered at home. After years of trial and error, the Chaplain General wrote to the Secretary at War, in 1805, that:

The largeſt allowance permitted where a ſeparate ſervice ſolely for the uſe of the military is not actually performed, is 10s. a-week for one Regiment, and if the Regiment be quartered in different cantonments and the Commanding Officer thinks fit to repreſent the expediency, there can be

no objection to this ſum being divided in ſuch manner as
may appear proper for the remuneration of more than one
clergyman. Seldom, however, except in fixed Military
Stations or unleſs a ſeparate ſervice is performed, is the full
extent of the above ſum required.[4]

Appendix 40 of the *Seventh Report of the Commissioners of
Military Inquiry* gives a list of all the clergy in Britain who were
paid for their services to the troops in quarters, and, it is clear
that the Chaplain General had been able to carry out this part
of his task, and had provided for the needs of the troops at home.
He was less successful in finding clergy who were willing to
accompany those sent on foreign service. His failure in this
respect is demonstrated by the rapid growth of the funds at his
disposal.

These funds were composed of the sums saved by the retiral
of the former chaplains, and it was intended that these should be
expended upon the new chaplains. In one year the balance on
hand was seven thousand pounds, and in 1805 it amounted to
£55,000, invested at three per cent. It is remarkable that no
arrangements were made to audit this fund until the Commissioners of Military Inquiry recommended that this should be
done, in 1807. This financial evidence is amply confirmed by
the complaint that in three military expeditions which left
Britain in 1805, there were only two chaplains in all.

The Commander in Chief complained of this dearth of chaplains, and also indicated that he was not satisfied with the system
of officiating chaplains who had the care of the garrisons at home.
He agreed that they might be conscientious in the reading of
prayers on Sunday, but that

there was no adequate proviſion made for the diſcharge of
their other duties, which cannot certainly be looked upon as
leſs important; nor were they calculated to eſtabliſh that
conſtant intercourſe and communication between the
Chaplain and the Soldier which is neceſſary to render the
ſervice of the former of real eſſential benefit or to impreſſ
the minds of the latter with that salutary influence which

ſentiments of religion and morality when inculcated by perſons duly authoriſed and ſpecially appointed to that duty, cannot fail to produce.[5]

This comment by the Duke of York is an early and shrewd appreciation of the necessity for close contact and for some community of interest between the chaplain and the soldier if the work of the former was to be really effective.

Indeed, there is evidence that the military authorities of Britain were anxious to secure the services of an adequate supply of good chaplains for the army at home and abroad.

When Major General Le Marchant was Lieutenant Governor of the Royal Military College, in 1802, he drew up an *Outline* of the duties of all the staff of an army, and included therein the first definition of the work of a military chaplain. Le Marchant's ideas were put into practice by some departments of the army, but his ideas for the Clerical Staff do not seem to have been publicised, although they have since been very largely adopted. He treats the clergy under the heading of 'General Staff, Section 2nd, No. 5.'

CLERICAL STAFF
Chaplain General
Assistant Chaplains

This Staff shall constitute a Branch of the Adjutant General's Department.

It shall consist of a Chaplain General whenever the Army amounts to a Division and Assistant Chaplains in the proportion of one to each Brigade and one to the permanent Hospital.

The duty of the Chaplain General will be to read Prayers at Head Quarters to the General Staff of the Army, and also to direct the duties of the Assistant Chaplains who are placed under his entire direction and control. He shall reside at Head Quarters.

The duty of the Assistant Chaplains shall be, generally to superintend the morals of the Army, and celebrate Divine Service at such times as may be specified in orders. They shall attend daily at the Ambulating Hospital, in order to converse and pray with the sick, and to bury the dead.

Each Assistant Chaplain shall send a weekly return to the Chaplain General of all casualties in their Brigade, under the Heads of Buried, returned to their Corps, or remov'd to the permanent Hospital. This is to act as a Check on the Hospital returns, and to secure Attendance.

The Assistant Chaplains shall in rotation visit the Goal [sic] and make a daily report of the Prisoners, and their conduct to the Chaplain General.

Hitherto there have been no Regulations, for the conduct of the Clerical Staff, which has prevented its being attended with those advantages to the Army, that may be expected from the proposed arrangement.

This if properly carried into effect will conduce much to the preservation of good order, by the Influence of Religion on the Conduct of Persons in the subordinate Stations of the Army, and by contributing to the Comfort and consolation of the Sick.[6]

The pious hopes of the author of this plan were disappointed by the chronic shortage of chaplains willing to accompany the army in the field.

The repeated complaints of the army induced the Church to set up a small committee of the two Archbishops and the Bishop of London, charged with the task of finding chaplains.

The *Army Lists* for 1810 show that the 'Staff Chaplains', as they were then called, numbered eighteen, in addition to Archdeacon Owen, the Chaplain General, and his assistant, Mr Dakins. These figures gradually improved until, in 1815, the Clerical Department numbered thirty-three in all. This crest was followed by a gradual decline and, in 1833, there were only eight commissioned chaplains with the army.

These years of transition and of experiment in the sphere of the military chaplain contain much of general interest, but this must be left for a more particular account of the position with regard to the soldiers of Scotland.

The effect of the new regulations of 1796 upon the troops quartered in Scotland was, on the whole, good. In addition to the long-established garrison chaplaincies, there were now a number of ministers in receipt of payment from army funds for their services to the troops quartered in their parishes. The *Seventh Report of the Commissioners* gives an official list of these gentlemen for 1807, as follows[7]

Rev. R. Grierson	Musselburgh	£40 per an.
Rev. Dr Dalrymple	Ayr	15s. per week
Rev. James Pate	Glasgow	do.
Rev. P. MacVicar	Dundee	do.
Rev. P. Carfrae	Dunbar	do.
Rev. R. Crawford	Edinburgh (2 Services)	do. each
Rev. Dr Gordon	Aberdeen	£30 per an.
Rev. R. Stirling	Dunblane	10s. per week
Rev. R. Dickson	South Leith	do.
Rev. J. Menzies	Lerwick	£10.10s. per an.
Rev. Dr Lloyd	Leith (attached to the artillery)	10s. per week.

These were all ministers of the Church of Scotland, except Messrs Grierson and Lloyd, who have not, so far, been identified. It would be more accurate to call Mr Pate a licentiate of the Church, for he was then Keeper of Stirling's Library in Glasgow.[8] The care of the troops in Scotland was thus largely, if not entirely, in the hands of the national Church, although a General Order, issued from the Head Quarters in Edinburgh in 1798, is markedly tolerant. It gave permission to Commanding Officers to permit

the Noncommissioned officers and men to attend Divine Worship in the Churches, chapels and Meeting Houses of that persuasion to which they belong when an opportunity shall offer.[9]

A typically military reaction to such an order is shown in the Order Book of the Gordon Highlanders, in 1809.

Officers and men who profess the Catholic religion will attend all church parades in future but, previous to the service commencing, they will be indulged by being allowed to fall out if they wish, but the commanding officer cannot see the propriety of their doing so.[10]

In spite of such indulgence, however, the troops in Scotland were attended by the ministers of the Established Church. Some of the sermons preached to these military congregations have been preserved, with texts ranging from 'Prepare war, wake up the mighty men',[11] to the more modest 'Lord, it is nothing to thee to help, whether with many, or with them that have no power'.[12]

One of these sermons contains the usual tribute paid to the soldier in every time of crisis.

In this part of the country, the military character uſed to be considered as a compound of profanity and licentiouſneſs; and if a young man enliſted in the army, he was conſidered from that day as abandoned to vice. . . . I hope it is now generally underſtood, that there is hardly any profeſſion which requires more ſtrict attention to decency, regularity and ſobriety, than that of a soldier.[13]

The practice of employing a deputy was not entirely abolished in fact, for Mr James McLauchlan, minister of the Gaelic Chapel, Edinburgh, from 1799, and officiating chaplain to the Militia regiment in garrison there, was sued by his assistant in the latter office for payment of half a guinea for preaching of each of fifty-nine sermons. The assistant lost the case on the grounds that he failed to prove that preachers of the Gospel are paid for occasional preaching.[14]

It may be said, however, that the new system worked reasonably well, for the soldiers stationed in Scotland, but for the Scottish regiments serving overseas the situation was different. There was nothing in the Royal Warrant of 1796 which prohibited the employment of Presbyterian chaplains, but the appointment of one chaplain for each Brigade or group of regiments raised an effectual barrier against their appointment.

In the unlikely event of Scottish regiments forming a complete
Brigade it would be possible to have a Presbyterian chaplain, but
in every other case, the vacancy must go to the Church of
England. The failure of the first Chaplain General to recruit a
sufficiency of chaplains led to the setting up of a committee
from the hierarchy of that Church, and they were not likely to
look to Scotland to supply their needs. Before this stage was
reached, however, the attention of the General Assembly had
been called to the subject, and at their last Sederunt of 1806, they

> appointed a Committee to confider the moſt effectual means
> of providing for the regular adminiſtration of the Ordi-
> nances of Religion to the Regiments on the Scottiſh eſtab-
> lishment, *when they ſerve in Scotland* [italics mine]; and to
> report to the next Aſſembly.[15]

In spite of a very weighty committee and in spite of the modest
limitations of their brief, little progress was made and the committee was continued in the following year. The failure of this
attempt seems to be indicated by the action of the General
Assembly in 1812, which set up a new committee with the
bolder instruction:

> to embrace every opportunity of ſtating the claims of the
> National Church to have it provided that ſome portion of
> the army chaplains ſhould be Preſbyterian clergymen, whoſe
> character ſhould be fully certified by the Moderator of the
> General Assembly.[16]

The fate of this effort does not seem to have been any happier,
for, in 1827, the matter was raised once again. This time Mr
Campbell of Carbrook proposed that an address be sent to the
King.

> praying him to take measures for securing to Protestant
> Officers and Soldiers the same protection which is afforded
> to their fellow-soldiers in communion with the Church of
> Rome.

The Assembly agreed that no action was necessary, having entire confidence that the Laws secured to all the full enjoyment of religious rights and privileges.[17]

In 1839 the Assembly proposed to petition Parliament that licentiates of the Church of Scotland be employed as chaplains to Presbyterian regiments. By that date, however, the chaplains branch in the army was at a very low ebb, the Church of Scotland was approaching a crisis in her history and nothing constructive was done.[18]

The effect then, of the Royal Warrant, coupled with the futility of the General Assembly, was to exclude Presbyterian chaplains from the army, without the slightest legal justification, and this over a period of years during which successive army commanders demanded more and better chaplains.

The reaction of the Scottish regiments to the complete withdrawal of Presbyterian chaplains varied considerably.

The Lowland regiments seem to have accepted the services of the English Brigade chaplain, when there was one, without much demur, but the Highland regiments found this more difficult. This difficulty arose in part from the score of language, for many of the rank and file had no fluency in English, but it was partly due to the very serious views which many of the Highland soldiers held of their religion. The Highland regiments reacted in diverse ways to the new system. In some cases they made vigorous protest against the proposed changes. This was done with some success by the Grant Fencible Regiment, whose Commanding Officer wrote to the Chaplain General requesting that they be permitted to retain the services of their Deputy Chaplain, Mr McGregor. He wrote that

> if the Regiment is deprived of a Gaelic instructor it will be very hard upon it at a time when the principles of the men are tampered with and it will give the Colonel much pain to have the Regiment left without a Pastor.[19]

After some correspondence, this plea was admitted and the Agents were authorised to make a payment of 2s. 6d. a day which the Colonel supplemented.

Another Fencible regiment, stationed at Fort George, augmented the official diet of worship by private arrangements.

It is said of them, that

> Many of the more religious characters in the regiment assembled regularly for worship in a building which they hired for the purpose not far from the barracks. At these meetings, which were frequently attended by the different ministers in the neighbourhood of Fort George as well as by others who chanced to be passing through the district, it was the custom to sing or recite the Gaelic hymns composed in the Reay country at that time.[20]

Among the Scottish regiments of the Line there were some who endeavoured to find acceptable forms of worship. The most successful of these attempts was made by the Sutherland Highlanders when stationed at the Cape of Good Hope in the early years of the nineteenth century. This corps engaged Mr Thom, a Presbyterian missionary to the Kaffirs, to act as their chaplain, paying his salary out of their own pockets. Their unofficial chaplain paid them a high tribute in 1814, when he wrote:

> The regiment was certainly a pattern for morality and good behaviour to every other corps. They read their Bibles; they observed the Sabbath; they saved their money in order to do good; 7000 rix dollars (£1400) they gave for books, societies and the support of the Gospel. . . . Their example had a good effect on both the colonists and the heathen. How they may act as to religion in other parts is known to God; but if ever apostolic days were revived in modern times on earth, I certainly believe some of these to have been granted to us in Africa.[21]

Such a tribute would be suspect if it stood alone, but, it can be reinforced by the golden opinions which the regiment earned when passing through Plymouth on its return from South Africa. It was then said of them:

> On such occasions it was no uncommon thing for soldiers to spend in taverns and gin shops the money they had saved.

In the present case the soldiers of Sutherland were seen in booksellers shops supplying themselves with Bibles and such books and tracts as they required. Yet, as at the Cape, where their religious habits were so free from all fanatical gloom, while expending their money on books, they did not neglect their personal appearance, and the haberdashers' shops had also their share of trade. . . . During the short period the regiment was quartered in Plymouth upwards of £500 was lodged in one banking house to be remitted to Sutherland, exclusive of many sums sent home through the post office and by officers.[22]

Some of the Scottish regiments found chaplains of the official stamp who gave them good service. The Gordon Highlanders, in the Peninsula, admired the courage of their Brigade Chaplain, Edward Cockayne Frith, though one man did say, 'He's the very man that should be there, He's prepared.'[23]

The 78th Highlanders (Seaforth's), when in Cawnpore in 1800, subscribed £700 for the building of a hospital at Inverness, and in the list of the subscribers is the name of Mr Tennant, their Episcopal chaplain.[24]

This acceptance of Episcopal chaplains is less surprising than the appearance of a Roman priest as the chaplain to the Glengarry Fencible regiment, having been commissioned 14th August 1794. The Glengarry regiment, which was largely Roman Catholic, was disbanded in 1802, and their former chaplain, Alexander MacDonell, accompanied many of them as emigrants to Canada. Many of the Glengarry men joined a regiment raised for the defence of their new country, and it is said that when they advanced across the ice towards Ogdensburg, in February 1813, MacDonnell marched on one flank holding up a Crucifix, while a Presbyterian minister carried a Bible at the other extremity of their line.[25]

A sergeant of the Black Watch pays tribute to the fine work done by the clergy in Ireland for the Scots stationed there in 1815. He speaks in particular of the parish of Tulleroan, and says:

and thou, the reverend coadjutor of the parish priest, wert

s

not remiss in encouraging that spirit of good-will, which sprang up after our arrival, and continued increasing until we departed. From thy hands we received such books as made the long winter nights pass pleasantly away; thy good sense made thee forbear to offer us volumes of divinity; thou gavest us, therefore, what some would call, 'the not needful'; but thou didst give us the truly acceptable; and I trust we are no further from the throne of grace yet, than if thou hadst loaded our table with all the works of the holy fathers of the church. Permit me in the name of all who survive of that party, to express our gratitude for that kindness. And were my thanks worthy of acceptance, they ought not to be the last of being offered to thee, our reverend curate of Kilmanagh; often hast thou visited our smoky barrack, called our attention to thy divine exhortations, kneeled down amongst us, and offered up thy prayers to heaven for our happiness. Ah! Mr Cauldfield, we, who kneeled around thee, had much need of thy intercession to heaven in our behalf . . . and if thy ministry has been cast away upon some, we hope it has had a good effect upon others; and wherever the fortune of war leads us, we shall gratefully keep in remembrance thy kindly visits and well-intentioned instructions.[26]

By such improvisations and acceptances the regiments of Scotland made good, in some measure, the absence of chaplains of their own Church. But the shortage of chaplains of any denomination with the army continued, and is underlined by a War Office letter of 1811, which authorises any officer, not below the rank of captain, to perform a chaplain's duties in the absence of a clergyman.[21]

The records of the Gordon Highlanders show that, on one occasion, the gravest of these duties fell to the lot of a 'schoolmaster sergeant'. A private of that regiment was sentenced to die for desertion to the enemy, in the Peninsula, in 1813.

The schoolmaster sergeant accompanied the poor lad to the fatal spot, and all the way from the village read portions of the scripture. On their arrival at the point assigned to them, the criminal joined very audibly in singing a few verses of a psalm and then, after spending a few minutes in prayer, the fatal cap was drawn over his eyes and the provost marshall with his party advanced from the rear to carry the sentence of the court into effect. At this awful affecting part of the scene the whole regiment, officers and men knelt down, and, on behalf of him who then stood on the verge of eternity, offered up humble supplications to the throne of mercy.[28]

It is unfortunate that we do not know more about this school-master sergeant, who might easily have been a licentiate of the Church of Scotland, but the tempting speculation that he was a Presbyterian chaplain 'incognito' requires more evidence, and there were, undoubtedly, many non-commissioned officers and men then in the army who could have done such duty willingly and well.

Regiment after regiment can show instances of religious enthusiasm in their ranks during these years. An extreme case was that of the hot-tempered soldier of the 94th, who obeyed literally the command to 'cut it off', by striking off his own right hand at a single blow.[29]

Less fanatical, but equally real was the religion of Sergeant Robert Butler of the Royal Scots, who noted that on Good Friday some refrained from eating meat, but could

vomit up a bellyful of oaths without any remorse.[30]

John Rae of the 71st (H.L.I.) was a noted Methodist, who single-handed fought and slew three French soldiers, a feat for which he received a decoration.[31]

One of the Scots Guards, John Stevenson, expressed the faith of these 'soldier-saints', when he wrote:

Standing between the enemy and my own men, with the shot ploughing up the ground all about me, the Lord kept me from all fear, and I got back to my place in the line without injury and without agitation. Indeed who should be so firm as the christian soldier, who has the assurance in his breast that to depart and be with Christ is far better than to continue toiling here below?[32]

George Fraser, also of the Scots Guards, has, in his Memoirs, a poem on the Second Coming, in which he speculates on that day:

> When Christ descends in glory from the skies,
> All nature in one conflagration dies[33]

The most ambitious piece of religious writing by a soldier of these days, comes to us in a MS. volume of 400 pages of Meditations, which is now in the Military Library of Edinburgh Castle. It is whimsically entitled

A few Scraps carefully gathered from the Dining Room Plates by Thos. Maltby, Scullion, whilst in ward in the Emperor's Prison, at Besancon, France.

The inscriptions on the fly-leaf show that it has come to us through a soldier in the Royal Scots Fusiliers. The first inscription says, simply,

> George Parish, 1st. Battn. 21st. Regt., Morlaiss, 23rd May, 1814.

The second urges:

> My friends take particular care of this book as it is a present from a worthy friend and a lover of the Lord Jesus. If ever I return I shall *need it.*

The closely written pages cannot be summarised here. They embrace about one hundred chapters, whose subjects range from 'The names and attributes of God' to a 'Caution against Slander'. From the latter chapter comes this illustration of the whole:

> Son take it not to heart if some people think ill of thee, and say of thee what thou art not willing to hear, thou ought to think worse of thyself, and to believe no one is weaker than thyself.

Thus did religious life continue in the regiments of Scotland throughout the lean years between 1796 and 1856.

The return of the Presbyterian chaplains to the commissioned ranks of the Army was mainly due to the shock of the Crimean War, with its revelation of inefficiency in this as in other departments of the Forces of the Crown. It does not, therefore, fall within our brief, but a word must be said of the changing situation in regard to the Officiating Chaplains which prepared the way for that return.

The early principle which governed these part-time chaplaincies was that the Established Church in each part of the British Isles should provide for the troops quartered therein.

This principle was gradually broken down in favour of the English troops quartered in Scotland. By the year 1825 payments for services to the army were being made to the Rev. Dr Russell, the Rev. Mr Routledge and the Rev. Mr Maclennan, Episcopal ministers, for conducting services for troops stationed at Piershill, Glasgow and Fort William.

In that year, however, the Secretary at War objected to similar payment being made to Dr Gardiner for taking services for the troops in the Castle of Edinburgh, although he seems to have been paid for this duty from 1821.

The epistolary war which followed, between the Chaplain General and the Secretary at War, lasted for two years.

The Secretary, Lord Palmerston, argued that the Established Church in each part of the realm was the fit and proper place of worship for the troops. Dr Hodgson was willing to agree to this with regard to the Scottish troops but pleaded that

> An exception may properly be made in favour of members of the Church of England which might reasonably be refused to persons of another persuasion.

The Secretary was not convinced by this and referred the matter to the Treasury, and in August 1827 he reiterated his decision

> that allowances for Divine Service to the troops shall be given exclusively to the Church Established by law in the country where the service is performed.

Dr Hodgson would not admit defeat and appealed to the

s*

Treasury and extracted from that authority a reversal of this decision. The letter is brief and worth repeating.

Treasury Chambers,
9th November, 1827.

My Lord,

With reference to the letter of this Board of 9th August last, respecting the performance of Divine Service to the troops in the United Kingdom, I am commanded by the Lords Commissioners of His Majesty's Treasury to acquaint Your Lordship that upon a further consideration of the subject they are of the opinion that Divine Service to English Regiments stationed in Scotland should be performed by clergymen of the Church of England wherever it may be practicable to engage clergymen of that establishment to perform the service.

Having won this victory, the Chaplain General pressed on, and in January 1828 he secured the right that English soldiers in Scottish regiments stationed in Scotland should have the services of a clergyman of the Church of England.

Dr Hodgson had fought a battle for toleration, though he may not have been conscious of it. A few years later, in 1835, the right of a Presbyterian minister to be paid for services taken for the Scottish 78th Regiment, stationed in Ireland, had to be conceded, because of the precedent established in 1828.

The next landmark of the return journey of the Presbyterian chaplains to full status with the army was a letter from the Chaplain General, or more correctly, from the Principal Chaplain, to the General Assembly of 1844.

Mr Gleig, the writer of this letter, was himself a Scot, and had had considerable service with the army, in the Peninsula and in America, as a combatant officer. His approach to the problems of the chaplaincy was, therefore, based upon the needs of the troops and not upon the needs of a denomination. He requested the co-operation of the General Assembly in the choice of Presbyterian ministers to act as chaplains for the Scottish troops in colonial stations.

The Assembly welcomed this approach and appointed a committee to deal with the business.

The stage was now set for the restoration of Presbyterian chaplains to the *Army Lists*. Their right to preach to the troops of their persuasion in any part of Britain had been won. They were now to be employed where necessary in the colonies. The outbreak of the war in the Crimea found the chaplains department reduced to some half dozen men, most of whom were too old for such service. Volunteers of all denominations offered their services, and, under pressure of necessity, were accepted. They were not yet permitted full status, but, having given excellent service under the burdensome title of 'Assistant Officiating Presbyterian Chaplains', they achieved the dignity of the *Army List*, with a proud 'P', to distinguish them from their brethren of the Church of England.*

The end of this unhappy chapter in the story of the Scottish military chaplains and the beginning of one that is more worthy of their long and honourable record was marked by the tribute paid by Lord Palmerston, in the House of Commons, to the work of the chaplains in the Crimea. In reply to a question, he said:

> The chaplains, whether of the Church of England, whether of the Presbyterian or of the Roman Catholic Churches, have vied with each other in the zealous performance of their duty, and the success which has attended their efforts has been attested by the unvariable good conduct of the troops. These gentlemen spared no pains to carry on their good work, and shrank from no exposure to the dangers of the hospital or of the field, while at the same time they displayed to the world the highest example of Christian charity.[34]

Sir Sidney Herbert expressed his entire concurrence in this tribute, and added the information that, during the brief period of the war, no fewer than twelve of the chaplains had died. He

* Cf. 'Moral Discipline of the Army', a long and authoritative article in the *Quarterly Review*, 1845, vol. 76; and, 'My Predecessors in Office', by A. C. E. Jarvis, in the *Journal of the Royal Army Chaplains Department*, January 1931, vol. iii, No. 31, pp. 444-520.

also asked that the Government find room for the appointment of a large number of commissioned chaplains.

The *Army Lists* for 1859 show that this was done, and that more than sixty chaplains held commissions in that year.

REFERENCES

1. *Royal Warrant*, dated 23rd September 1796, and signed by His Majesty's Command, W. Windham.
2. *The Gentleman's Magazine*, 13th October 1796, p. 918.
3. *The Seventh Report of the Commissioners of Military Inquiry* (1809), p. 26. Charles Dupin, *View of the History and Actual State of the Military Force of Great Britain* (1822), vol. ii, p. 11.
4. Clode, *Military Forces*, vol. ii, p. 375.
5. *Seventh Report of the Commissioners*, Appendix 41, p. 120; cf. C. W. C. Oman, *Wellington's Army, 1809-1814* (1912), p. 326.
6. Major General Le Marchant, MSS. *Outline—The Field Staff of an Army*, pp. 108-12.
   This MS. is in the Library of the Royal Military Academy, Sandhurst. The extract was contributed by the Librarian, Lt. Col. G. A. Shepperd (rtd.).
7. *Seventh Report of the Commissioners*, Appendix 40.
8. *Fasti*, vol. ii, p. 243.
9. Mackintosh, *The Grant Fencibles*, p. 78.
10. C. Greenhill Gardyne, *The Life of a Regiment* (1929), vol. i, p. 170.
11. *Address to the men belonging to the Royal Athole Regiment of Volunteers by the Rev. A. Stewart* (1804).
12. *A Sermon preached before the Clydesdale Volunteers . . . Rev. Bryce Little* (1804).
13. *Address to the Athole Volunteers.*
14. *Fasti*, vol. i, p. 78.
15. *Acts of the Assembly*, Sess. ult., 1806 and 1807.
16. ibid., Sess. 4, 1812.
17. ibid., 22nd May 1827.
18. ibid., Sess. 11, 1839.
19. Mackintosh, *The Grant Fencibles*, p. 78.
20. I. H. Mackay Scobie, *An Old Highland Fencible Corps* (1914), pp. 70f.
21. *The Christian Herald*, October 1814.
22. Stewart, *Highlanders*, vol. ii, pp. 250f.
23. Gardyne, *Life of a Regiment*, p. 306.
24. H. Davidson, *The History and Services of the 78th Highlanders* (1901), p. 41.

25. *Army Lists.*
    W. T. Steven, *In This Sign* (Toronto, 1948), pp. 3f.
26. James Anton, *Retrospect of a Military Life* (1841), pp. 168f.
27. Public Records Office, W.O.4.345, pp. 122 and 134.
28. Gardyne, *Life of a Regiment*, p. 268.
29. Joseph Donaldson, *Recollections of an Eventful Life* (1825), pp. 219f.
30. *Narrative of the Life and Travels of Sergeant Robert Butler* (of the Royal Scots) etc. (1823), chapter xi.
31. Anonymous, *Vicissitudes in the Life of a Scottish Soldier* (1827).
32. James Stevenson, *Twenty-one Years in the British Foot Guards* (1830).
33. *Memoirs in the Life and Travels of George Fraser* (1808), p. 130.
34. *House of Commons Journals*, 11th April 1856.

BIBLIOGRAPHY

ABERCROMBY, PATRICK, *The martial achievements of the Scottish nation* (1762)
Accounts of the Lord High Treasurer for Scotland, Record Series (1877-1907)
Active testimony of the true Prefbyterians, An (1749)
ADAIR, PATRICK, *A true narrative of the rise and progress of the Presbyterian government in the North of Ireland*, ed. W. D. Killen (1866)
ADAMNAN, *Prophecies, Miracles and Visions of St Columba*, ed. J. T. Fowler (1895)
AGAR, WILLIAM, *Military devotion . . . fourteen sermons preached at the camps near Blandford* (1758)
AITON, WILLIAM, *A history of the rencounter at . . . Bothwell Bridge* (1821)
ANDERSON, A. O., *Early sources of Scottish history, A.D. 500—A.D.1286* (1922)
ANDERSON, A. O., *Scottish annals from English chroniclers* (1908)
ANDERSON, JOSEPH, *Scotland in early Christian times* (1881)
ANDREW of Wyntoun, *The orygynale chronykil of Scotland*, ed. D. Laing (1872)
Annals of King George year the second, being a faithful history of the affairs of Great Britain for the year MDCCXVI (1717)
ANTON, JAMES, *Retrospect of a military life* (1841)
Articles of militarie discipline (1639), printed by James Bryson
BACHILER, SAMUEL, *The campe royal, set forth in brief meditations . . . preached in the army at the Leaguer* (1629)
BAILLIE, ROBERT, *The letters and journals of Robert Baillie*, ed. David Laing (1841)
BANNATYNE, RICHARD, *Transactions in Scotland* (1806)
BARBOUR, JOHN, *The Bruce compiled by master John Barbour*, ed. W. W. Skeat (1870, 1889)
BARRETT, C. R. B., *The 7th Hussars* (1914)
BARRON, E. M., *The Scottish war of Independence* (1934)
BELLESHEIM, ALPHONS, *The history of the Catholic Church in Scotland* (1887-1890)
BERNARD, NICHOLAS, *The whole proceedings of the siege of Drogheda in Ireland* (1736)
BERNARD, RICHARD, *The Bible-battels or the sacred art military* (1629)
BLACKADER, Rev. JOHN, *Memoirs of the Rev. John Blackader*, ed. A. Chrichton (1823)
BLACKADER, Col. JOHN, *Select passages from the diary and letters of the late John Blackader, Esq., formerly colonell of the XXVIth or Cameronian Regiment of Foot* (1806)
BLAIKIE, W. B., *The origins of the 'Forty-Five* (Scottish History Society)

BOECE, HECTOR, *The history and chronicles of Scotland*, trans. John Bellenden (1821)

BOWLES, EDWARD, *Manifest truths . . . containing a narration of the proceedings of the Scottish army*, etc. (1646)

BOYD, ZACHARY, 'The battel of Newburne', in *Various Pieces of Fugitive Scots Poetry*, Second Series (1853)

BOYD, ZACHARY, *The sword of the Lord and of Gideon* (1643)

BOYSE, J., *A vindication of the Reverend Mr Alexander Osborn* (1690)

BROWN, PETER HUME, *Scotland before 1700* (1893)

BUCHAN, JOHN (Lord Tweedsmuir), *The history of the Royal Scots Fusiliers* (1925)

BUCHAN, JOHN (Lord Tweedsmuir), *Montrose* (1928)

BUCHANAN, G., *Rerum Scoticarum Historis*, trans. J. Aikman (1827)

BULLOCH, J. M., *Territorial soldiering in the north east of Scotland*, Spalding Club (1914)

BURTON, J. H., *The Scot abroad* (1898)

BUTLER, Sgt. ROBERT, *Narrative of the life and travels of Sergeant Robert Butler (of the Royal Scots)* (1823)

Calendar of documents relating to Scotland, 1108-1509, ed. J. Bain, Record Series

CAMERON, Sir EWEN, *Memoirs of Sir Ewen Cameron of Lochiel*, Abbotsford Club (1842)

CARLYLE, ALEXANDER, *Autobiography of Dr Alexander Carlyle* (1910)

Carmen de morte Sumerledi, Rolls Series, No. 75

CHAMBERS, ROBERT, *History of the Rebellion of 1745-6* (1869)

The Chaplains petition to the honourable House for Redress of grievances. By one of the camp chaplains (1693)

CHAPMAN, BENJAMIN, *The history of Gustavus Adolphus and of the Thirty Years War* (1856)

CHARLES, GEORGE, *History of the Transactions in Scotland in the years 1715-16 and 1745-46* (1817)

CLODE, C. M., *Military forces of the Crown* (1869)

COCKLE, Capt., *Bibliography of English military books up to 1642 and of contemporary foreign books* (1900)

Compendium of the laws of Scotland (1840)

Compleat History of the Lives and reigns of Mary Queen of Scotland and her son, A (1648)

Complete history of the wars in Scotland (1720)

Concilia Scotiae. Statuta Ecclesiae Scoticanae, Bannatyne Club

COWAN, HENRY, *The influence of the Scottish Church in Christendom* (1896)

CRAWFORD, DAVID, *Memoirs of the affairs of Scotland* (1753)

Cronikill of the Kingis of Scotland, Ane, Maitland Club

CRUSO, JOHN, *Castrametation, or the measuring out of quarters for the encamping of an army* (1642)

CUNNINGHAM, J., *Strictures on military discipline, by an officer* (1774)

DALRYMPLE, Sir DAVID (Lord Hailes), *Annals of Scotland, 1057-1370* (1819)

DALTON, CHARLES, *English Army Lists and Commission Registers, 1661–1714* (1896)

DALTON, CHARLES, *George the First's Army* (1910)

DALTON, CHARLES, *The Scots Army 1661–1688* (1909)

D'ALTON, JOHN, *King James's Irish Army List, 1689* (1861)

DAVIDSON, H., *The history and services of the 78th Highlanders* (1901)

Declaration of the Committee of the Estates of the Kingdome of Scotland held at Edinburgh the 15 October 1647

Declaration of the proceedings of the new moddel'd army in the kingdome of Scotland (1647)

DEFOE, DANIEL, *Memoirs of the Church of Scotland* (1717)

DELAVOYE, A. M., *Records of the 90th Regiment, Perthshire Light Infantry* (1880)

Diurnal of remarkable occurrents, A, Bannatyne Club (1833)

Divers papers presented to the honourable Houses of Parliament by the Commissioners of . . . Scotland (1645)

DODSWORTH, WILLIAM, *An historical account of the Episcopal See and cathedral church of Salisbury* (1814)

DONALDSON, JOSEPH, *Recollections of an eventful life* (1825)

DOUGLAS, ROBERT, *The diary of Mr Robert Douglas, in Historical Fragments Relative to Scottish Affairs* (1833)

DOUGLAS, W. S., *Cromwell's Scotch campaigns* (1898)

DOWDEN, JOHN, *The Celtic Church in Scotland* (1894)

DRUMMOND, WILLIAM, *The loadstar or directory to the new world* (1711)

DUDGEON, R. C., *The history of the Edinburgh or Queen's Regiment* (1882)

DUNCAN, FRANCIS, *The history of the Royal Regiment of Artillery* (1872)

DUPIN, CHARLES, *View of the history and actual state of the military force of Great Britain* (1822)

DYOTT, WILLIAM, *A selection from the Journal of William Dyott sometime General in the British Army*, ed. R. W. Jeffrey (1907)

Exercise for the Horse, Dragoons and Foot Forces (1740)

FARQUAR, G. T. S., *The Episcopal History of Perth* (1894)

FARRER, J. A., *Military Manners and Customs* (1885)

FINDLAY, J. T., *Wolfe in Scotland* (1928)

FIRTH, C. H., *Cromwell's Army* (1902)

FIRTH, C. H., *Scotland and the Commonwealth*, Scottish History Society

FIRTH, C. H., *Scotland and the Protectorate*, Scottish History Society

FISCHER, TH. A., *The Scots in Germany* (1902)

FISCHER, TH. A., *The Scots in Prussia* (1903)

FISCHER, TH. A., *The Scots in Sweden* (1907)

FORBES, ROBERT, *Journals*, ed. J. B. Craven (1886)

FORBES, ROBERT, *The lyon in mourning*, Scottish History Society (1887 etc.)

FRANCISQUE-MICHEL, R., *Les Écossais en France* (1862)

FRASER, GEORGE, *Memoirs in the life and travels of George Fraser* (1808)

FRASER, COL. SIMON, *Standing rules . . . of the Fraser Fencibles* (1798)

GARDYNE, C. GREENHILL, *The life of a regiment, the history of the Gordon Highlanders* (1929)

GODWIN, E., *A brief account of the late work of God in the British army in Flanders* (1746)

GRANT, JAMES, *British battles* (1899)

GRANT, JAMES, *Memorials of the castle of Edinburgh* (1850)

GROSE, FRANCIS, *Military antiquities* (1786-8)

GRUB, GEORGE, *Ecclesiastical history of Scotland* (1861)

GUTHRY, HENRY, *Memoirs of Henry Guthry . . . late Bishop of Dunkeld* (1747)

HAYES-McCOY, G. A., *The Scots mercenary forces in Ireland* (1937)

HENDERSON, G. D., *Mystics of the North East* (1934)

HENDERSON, G. D., *Religious life in seventeenth century Scotland* (1937)

HENDERSON, T. F., *The casket letters* (1889)

HENRY the Minstrel, *The actis and deidis of Schir William Wallace*, ed. W. A. Craigie (1940)

HEWISON, J. K., *The Covenanters* (1913)

Highland Papers, Scottish History Society

Historical papers relating to the Jacobite period, 1699-1750, New Spalding Club

Historical record of the Royal Regiment of Scots Dragoons . . . called the Scots Greys (1840)

Historie of King James the Sext, The, Bannatyne Club

History of Scottish Affairs, Spalding Club

HOGG, JAMES, *Jacobite relics of Scotland*, Second series (1821)

HOME, JOHN, *The history of the rebellion* (1802)

HOWIE, JOHN, *Biographia Scoticana . . . Scots Worthies* (1816)

INNES, COSMO, *Scotland in the Middle Ages* (1860)

INNES, COSMO, *Sketches of early Scottish history* (1861)

IRVING, JOHN, *Dumbarton Castle* (1917)

Jacobite attempt of 1719, The, Scottish History Society

JOANNIS de Fordun, *Scotichronicon*, cura Walteri Goodall (1859)

JOHNSTON, Sir ARCHIBALD, *Diary of Sir Archibald Johnston of Wariston*, Scottish History Society (1919)

KEITH, ROBERT, *History of the affairs of Church and State in Scotland*, Spottiswoode Society (1845)

KERR, ROBERT, *History of Scotland during the reign of Robert I* (1811)

KERR, Sir ROBERT, *Correspondence of Sir Robert Kerr, first Earl of Ancram and his son, etc.* (1875)

KIRKTON, JAMES, *The secret and true history of the Church of Scotland*, ed. C. K. Sharpe (1817)

KNOX, JOHN, *The history of the Reformation in Scotland*, ed. David Laing (1846)

LAMONT, JOHN, *The chronicle of Fife being the Diary of John Lamont*, Maitland Club (1830)

LANG, ANDREW, *Companions of Pickle* (1898)

LANG, ANDREW, *Prince Charles Edward Stuart* (1903)

LANKESTER, EDWIN, *Memorials of John Rae* (1846)

Lauderdale Papers, ed. O. Airy, Camden Society (1884)

LEASK, J. C., *The regimental records of the Royal Scots* (1915)

LEDIARD, THOMAS, *The life of John Duke of Marlborough* (1736)

LEITH, WILLIAM FORBES, *Memoir of the Scottish Catholics* (1909)

Letters and State Papers during the reign of King James VI, chiefly from the collection of Sir James Balfour (1838)

List of persons concerned in the Rebellion, Scottish History Society

LIVINGSTONE, JOHN, *A brief historical relation of the life of Mr John Livingstone* (1736)

McCARMICK, WILLIAM, *A farther impartial account of the actions of the Inniskilling men* (1691)

McCORMICK, JOSEPH, *State Papers and letters addressed to William Carstares* (1774)

McCRIE, THOMAS, *The life of Mr Robert Blair, minister of St Andrews*, Wodrow Society (1848)

McCRIE, THOMAS, *Memoirs of Mr William Veitch and George Brysson* (1825)

McCRIE, THOMAS, *The story of the Scottish Church* (1875)

MACEWEN, A. R., *A history of the Church in Scotland* (1915)

MACINTOSH, ALEXANDER, *Forfarshire or Lord Ogilvy's Regiment, 1745-6* (1914)

MACKAY, ANGUS, *The book of Mackay* (1906)

MACKAY, JOHN, *The life of Lt. Gen. Hugh Mackay*, Bannatyne Club

MACKENZIE, AGNES M., *The Scotland of Queen Mary* (1936)

MACKENZIE, GEORGE, *The Royal Naval and Military Calendar and National Record for 1821*

MACKENZIE, JOHN, *A narrative of the Siege of Londonderry* (1690)

McKERROW, JOHN, *History of the Secession Church* (1841)

MACKINTOSH, H. B., *The Grant, Strathspey or First Highland Fencible Regiment, 1793-1799* (1934)

MACKINTOSH, H. B., *The Inverness-shire Highlanders or 97th Regiment of Foot* (1926)

MACKINTOSH, H. B., *The Northern or Gordon Fencibles, 1778-1783* (1929)

MACLEAN, DONALD, *The Counter-Reformation in Scotland, 1560-1930* (1931)

MACPHERSON, HECTOR, *The Cameronian Philosopher, Alexander Shields* (1932)

MARSHALL, STEPHEN, *A plea for defensive arms, or a copy of a letter written by Mr Stephen Marshall to a friend* (1642)

MAURICE, F., *The history of the Scots Guards* (1934)

MAXWELL, Sir HERBERT, trans. *The chronicle of Lanercost* (1913)

Medecina Magnetica or the rare and wonderful art of curing by sympathy, etc. (1656)

MELVILL, JAMES, *The autobiography and diary of James Melvill*, ed.. Robert Pitcairn, Wodrow Society (1842)

Memoirs of the insurrection in Scotland in 1715, Abbotsford Club (1858)

Memorials of John Murray of Broughton, Scottish History Society

MICHELL, THOMAS, *History of the Scottish expedition to Norway in 1612* (1886)

Military memoirs of the great Civil War . . . and an account of the Earl of Glencairn's expedition (1822)

Minutes of the Synod of Argyll, Scottish History Society

Miscellany of the Maitland Club (1842)

MITCHELL, THOMAS, *The history of Thomas Mitchell, born and educated among the gipsies of Scotland, afterwards a soldier in the 21st Regiment of Foot* (1826)

Monro his expedition with the worthy Scots regiment (called Mac-Keyes regiment), (1637)

MORER, THOMAS, *A short account of Scotland* (1702)

MORREN, NATHANIEL, *Annals of the General Assembly* (1840)

NAPIER, MARK, *Memoirs of the Marquis of Montrose* (1864)

NAPIER, MARK, *Memorialls of Montrose and his times* (1862)

NAU, CLAUDE, *The history of Mary Stewart*, ed. Joseph Stevenson (1883)

NEVAY, JOHN, *The nature of the Covenant of Grace opened and applied in LII sermons* (1748)

NORUELL, ROBERT, *The meroure of an Christiane* (1561)

OMAN, C. W. C., *Wellington's Army, 1809-1814* (1912)

ORMSBY, JAMES W., *An account of the operations of the British army . . . during the years 1808-09* (1809)

OWST, G. R., *Literature and Pulpit in medieval England* (1933)

PALGRAVE, FRANCIS, *Documents and records illustrating the history of Scotland* (1837)

Papers about the rebellions of 1715 and 1745, ed. Henry Paton, Scottish History Society (1893)

Papers illustrating the history of the Scots Brigade in the service of the United Netherlands, 1572-1782, Scottish History Society

Papers relating to the Scots in Poland, Scottish History Society

PARIS, MATTHEW, *Chronica majora*, ed. H. R. Louard (1877)

PATTEN, ROBERT, *History of the late rebellion with original papers . . . by the Rev. Mr Robert Patten, formerly chaplain to Mr Forster* (1717)

PATTEN, ROBERT, *Rebel convinc'd and liberty maintain'd* (1718)

PATTEN, W., *The expedicion into Scotlande of the most worthely fortunate prince Edward, Duke of Somerset* (1548)

PETERKIN, A., *Records of the Kirk of Scotland, 1638-50* (1837)

PINKERTON, JOHN, *The history of Scotland* (1797)

Principal passages of Germany, The (1636-9)

PRINGLE, JOHN, *Observations on the diseases of the army* (1765)

RAE, PETER, *The history of the late rebellion* (1718)

RAY, JAMES, *A compleat history of the rebellion from its first rise in 1745* (1758)

Records of the Commissions of the General Assembly of the Church of Scotland, Scottish History Society

Records of the Presbyteries of Inverness and Dingwall, 1648-88, Scottish History Society

REID, H. M. B., *One of King William's men (Col. William Maxwell of Cardoness)* (1898)

REID, J. S., *History of the Presbyterian Church in Ireland* (1867)

Report of the Committee appointed to consider the state of H.M. Land Forces . . . 6th day of June 1746

ROSE, D. M., *Prince Charlie's friends or Jacobite Indictments* (1896)

ROUTH, E. G. M., *Tangier, England's last Atlantic outpost* (1912)

RULE, WILLIAM HARRIS, *Wesleyan Methodism in the British Army* (1883)

Rules and orders for the better government of His Majesty's forces employed in foreign parts (1747)

RYMER, THOMA, *Foedera, conventiones, literae* (1727)

SCOBIE, I. H. H., *An old Highland Fencible Corps* (1914)

Scotch Presbyterian eloquence displayed (1694)

SCOTT, HEW, *Fasti Ecclesiae Scoticanae* (1869)

SCOTT, SIBBALD D., *The British Army, its origin etc.* (1868–80)

Scottish correspondence of Mary of Lorraine, The, Scottish History Society

Selections from the registers of the Presbytery of Lanark, Abbotsford Club (1839)

Seventh report of the Commissioners of Military Inquiry, appointed by Act of 45 Geo. III. c. 47. The Departments of Foreign Accounts and the Chaplain General, ordered to be printed 20th January, 1809

SHIELDS, ALEXANDER, *A hind let loose* (1687)

Siege and history of Londonderry, The, ed. John Hempton (1864)

Siege of Edinburgh Castle, MDCLXXXIX, Bannatyne Club

SIMES, THOMAS, *A military guide* (1776)

SLINGSBY, Sir HENRY, *Original memoirs . . . the life of Sir Henry Slingsby* (1806)

SPALDING, JOHN, *Memorialls of the trubles in Scotland and England*, Spalding Club

STEUART, A. FRANCIS, *Newsletters of 1715 and 1716* (1910)

STEVEN, WILLIAM, *The history of the Scottish Church in Rotterdam* (1833)

STEVEN, W. T., *In this sign* (Toronto, 1948)

STEVENS, JOHN, *The journal of John Stevens containing a brief account of the war in Ireland*, ed. R. N. Murray (1912)

STEVENSON, J., *Twenty-one years in the British Foot Guards* (1830)

STEWART, DAVID, *Sketches of the Highlanders* (1822)

STORY, GEORGE, *A continuation of the impartial history of the wars in Ireland by George Story, chaplain to the regiment, etc.* (1693)

STORY, R. H., *William Carstares* (1874)

STOTHERT, WILLIAM, *A narrative of the principal events of the campaigns of 1809, 1810 and 1811* (1812)

System of Camp Discipline, A (1757)

TAYLER, A. and H., *Jacobites of Aberdeenshire and Banffshire* (1928)

TAYLER, A. and H., *1715, The story of the Rising* (1936)

TAYLOR, JAMES, *Operations of the campaign of 1743, by James Taylor, Rector of Broadway . . . and chaplain to His Majesty's Own Regiment of Horse*

TERRY, C. S., *John Graham of Claverhouse* (1905)

TERRY, C. S., *Life of Alexander Leslie* (1899)

TERRY, C. S., *Papers relating to the army of the Solemn League and Covenant* (1917)

TERRY, C. S., *Pentland Rising and Rullion Green, The* (1905)

THOMSON, T. B. STEWART, *The chaplain in the Church of Scotland*, Lecture III (1947)

TRINTERUD, LEONARD J., *The forming of an American tradition* (1949)

True account of the great victory obtained . . . by His Majesties forces under the command of the Duke of Monmouth (1679)

True account of the proceedings at Perth by a rebel (1716)

True and impartial history of the occurrences in the Kingdom of Ireland . . . by an Eyewitness (1691)

True relation of the happy successe of His Maiesties forces in Scotland under the conduct of Lord James, Marquise of Montrose (1644)

True relation of the proceedings of the English army now in Scotland . . . contained in letters (1650)

True relation of the routing of the Scottish army near Dunbar, Sept. 3 (1650)

TULLIBARDINE, The Marchioness of, *A military history of Perthshire*

TURNER, *Sir* JAMES, *Memoirs of his own life and times*, Bannatyne Club (1829)

TURNER, *Sir* JAMES, *Pallas armata* (1683)

VAUGHAN, ROBERT, *Life of Wycliffe* (1831)

Vicissitudes in the life of a Scottish soldier (1827)

WALKER, JAMES, *The theology and theologians of Scotland* (1872)

WALTON, Col. CLIFFORD, *History of the British Standing Army from 1660–1700* (1894)

WARD, ROBERT, *Animadversions of warre* (1639)

WEDGEWOOD, C. V., *The Thirty Years War* (1938)

WHITTIE or WITTEL, JOHN, *An exact diary of the late expedition of . . . the Prince of Orange. By a minister, chaplain in the army* (1689)

WHITTIE or WITTEL, JOHN, *Constantius redivivus, or a full account of the successes . . . of the heroical Prince William, etc.* (1693)

WHITTLE, SETH, *A sermon preached before the garrison, etc.* (1689)

WILSON, ARTHUR, *The history of Greater Britain* (1653)

WILSON, WILLIAM, *A true and impartial relation of the . . . defeat at Bothwell Bridge* (1797)

WISHART, GEORGE, *The memoirs of James Marquis of Montrose* (1893)

WODROW, ROBERT, *Analecta* (1842)

WODROW, ROBERT, *The history of the sufferings of the Church of Scotland* (1722)

MANUSCRIPT SOURCES

Use has been made, and acknowledged in the references of the *Clarendon, Clarke, Hare* and *Laing* collections of manuscripts.

Use has also been made of the following manuscripts:

Acts of the General Assembly of the Church of Scotland
> These may be consulted in the General Assembly Library, New College, Edinburgh.

General Orders of the Madras Presidency, 7th April 1786—25th November 1794
> These may be consulted in the Naval and Military Library, The Castle, Edinburgh.

Minutes of the Committee for the Management of the Royal Bounty
> These may be consulted in the General Assembly Library.

Order Book of the Stewart of Appin, Clan Regiment—1745
> This may be consulted in the Naval and Military Library, The Castle, Edinburgh.

Outline—The Field Staff of an Army, by Major General le Marchant
> This may be consulted in the Library of the Royal Military Academy, Sandhurst.

Pocket Book of Dr Samuel Noyes
> This may be consulted in the Naval and Military Library, The Castle, Edinburgh.

INDEX

Aberdeen, 77f, 84
Abergeldie, 176
Adamson, Thomas, 247
Agar, William, 226, 235
Aird, John, 138
Alexander, John, 195, 197
Anderson, George, 71f, 186, 241
Arbroath, Abbot of, 6f, 10
Archer Guard, 30, 51
Articles for War, 19, 45, 57f, 87, 89, 154f, 188 224, 228
Ashe, Simeon, 93f
Assembly, The General, 53, 84, 89f, 92, 108f, 178, 181, 183f, 188, 229, 235f, 245, 262f, 270f
Associate Church, 214f
Auld Alliance, 49f

Bachiler, Samuel, 64
Baillie, Robert, 1, 78f, 108, 131, 139
Baird, John, 138
Balcanqual, Walter, 42
Balliol, John, 8f
Balnaves, Henry, 30f
Balnevis, Alexander, 170
Bane, Donald, 71f
Barclay, Alexander, 196
Barclay, George, 167
Barclay, John, 156
Baston, Friar, 16
Bat-horse, 225
Batta, 225f
Battles & Skirmishes
  Ayrsmoss, 166
  Balrinnes, 42
  Bannockburn, 14f
  Blenheim, 184f
  Bothwell Bridge, 165f
  Brunanburgh 3
  Carham, 3
  Corbiesdale, 102
  Culloden, 205, 208f, 218

Dettingen, 230
Drumclog, 163f
Dunbar, 125f
Dunkeld, 171
Edgehill, 88
Falkirk, 205, 209, 214, 216f
Flodden, 24
Fontenoy, 231f
Gladsmuir, 205f, 213f
Halidon Hill, 18
Kilsyth, 103
Langside, 38
Largs, 7
Lutzen, 60f
Marston Moor 92f, 103
Mauchline Moor, 117f
Methven, 14
Neville's Cross, 18
Newburn , 83
Ogdensburg, 265
Otterburn, 20
Pinkie, 31f
Preston, 199f
Prestonpans, 205f, 213f
Rullion Green, 161f
Sherriffmuir, 196
Solway Moss, 29
Steinkirk, 177
Stirling Bridge, 11
The Standard, 4f
Tippermuir, 102
Verneuil, 50
Witstock, 60
Worcester, 130
Baty, James, 139, 141
Bayne, Donald, 233
Beadle, rebel, 211f
Bede, 2
Beevor, Miles, 226f
Bells, Church, 208
Bennet, David, 129
Bennet, Robert, 92

Bernard, Richard, 45f
Berwick on Tweed, 11, 18, 33, 190
Bible, The, 7, 179, 265
Blair, John, 10f
Blair, Robert, 80, 92, 103, 139
Blair, William, 189
Borthwick, Alexander, 183f
Boyd, William, 169
Boyd, Zachary, 83
Brand, John, 39f
Brecbennoch, The, 6f
Brodie, David, 206
Brodie, William, 190
Brown, Andrew, 245
Brown, John, 156
Brown, Robert, 119, 121
Bruce, *Hon.* James, 230
Bruce, Robert the, 12f
Burnet, Gilbert, 169
Burns, Robert, 227

Cameron, Alexander, of Findron, 243
Cameron, Alexander, priest, 209
Cameron, John, 210
Cameron, Richard, 166
Campbell, Neill, 42
Campbell, Pryse, 239
Campbell, William, 237
Campbelltown, 167
Campfollowers, 89f, 226
Canada, 265
Cant, Andrew, 84, 92, 95, 103, 112
Cape Colony, 264
Cappock, Thomas, 207f
Captain and Chaplain, 149
Cargill, Donald, 163, 166
Carlisle, 6, 208
Carlyle, Alexander, 213f
Carmichael, Frederick, 91, 102f
Carmichael, John, 50
Carrickfergus, 138f, 144
Carstares, William, 169, 177, 188f
Cathach, 7
Cathcart, *Hon.* Archibald, 230
Cathedral roofs, 12
Chalmers, John, 180
Chapel, portable, 12, 23
Chaplain General, 177, 185, 205, 255, 258, 269f
Character of Chaplains, 45f, 66, 73f, 79f, 134, 182f, 233, 227f, 271
Charlemagne, 1, 49f
Church parade, 181, 223f

Claverhouse, John Graham of, 169f, 216
Clerk, Alexander, 100
Clerk, George, 65
Commissions, 40, 72, 82, 153f, 190
Communion, 6, 8f, 15, 95f, 99, 163, 200
Conventicles, 162f
Coote, Charles, 202
Crane, James, priest, 208
Crimean War, 271f
Cromwell, Oliver, 93, 125f
Cruikshank, John, 92
Cunningham, Hugh, 138

Dalyell, Thomas, 155
Danzig, 61
D'auvergne, Edward, 180
Davidson, John, 41
Deacons, regimental, 85f
Denmark, 54f
Deputy chaplains, 244, 261
Discipline, Kirk, 85, 111
Dissenters, 201f, 212, 216
Donaldson, Thomas, 92
Douglas, John, Scots Brigade, 63
Douglas, John, Scots Guards, 231
Douglas, Robert, 59, 90, 92f, 96, 127, 131, 246
Douglas, Thomas, 163
Dress, clerical, 19
Drogheda, 137f
Druids, 2
Drummond, Henry Hay, 229f
Drums for Church, 57, 86 and n., 87
Drysdale, John, 139
Duart Castle, 240
Dumbarton, 21f, 38, 100, 189
Dunavertie, 114f
Dundee, 130, 215
Duns, 78f, 81f
Durie, John, 39f
Duty of chaplains, 191f, 258f

Eades, Martin, priest, 208
East India Company, 225f
Edinburgh, 9, 12, 39f, 123, 127, 132f, 156, 160, 169f, 189f, 205f, 212f, 235f, 261, 269
Eileen Donan Castle, 202f
Elder and rebel, 211
Engagement, The, 117ff
Engineers, military, 11f, 23

English chaplains in Scotland, 188f, 223, 229f, 248, 269f
Erskine, Ebenezer, 119, 216
Erskine, Henry, 119ff
Examination by Presbytery, 143f
Execution, military, 202, 215, 244, 266f
Exercise of Edinburgh, 40
Expenses, Communion, 95, 99

Families, military, 226
Fencible regiments, 242ff
Ferguson, Adam, 231, 245
Ferguson, John, 246
Feudal duty, 22f
Fleming, John, 190
Forbes, Robert, 204, 210
Forme, James, 66
Forrester, Charles, 156, 169f
Forsyth, Morris, 246
Fort Augustus, 241f
Fort George, 238f, 264
Fort William, 189f, 241f, 269
France, 49ff
Fraser, Alexander, 241f
Friar Tuck, 9
Funeral arrangements, 225

Gaelic, 190, 230
Gaittis, John, 82
Galloway, Patrick, 42f
Gamble, John, 256
Garrison chaplains, 189f, 235-42
Gib, Adam, 214
Gibson, John, 238
Gilchrist, James, 241
Gillespie, George, 87
Gillespie, Patrick, 91f, 126
Glasgow, 3f, 10, 130, 223
Glasgow, James, 235
Gleig, George Robert, 270
Good, John, 180
Goodman, Christopher, 36
Gordon, Alexander, priest, 209
Gordon, Alexander, 239
Gordon, George, 239
Gordon, Henry, 238
Gordon, James, Comber, 145
Gordon, James, Rothiemay, 80
Gordon, James, Bellie, 232, 239, 245
Gordon, John, Scots Brigade, 67
Gordon, John, priest, 203
Gordon, Robert, 243
Graham, Father, 206f

Grant Fencible Regiment, 263
Grant, James, Laggan, 242
Grant, James, Urquhart, 243f
Grant, John, 210f
Gray, Thomas, 11
Green Book, 62
Greig, Patrick, 61
Groves, Samuel, 191
Gustavus Adolphus, 55/61
Guthrie, David, 176

Haig, William, 236
Hakon of Norway, 7f
Halyburton, George, 87
Hamilton, James, 127, 141
Hamilton, John, 52
Hardie, Thomas, 247
Hare, Francis, 185
Harper, William, 209
Harry, Blind, 10f
Hartlepool, 109
Henderson, Alexander, 83
Henderson, Hugh, 159
Hepburn's Regiment, 52
Hepburn, Thomas, 37
Herbert, Henry, 191
Home, Alexander Earl, 230
Home, John, 213, 217, 237
Home, Robert, 237
Home, William, 237
Hospital, 149, 218, 259
Houston, James, 140
Hume, David, 164f
Hume, William, 94
Hunter, Andrew, 43f, 62f
Hunter, James, Dornoch, 202
Hunter, James, 247

Independency in Scotland, 130f
India, 233, 265
Innes, Alexander, Rothiemay, 101
Innes, Alexander, 158
Innes, William, 238
Inniskillen, 148
Inverlochy, 133, 181
Inverness, 170, 204
Ireland, Presbytery in, 138ff
Irvine, William, 170, 200

Jack, Robert, 234
James III, 22
James IV, 22
James VI, 40ff

Jeffrey, Andrew, 195
Joan of Arc, 50
Johnstone, John, 235f
Johnstone, Lachlan, 233

Kay, George, 237
Ker, Alexander, 190
Ker, Robert, 87, 91, 127
Keyden, James, 247
Kid, John, 163f
Kinamond, William, 102
King, John, 163, 165
Kirk, Robert, 218
Kissing the ground, 15f
Knox, Andrew, 44
Knox, Harry, 128
Knox, John, 31, 33f, 35
Knox, John, North Leith, 128

Langlands, Robert, 167
Law, Alexander, 195
Law, George, 209
Law, Mungo, 92, 113, 122, 127
Lennox, Regent, 38f
Leofgar of Hereford, 3
Leslie, David, 93, 112, 114f, 125f
Lists called for, 90f, 109f, 127f
Littleton, Father, 200
Livingstone, Andrew, 195
Livingstone, John, 80f, 83, 87, 139, 143
Londonderry, 146f
Lorimer, Robert, 247
Lumsden, Charles, 129
Lyon, Robert, 204f

Macauley, Alexander, 233
Macauley, Angus, 72
Macbean, Alexander, 218
McCaskill, Malcolm, 241
McCra, Donald, 203
McCra, John, 128
Macdonald, Alan, 209f
Macdonald, Hugh, 203
Macdonell, Alexander, 265
McFarlane, Alexander, 240
McGhie, John, 111
McGhie, Thomas, 40
McGill, John, 122
McGilligan, Daniel, 202
McGregor, Alexander, 244, 263
McGregor, Robertson, 244
McKail, Hugh, 162

McKay, Daniel, 189f
Mackay, General Hugh, 183
McKenzie, George, 246
McKenzie, Murdoch, 66f, 101
McKenzie, Roderick, 158
Mackintosh, Alexander, 158
McLachlan, John, 205
Maclagan, James, 233f
McLauchlan, James, 261
McLeod, Murdoch, 240
McMurdo, John, 202
McNicol, Donald, 246
Macpherson, Robert, 233
McSweyn, Sweyn, 170
McVicar, Neil, 190, 207
Maitland, John, 209
Maitland, William, 101
Man, Thomas, 211
Marchant, Maj. General Le, 258f
Marriage of soldiers, 224f
Martin, William, 238
Mary, Queen of Scots, 36f
Matthew of York, 9
Melvill, Andrew, 41f
Melvill, James, 41f
Middleton, John, 116
Milling, John, 180
Ministers' regiment, 89
Minute Book lost, 87
Mitchell, Thomas, 234
Moncrieff, John, 91
Monro, Col. Robert, 70
Monteith, Robert, 214
Montrose, James Graham, Marquis of, 97f
Moodie, Robert, 238
Morrison, Walter, 239
Murray, Gideon, 229
Muschet, John, 238
Mylne, James, 246

Nasmyth, James, 109, 112f
Netherlands, 62ff
Nevey, John, 87, 113, 114f, 118
Newcastle, 41, 83f, 94f
Newman, Samuel, priest, 208
New Model Army, 112
Newton, Archibald, 129
New York, 158
Nicholson, James, 43
Norville, Robert, 51
Norway, 7f, 55f
Noyes, Samuel, 180, 185

Officiating chaplains, 183f, 254, 256, 257f, 260, 265f
Ordination as chaplain, 63, 189f, 244ff
Organ, portable, 23

Palmerston, *Lord*, 269f
Parade for Church, 181, 186f, 223
Paris, Matthew, 6
Pate, James, 260
Patten, Robert, 195, 198f
Patten, William, 32f
Paul, William, 199f
Pay of chaplain, 17, 53, 59, 61f, 64f, 71f, 83, 91, 121, 176, 190, 225, 242, 244, 254, 256, 260f, 269
Pearson, John, 195
Peat, Samuel, 246
Peebles, Thomas, 138
Pentland Rising, 159ff
Perth, 9, 34, 196, 204
Petition, The Chaplains', 182f
Pirate's chaplain, 45
Pitcairn, Alexander, 69f
Pitcairn, David, 185
Plague, 19, 60
Playfair, James, 246
Pluralities, 183f
Poland, 61f
Pollock, John, 202
Poor, care of the, 85
Prayers, daily, 56, 86f, 224, 234
Presbytery of the Army, 58f, 83-86, 87, 89, 108, 110, 129f, 133, 138, 141f, 150f
Prison, chaplains in, 13, 103, 141f, 197, 199f, 209
Purchase, 190, 226f, 255f
Purging the Army, 122, 124f

Quigrich, The, 15

Rae, John, 165f
Ramsay, James, 162
Ramsay, James, Kelso, 201
Recruiting by chaplains, 243f
Refusal to appoint chaplains, 39, 117
Regiments in alphabetical order
  Argyll and Sutherland Highlanders, 264f
  Black Watch, 229, 231, 233, 245, 265f
  Cameronians, 166, 171f, 176-9, 185, 191

Gordon Highlanders, 230, 265, 266f
Highland Light Infantry, 267
Kings Own Scottish Borderers, 176, 180, 190, 230
Royal Scots, 54, 157, 180, 185, 191, 267
Royal Scots Fusiliers, 157, 178, 232, 234f, 247f, 268
Royal Scots Greys, 176, 201
Scots Brigade, 62, 246, 247f, 267
Scots Guards, 153, 180, 231, 267f
Seaforth Highlanders, 265, 270
Seventh Hussars, 176, 201
Regulations for French chaplains, 191f
Reiley, James, priest, 208
Relics, Sacred, 2, 9, 15, 18
Revolution, The, 167/9
Richardson, James, 240
Riddell, Simon, 202
Ritchie, David, 247f
Robertson, Alexander, 160, 162
Robertson, James, 102, 129
Robertson, John, 195
Robertson, William, 237
Roger, Bishop of Salisbury, 4
Roman Catholic chaplains, 97ff, 150, 197, 200, 206f, 208ff, 265
Ross, John, 44
Rough, John, 30f
Royal Bounty Committee, 238ff
Royal Warrant, 252, 261ff
Ruthven of Badenoch, 116, 189, 241

Sage, Aeneas, 217
St Andrew, 19
St Andrews town, 12, 30f, 132
St Botulph, 9
St Columba, 2f, 7
St Comgall, 2
St Fillan, 15
St Giles Church, Edinburgh, 35
St Gorgon, 32
St Kentigern, 4
St Mungo, 19
St Romayn, 19
St Sunday, 32
Sandilands, Andrew, 101
Scandals, 89, 104, 116
Scott, John, 138
Scot, John, Oxnam, 162
Scot, Thomas, 64
Semple, Gabriel, 159f

Sermons, 4, 19, 35f, 62, 64f, 70f, 83, 93, 103, 157f, 190, 198, 204, 206, 222, 232, 235, 261
Session, Regimental Kirk, 53, 68ff, 85f, 89, 111, 133f, 138
Sharp, James, 127
Sherriff, Francis, 246
Shields, Alexander, 171, 177ff, 189
Shortage of chaplains, 84. 90, 92, 97, 108, 113f, 127, 141, 144, 181f, 248, 257, 259
Short service, 83, 90, 92
Sibbald, Patrick, 129
Sick, care of, 89
Simony, 184
Simpson, Gilbert, 156
Simpson, James, 92
Simson, Patrick, 214, 217
Sinecurists, 226-9, 237f, 243f
Single combat, 5
Smith, Alexander, 156
Smith, John, 127
Smith, Walter, 190
Societies, religious, 234
Soldiers' character, 88, 103f, 108, 116, 124, 148, 178f, 185f, 187f, 232f, 235, 261, 264f, 267f
Staff chaplains, 17, 91, 259
Stalker, James, 239
Stewart, Alexander, 217
Stewart, James, 245
Stewart, John, 247
Stewart, Robert, 170
Stickit minister, 243
Stirling, 35, 42, 129, 189, 216, 237f
Story, George, 148f
Stuart, Alexander, 245
Student rebel, 211
Sumerled, 3f
Sweden, 55/61
Syme, Thomas, 209
Synod in Netherlands, 68

Tangier, 157f

Taylor, James, 170
Thanksgiving services, 42, 60, 83f, 94, 96, 169, 185f, 196, 230
Thomson, James, 191
Thomson, Thomas, 109
Toleration, 260f, 269ff
Traill, Robert, 110, 112
Tranent, 111
Transport money, 91
Tremblay, Father Joseph de, 52
Trumpet for church, 57, 86f
Turner, Andrew, 201
Turner, Archibald, 129
Turner, Sir James, 115, 117, 156, 159f
Tyrie, John, priest, 209

Vatass, Peter, 228
Veitch, William, 162, 167

Wallace, Sir William, 9ff
Weapons blessed, 42, 57
Webster, Alexander, 214
Weir, John, 141f
Welch, John, 52
Welsh, John, 159f, 164
Wesley, John, 233
Western army, 130
Whitestone, Walter, 64
Whitford, David, 157
Whittie, John, 167f
Wickhart, John, 177
Willis, Richard, 177, 180
Winster, Alexander, 170
Wishart, George, 96, 101f, 162
Wither, George, 88
Witherspoon, John, 217
Wolfe, General, 222f
Wood, James, 100f
Wordsworth, William, 227f
Wycliffe, 21

York, 94